IN THE COMPANY
OF OTHERS

IN THE COMPANY OF OTHERS

A DIALOGICAL CHRISTOLOGY

DAVID H. JENSEN

THE
PILGRIM
PRESS
Cleveland

For Molly

The Pilgrim Press, Cleveland, Ohio 44115
www.pilgrimpress.com

Copyright © 2001 David H. Jensen.

Printed in the United States of America on acid-free paper

06   05   04   03   02   01   5   4   3   2   1

Library of Congress Cataloging-in-Publication Data
Jensen, David Hadley, 1968-
 In the company of others : a dialogical christology / David H. Jensen.
  p.   cm.
 Includes bibliographical references and index.
 ISBN 0-8298-1420-5 (alk. paper)
 1. Jesus Christ – Person and offices. 2. Christianity and other religions.
3. Incarnation.   I. Title.

BT203 .J46 2001
232 – dc21

2001018558

CONTENTS

FOREWORD

WRITING A THEOLOGICAL ESSAY these days is not easy. It
probably never was. Nonetheless, the postmodern Scylla
and Charybdis is a particularly unnerving one: say something
big with conviction and be accused of essentialism or universalism; say something small with modesty and be accused
of insignificance or triviality. The postmodern alternatives,
however, hide a greater calling: say something small with
conviction—and listen to others.

David Jensen's *In the Company of Others* attempts this last task.
This essay stands firmly on the particularity of Christianity—the
incarnation and resurrection of Jesus Christ—and finds in this
singularity the conditions for radical openness to others. This is
a "back to Jesus" move that allows for a different kind of interreligious dialogue. Over the last several decades, Christians have
modified their claims about Jesus in an effort to find a common
denominator with other religious traditions. This has been a
noble work in many ways and has certainly tempered some of
the deserved criticisms of Christianity as absolutistic and imperialistic. It has also opened the possibility of joint efforts on
such planetary issues as human rights and environmental sus-
tainability. But it has watered down the distinctiveness—and the
rich benefits—of different religious traditions.

David Jensen suggests another way: not the way of the one
Savior for all time and for all people, but the way of the One
who emptied himself to become incarnate and who is risen as
an absent presence. This is a Christology that makes way for
others—other people, other religions. This Christology gives
"space" to all creatures. It is a Christology that seeks not its
own power and place but the abundant life for all.

At the heart of Jensen's thesis is the ancient notion of kenosis—self-emptying. But unlike many in the Christian tradition,

vii

he does not understand it to be world-denying—not for God, or Christ, or us. In fact, just the opposite: it is the way to love another. As Iris Murdoch puts it, "Love is the extremely difficult realization that something other than oneself is real. Love . . . is the discovery of reality."[1] When God creates the world and says, "It is good"; when Jesus Christ is seen as thoroughly embodied and especially intimate with the poor, the sick, and the outcast; when we are called to love God totally and our neighbor as ourselves—all of these confessions are ways of loving or, what is the same thing, "the extremely difficult realization that something other than oneself is real." God does this in creating the world; Christ does it in being bodily with the despised; *we* do it when we try to live the great commandments. It is nothing special—it is simply the discovery of reality.

So, Jensen's Christology, centered as it is on this recognition, is ipso facto a different basis for interreligious dialogue—one that says the particular Christian thing with conviction and is *for that reason* radically open to others. It is a significant accomplishment. It is thoroughly Christian yet not absolutistic; it is profoundly appreciative of others but not trivial in its claims.

In other words, it is a model of good public theology, and by that I mean theology that enters the conversation concerning the most pressing issues of the day. Such theology is not merely for individuals or even only for one's own community; rather, it assumes that theology is concerned with human and planetary flourishing. Our planet and its people cannot flourish when religions war with one another, when instead of working for the well-being of all, they engage in acts ranging from exclusion to genocide in support of their "truth" and in opposition to everyone else's "error." Christianity has been a big contributor to this practice, and at the heart of Christian absolutism is Jesus Christ as the world's one and only Savior. David Jensen's deconstruction and reconstruction of the christological symbol seeks to remove support for this Christian imperialism. More than that, it offers a portrait of Christ that, while retaining its distinc-

---

1. Iris Murdoch, "The Sublime and the Good," *Chicago Review* 13 (autumn 1959): 51.

tiveness and centrality for Christians, welcomes others in the heartiest fashion possible: the self-emptying Christ is an open invitation to others. That is what self-emptying *means:* giving space for others to be; acknowledging that reality is made up of others; loving others by appreciating their differences. Jensen is claiming that Christology is acknowledging the other as other; Christology is the way toward the discovery of reality.

A more fruitful basis for interreligious dialogue as well as the mediation of universalist claims is difficult to imagine. This is a substantial public theology. But it is also a *Christian* theology, firmly grounded in an ancient tradition of christological interpretation, reconstructed for just and sustainable living on planet Earth in the twenty-first century.

SALLIE MCFAGUE
Carpenter Professor of Theology, Emerita
Vanderbilt University

PREFACE

I N ORDER TO BECOME more faithful disciples, Christians need the insights of persons who profess distinctly different religious commitments. Too often, however, most Christians act as if the opposite were the case. For many contemporary churchgoers, dialogue appears more as a peripheral than a central concern. Conversation with the religious Other, according to this common perspective, dilutes Christian commitments rather than affirms them; it represents the gradual withering away of the Christian worldview, its monotheism and ethical stance in the search for an elusive least common religious denominator. Jesus Christ, as a result, soon vanishes in a fog of religious generality and is relegated to the margins of interreligious encounter.

In contrast, "interreligious dialogue" has become something of a catchphrase within many contemporary theological circles. To say that today's Christian theologian lives in an age of global conversation is certainly an understatement, given the plethora of recent approaches that grapple with the thorny issues of Christian particularity in a context of religious diversity. Religious difference, it seems, can no longer be ignored either in the Christian life or within the discipline of theology itself. Indeed, the more Christians survey this difference, the less satisfied we become with our own stock answers, and the more we become convinced that we need *others* who are different from us in order to better formulate questions of meaning and survival on our increasingly threatened planet. The primary call in this atmosphere is not to convert one's neighbors, but to understand and learn from them. The practice of dialogue—the mutual sharing of religious confessions and the critical engagement of each other's commitments and worldviews in a setting that resists the forcible imposition of one way of life and belief over another—is one promising avenue for the engagement of interreligious difference. Its practitioners among the ranks of Christian theologians (not to mention Buddhist, Jewish, and Hindu thinkers) are certainly growing in number.

In an age in which interreligious misunderstanding has contributed to so much suffering—from war in Palestine to murder in Northern Ireland, from ethnic feuding in Sri Lanka to ethnic genocide in Bosnia—dialogue is no longer a luxury for the privileged academic few; it is a *necessity* for any who find themselves immersed in our world of difference. We need to better understand each other and learn to appreciate each other's commitments if we are ever to stop the inexorable cycle of violence and hatred. Too often in Christianity's history has religious difference given rise to crusading triumphalism and the obliteration of otherness; too little has it been celebrated as one facet of the abundant life of creation Christians are wont to proclaim. In the name of preserving this life—and ourselves— dialogue presents one avenue of hope. Tom Driver addresses our current situation poignantly: "Pluralism is not an ultimate concern. It is something more serious. It is an immediate concern."[1] Dialogue, as Driver would maintain, is not an end in itself, but a means toward enhanced understanding of difference and toward the more equitable sharing of life's resources on this one Earth, in which all actions—for good or for ill—are inextricably intertwined.

The discipline of Christian theology, in other words, cannot be conducted as if it were a private affair. Christian thought is no longer (if it ever was) an "in-house" conversation intended only for those immersed in its symbols and language. For the ruminations of those who make sense of the faith invariably ripple outward as Christian practice in the company of others. In this polyglot environment, we who are Christians need others to hold us accountable to our traditions, to criticize the instances in which our thinking and acting have denigrated others, and to express appreciation for how our traditions have

---

1. Tom Driver, "The Case for Pluralism," in *The Myth of Christian Uniqueness,* ed. John Hick and Paul F. Knitter (Maryknoll, N.Y.: Orbis, 1987), 207.

affirmed other ways. Christians need others not simply to become more responsible theologians, but, more pointedly, to
become more authentic followers of the One from Nazareth
who placed others at the center of his ministry and message.

The approach that I offer issues a stern challenge to any view
that considers the commitment to dialogue as being antithetical
to the traditions, symbols, and confessions that have gathered
around Jesus Christ. This project, in short, is a *christological
exploration*, a sustained grappling with the claims Christians
have made about the Nazarene. Through this reexamination
of Christology, dialogue and the religious Other emerge not on
the fringes of Christian confession, but at its very core. As we
will see, it is not simply Christian theology that demands difference, but the *figura*[2] of Jesus Christ himself. Faithfulness to
Jesus Christ issues forth in the invitation of the religious Other.

This focus upon Christology is doubtless intentional. For if
Christian obstacles to interreligious encounter ever did exist,
our classical interpretations of Jesus Christ would surely constitute one of them. He whom Christians proclaim as the Way, the
Truth, and the Life, generally is presented as the *only* Way. In the
face of this ultimate religious trump card, it has been more characteristic of the theological tradition to assert that others need
Christ than to claim that Christians need others. One hope of
this project is to show that such "Christomonism"—the proclamation of Jesus Christ at the expense of everything else—is a
distortion of the life of discipleship and not its faithful execution. Indeed, conformity to Christ involves *being claimed by others*,
and not claiming others as our own.

This project in "dialogical Christology" comprises six chapters. The first, "Christian Responses to the Religious Other,"

---

2. By employing the term *figura*, I am underscoring the recognition that there
is no immediate access to the historical Jesus. The earliest portrayals of Jesus, the
Synoptic Gospels, are less concerned with biography than they are with document-
ing the continuing influence and sustaining power of the Incarnate and Risen One.
Accordingly, the "facts" of Jesus' life are often inseparable from the memory and interests of those gathered in his name. Since the details of this life are comparatively
thin, the task of each generation of Christians is to ask christological questions anew,
to reconstruct this *figura* in faithfulness to the memories and traditions of those
who gathered in his name before us. Only in this manner do Christians continue
to participate in a *living* tradition.

offers an introduction to the spectrum of Christian responses to the religious Other. After constructing a typology that addresses the insights and pitfalls of five historical approaches to our religious neighbors, I argue for the necessity of a *christological* focus to the difficult cluster of issues surrounding Christian identity in our pluralistic milieu. Such a chapter is doubtless wide in scope, but necessary for anchoring my subsequent contributions to the interreligious conversation.

The second chapter, "The Incarnate, Emptying Christ," presents the exegetical and historical underpinnings of my alternative christological approach. In it, I introduce the image of kenosis, or self-emptying, as a possible interpretation of incarnation in our pluralistic age. The chapter begins with a brief study of the New Testament hymn from which this image is drawn, found in Philippians 2, suggesting that christological confession and hymnic adoration are continually bound up with the *life of discipleship*. The chapter moves toward its more explicitly theological task by examining the kenotic Christologies of G. W. F. Hegel and Gottfried Thomasius. Grappling with the shortcomings and brilliance of these two nineteenth-century approaches, I ask how their doctrinal concerns might be framed in our age.

The following two chapters form the heart of my christological argument. Chapter 3, "Professing Christ and Encountering Buddhism," offers a constructive articulation of Christ's kenosis. I begin the chapter by suggesting how a profession of the *Emptying Christ* draws Christians into encounter with a particular tradition, Zen Buddhism. This "experiment" in dialogical openness has significant consequences for how Christians envisage the relational God of their own tradition. In light of this encounter, and the scriptural and theological resources uncovered in chapter 2, I present a constructive incarnational theology for our pluralistic age. Jesus Christ is the *One who embodies openness to others*. He is the One who empties himself on behalf of us, enfleshing our right relation with each other and humanity's relation with God. As those who confess Jesus as the Christ, Christians are likewise called to open themselves to others, particularly those who profess different religious commitments.

Chapter 4, "The Absent Presence of the Risen Christ," suggests that the dynamic of kenosis is not exhausted by Christ's incarnation, nor does it disappear with Jesus' death. Rather, it continues wherever the church professes Christ as risen and alive today. The image that focuses this discussion is Mark's narration of the empty tomb. Beginning with a brief exegetical study, the chapter probes Mark's perplexing ending, paying close attention to the role of *proclamation, silence,* and the Risen Christ's *absence* from the places where his followers seek him. The discussion progresses to a further examination of the provisionality of narrative endings and the juxtaposition of absence and presence, closure and openness, in Mark's Gospel. The chapter concludes with my own constructive articulation of Christ's resurrection. Jesus Christ, as the Risen One, resists those very spaces that would claim him as theirs alone. He is the One who goes on *ahead* of all who would enclose him, manifesting himself throughout time whenever openness to others is embodied in love. As the One who whispers the "absent presence" of God, the Risen Christ opens Christians to a world of difference.

Chapter 5, "And We Shall Be Changed," shifts our attention to more practical concerns. Here I explore the pervasive change that this kenotic Christology effects in three forms of Christian praxis: *discipleship, dialogue, and doctrine.* First, a kenotic approach adjusts the focus of discipleship from a relatively straightforward moralism of "following" Jesus to a deeper concern with the *ethical* claim of others and the demand of difference in the Christian life. Secondly, dialogue itself is questioned as an adequate model for interreligious encounter, if what is meant by it is the detached exchange of competing religious truth claims. What a kenotic approach suggests, rather, is not the dialogical quest for "truth," but recognition of the *beauty and sacredness* of others as unique persons of difference. Finally, Christian articulation of doctrine is transformed from an intra-Christian enterprise to an "ec-centric" discipline. What stands at its center, is not the self, the church, or even the One we profess as incarnate and risen, but the new life promised through him in the company of others. Christian doctrine, in other words, exhibits difference at its very core.

Chapter 6, "Called by the Other," concludes the study by acknowledging the constructed nature of reality and the importance of theological models. Although this study advocates one interpretation of kenosis, broadly consonant with Rahner's and Hegel's understanding of the relational God and the relational cosmos, other possibilities abound, some of which might be more amenable in different contexts. This wide variation of interpretive options, I would suggest, points to kenoticism's continued relevance in a world of difference.

What this study will *not* effect is a gigantic interreligious leap forward. In response to the bewildering number of religious voices that confront persons today, I will not be offering a kind of theological Grand Unifying Theory. However much many on the contemporary scene may yearn for it, such a leap is neither desirable nor possible. For such a leap would invariably obscure the difference it sought to explicate. Situated in the midst of a thoroughly pluralistic world, one can, however, encourage the development of subtle shifts in thinking, especially when these shifts are directed at a particular religious community. Such a move is what this project seeks to inaugurate: for Christian theology to perceive the religious Other no longer at the periphery of its enterprise, but at its very center. Small as this shift may seem, it has enormous consequences, liberating countless voices that have heretofore been suppressed in the tradition.

Given this wide range of voices, my hope is that this study will interest a broad spectrum of readers. For Christian theologians and pastors grappling with the issue of Christian particularity in a pluralistic age, these reflections may offer one possibility for affirming Jesus Christ as the Incarnate and Risen One while at the same time opening such affirmation to the wisdom of the religious Other. Yet my hope is that this study will engage not only these professionals, but also any person who is asking the questions "How can I be a Christian without ignoring my religious neighbor? How might I engage this difference beyond blatant prosyletization or the banal claim 'I have my truth, others have theirs, and never the twain shall meet?' " Because this latter question concerns not only Christians, but also anyone who inhabits planet Earth, this project may be of interest to Buddhists, Jews, atheists, and Muslims as well. For as an ec-centric discipline, Christian theology fails if it engages only those within the confines of Sunday sanctuaries. This study of the Emptying Christ, I would argue, offers one example of how a particular community can take its own commitments seriously while acknowledging that they alone do not constitute the search for the final word. We need *others* to make that journey possible.

A project of this magnitude is never really completed. Like most work in theology, this manuscript will always remain a work in progress. At a certain point, however, theologians feel prepared—even compelled—to offer their voices to an ongoing conversation in the hope that they might add yet other refrains to the living theological chorus. After several years of study and composition, I find myself at such a juncture and in the debt of several people who have helped me arrive at this stage. Work on this project began in earnest in the spring of 1997, as I began to write my doctoral dissertation. My first two readers, Peter Hodgson and Sallie McFague, proved to be exacting critics and excellent motivators as I strove to find my own theological voice. At numerous stages along this journey, they helped me refine my ideas, sharpen my prose, and venture bolder moves in my thinking. Those readers familiar with their work will find much of their influence in the pages that follow. For their unflagging interest and commitment to this project, I cannot offer enough thanks; along this long and rocky path of writing, both of them have been steadfast companions and strong mentors for me. Gene TeSelle offered an extremely helpful reading of an earlier draft. His careful observation and penetrating knowledge of the Christian theological tradition enabled me to redirect my course at a stage when I was foundering. David Buttrick and Jeffrey Tlumak guided and broadened my reading at various stages of this project, helping me uncover theological and philosophical voices I had heretofore ignored. To my entire dissertation committee I owe many heartfelt thanks.

Without the interest and support of George R. Graham of the Pilgrim Press, I doubt whether this work would be appearing in its present form. His enthusiasm for my project was apparent from our initial phone conversation, and has continued unabated. Pilgrim's willingness to take a risk with a young, unknown theologian like me is clear evidence of its commitment to bring fresh voices to the contemporary theological conversation.

My parents, John and Gretchen Jensen, have often expressed their interest in my work and support for my seemingly endless educational odyssey. Along a journey that others have undoubtedly questioned in terms of its practicality and length, they have always nurtured my eros for learning.

As this project came to fruition, Hannah Grace Jensen entered the world. Words can hardly describe the joy that has come in the nineteen months since her birth. To watch the world unfold through my daughter's eyes, to hold her hand as we run through the grass, is a reminder of the graciousness of life itself.

The person to whom I owe the greatest thanks is my partner and wife, Molly Hadley Jensen, to whom this book is dedicated. Molly has nurtured my mind, body, and soul in ways that I could have never imagined before I met her. Her theological thinking has cultivated my own in countless conversations and letters. As we have walked hand-in-hand over the past five years, I have learned that a life shared—in all its struggles, laughter, tears, and joy—is a life well-lived. Nothing else has opened my life to the world, to others, and to God in such a radical way as has the love that we share. In the reflections that follow, her presence is on every page. Life in our little apartment that housed two graduate students (and now the little apartment that houses three) has surely been full of challenges—particularly financial ones—but in the midst of it all grace continues to emerge. Not a day goes by when I do not thank Molly for all that she brings to the world, and for all that we have yet to share.

Karl Rahner wrote, "The first thing therefore that the theologian must do is ask himself some questions.... [These questions] do not of course appear...for the first time. They are in fact questions which the faith and theology of the Church as a whole have always been answering in chorus. It is however the task...of the theologian in particular to repeat the old questions in a new way, so that they may really have a new and vital understanding of the old questions."[3] In the pages that follow I will attempt to ask an age-old question, "Who is Jesus Christ?" in a manner attuned to our pluralistic milieu. For the ways in which I ask that question effectively, I have many to thank; for the ways in which the approach to that question falls short, the fault is solely my own.

---

3. Karl Rahner, "Dogmatic Questions on Easter," in *More Recent Writings*, Theological Investigations 4, trans. Kevin Smyth (Baltimore: Helicon, 1966), 121–22.

CHAPTER I

CHRISTIAN RESPONSES TO THE RELIGIOUS OTHER

THE CURRENT PROLIFERATION of work focusing on inter-religious dialogue often suggests that the question of the "religious Other" has emerged only recently in Christian theology. A loud chorus of voices—from the documents of Vatican II to the writings of Christians in South Asia, from Christian "pluralists" such as John Hick to more traditional "confessionalists" such as Wolfhart Pannenberg—urges contemporary Christians to acknowledge the cultural location of our own most cherished convictions, to recognize the legitimacy of other traditions and persons who embody different claims, and to open ourselves to those others in both conversation and life.[1] As participants in a *living* tradition enmeshed in a culturally complex and religiously pluralistic world, many thinking Christians have recognized that we can neither stomach the exclusivism of our collective past nor overcome religious difference in a solidarity of sameness. Difference is *real,* and one task of all persons on this planet, whether religious or not, is to live in ways that promote peace and the well-being of each irreducible Other. To refuse this encounter is a cowardly retreat that ignores the complexity of creation and the invitation of my neighbor. At the dawn of the twenty-first century, moreover, this neighbor can be almost anyone, both the person with whom I share my

---

1. A recent article by Anselm Min offers a helpful typology of recent Christian approaches to the issue of religious pluralism: "Dialectical Pluralism and Solidarity of Others: Towards a New Paradigm," *Journal of the American Academy of Religion* 65, no. 3 (1997): 587–90. For examples of the "pluralist" and "confessionalist" approaches, see, respectively, John Hick, *A Christian Theology of Religions* (Louisville: Westminster John Knox, 1995), and Wolfhart Pannenberg, "Religious Pluralism and Conflicting Truth Claims," in *Christian Uniqueness Reconsidered,* ed. Gavin D'Costa (Maryknoll, N.Y.: Orbis, 1990), 96–106.

deepest religious commitments and the person whose practice embodies foreign claims and worldviews.

For Christians, this recent stress upon dialogue and difference may suggest that the religious Other has come to the fore as a result of external forces—immigration and global communication. Otherness is an immediate, contextual concern that faces us in a techno-ecological age. Difference, according to this view, has recently emerged as an issue because of the polyglot environment in which most Christians find themselves; it is neither intrinsic to Christian thought nor a necessary component of the life of discipleship. Although I would hardly dispute the urgency with which our age has focused the question of the religious Other, I also would suggest that difference is more than a contextual concern for Christians. Indeed, our approach to the religious Other gets to the heart of the claims and commitments by which we live. For the Christian faith becomes irrelevant or mere religious privatism unless it is lived out in the company of others, unless thought meets practice. The sustained argument of this work is that the religious Other stands at the center of our most distinctive affirmation—proclaiming Jesus as the Christ—and that faithfulness to this confession turns our attention outward, allowing us to be captivated by the beauty and detail of *all* persons of difference.

As we will see in this chapter, the question of the religious Other is hardly new to Christian theology; indeed, it has been asked with varying degrees of appropriateness throughout the history of the church. In our ambiguous tradition, the Other has represented both the one to whom we are summoned in love and the one against whom we must battle in the name of truth. Each of these attitudes, moreover, has been framed in response to the claims Christians have made about Jesus of Nazareth. Confessing Christ and confronting the Other appear as two prongs of the same religious commitment. As we will see, the degree of openness that Christians have exhibited toward the religious Other has often paralleled the degree to which Christianity is or is not a disestablishment religion. The task of this chapter, then, is to construct a brief typology of Christian attitudes toward the religious Other, to connect these attitudes with perhaps the most distinctive affirmation of the Christian faith—proclaiming Jesus as the Christ—thus clearing the space for an alternative Christology that does justice to incarnational claims and takes with seriousness voices heretofore ignored. Whether Christians have regarded them or not, these others have always stood in our midst.

THE OTHER TO WHOM WE ARE SUMMONED IN LOVE

Those who see pluralism as a new concern are surprised that some of the oldest traditions to which the church lays claim offer the widest embrace of the Other. Witnessed primarily in the Hebrew Bible's prophetic voices, this attitude is also grounded in Torah, and is subsequently echoed in some of the Synoptic traditions. The Other, according to this scriptural theme, is the one to whom we are summoned in love. Those who are different or alien, particularly those who are vulnerable, are afforded a distinct privilege: they are not regarded as "lesser" citizens, beyond the pale of redemption, but as neighbors who are worthy of love *in themselves,* by the sheer fact that *they are.*[2]

This legal privileging of the alien Other is grounded in the recognition that Israel was once held captive in a foreign land: "When an alien resides with you in your land, you shall not oppress the alien. The alien who resides with you shall be to you as the citizen among you; you shall love the alien as yourself, for you were aliens in the land of Egypt: I am the Lord your God" (Lev. 19:33–34). Some strands of the legal tradition even speak of an equality between God's covenantal people and those perceived as "strangers" in the land: "There shall be for you and

---

2. The idea of the *religious* Other is undoubtedly foreign to the authors of the Hebrew Bible. For the Israelites, "religious" difference could not be isolated from the complex weave of national, ethnic, and linguistic identity. A different "religion" (to use an anachronistic term) was not the chief concern of the writers of Torah, except in cases where they denounced idolatry (e.g., Baal worship). Their task, rather, was to describe Israel's covenant with God and to document whether or not Israel maintained faithfulness to that promise. A recognition of "otherness" and election, however, formed a part of that narration. The Hebrew mind was no less attuned to difference, but constructed it along lines foreign to modern persons concerned with "religious difference."

the resident alien a single statute, a perpetual statute throughout your generations; you and the alien shall be alike before
the Lord" (Num. 15:15).[3] Benign, modern-day toleration is not
what this tradition underscores, but love of the alien neighbor
as oneself. For the writers of Torah, Israel's relationship with its
God was lived out in its relations with others: a reflection of that
covenant could be glimpsed in the face of the alien sojourner.

It is no coincidence, then, that one of the ruptures in covenant that the prophets decried is the community's disregard for
and rejection of the Other. A recurrent theme in this corpus is
the binding together of love of stranger and love of God. Where
Israel stumbles in the former, it has surely failed in the latter.
For the prophets, the record of covenant is marked as much
by failure as by faithfulness: "Father and mother are treated
with contempt in you; the alien residing within you suffers ex-
tortion; the orphan and the widow are wronged in you. You
have despised my holy things, and profaned my sabbaths" (Ezek.
22:7–8). Oppression of the alien and blasphemy are mentioned
by several prophets in the same breath. Indeed, it is a mockery
of covenant for Israel to continue its festivals and priestly rituals
while ignoring the plight of those suffering in its midst (Amos
5:21–24). The covenant, in short, cannot be maintained unless
love of vulnerable others is made real.

With no uncertain emphasis, the Synoptic Gospels resume
this theme from the law and prophets. Matthew, for example,
accords a high recognition to love of neighbor as the second
"great commandment" (Matt. 22:39–40), and the way in which
love of God is made manifest: "I was hungry and you gave
me food, I was thirsty and you gave me something to drink,
I was a stranger and you welcomed me, I was naked and you
gave me clothing, I was sick and you took care of me, I was
in prison and you visited me" (Matt. 25:35–36). For the writers of the Synoptic Gospels, others—particularly those who are

---

3. Examples of this privileging of the Other abound throughout the legal tradition. See also Exod. 23:9; Deut. 10:19; 24:21–22. This regard for the Other,
however, does not run unambiguously throughout the Hebrew Bible. The con-
quest of Canaan, for example, affords no privilege whatsoever to those outside the
covenantal fold. Obliteration of otherness and the triumph over foreign peoples
are the tragic results of the settlement of the promised land. See Josh. 8:1–29.

most vulnerable—are neighbors to whom I am called in love. Even though this difference is not construed along *religious* lines, the call of the Other is no less real.[4] Difference is not simply a religious distinction, but a matter of the well-being and sacredness of those to whom we are summoned in love.[5] Insofar as contemporary Christians are heirs to these biblical traditions, a historical warrant for the embrace of the religious Other certainly is plausible.

THE OTHER AS CONVERT WHO STANDS IN NEED

The second posture vis-à-vis the religious Other percolates to the surface as the Jesus movement spreads to the Gentile world. Presenting itself often in terms of Christian *apology*, this attitude assumes the wisdom of the Other in a grand sweep of inclusivity, but also claims that such wisdom is incomplete without Christ's culmination. The Other, accordingly, stands not so much as my neighbor on his or her own terms, but only as a foreshadow of what is fully embodied in Christian claims, in other words, what I myself embody. If the first type considered the Other as *neighbor*, this alternative views the Other as *my pupil or convert.*

Justin Martyr is one of the earliest exponents of this attitude. In his *Second Apology*, he captures the gist of Christian inclusivism: "Whatever things were rightly said among all men, are the property of us Christians. For next to God, we worship and love the Word who is from the unbegotten and ineffable

---

4. Indeed, in its inaugural stages, the Jesus movement placed little emphasis on "religious difference." For the Lukan community, Jesus' followers are often found in the temple (cf. Luke 19:45–21:38; 24:50–53; Acts 1–4), while the synagogue figures prominently in the Gospel of John. Only in subsequent *disputes* with the synagogues does "religious difference" emerge as an issue for John. See Norman Perrin and Dennis C. Duling, *The New Testament: An Introduction*, 2nd ed. (San Diego: Harcourt Brace Jovanovich, 1982), 339–40.

5. Several liberation theologians have reappropriated this biblical theme. For Gustavo Gutiérrez, love of God is made real in relation to the other. Gutiérrez uses the language of *metanoia* to describe this relationship: "A spirituality of liberation will center on a *conversion* to the neighbor, the oppressed person, the exploited social class, the despised ethnic group, the dominated country. Our conversion to the Lord implies this conversion to the neighbor" (*A Theology of Liberation*, rev. ed., trans. Sister Caridad Inda and John Eagleson [Maryknoll, N.Y.: Orbis, 1988], 118).

God, since also He became man for our sakes, that, becoming a partaker of our sufferings, He might also bring us healing."[6] The Other, according to Justin, is not a benighted soul, but sagacious, possessed of rich cultural traditions and intellectual resources that summon our reverence. Justin's stance encourages Christians to recognize the integrity of these traditions, to learn from Plato and Aristotle, and to claim them as an arm of Christian truth. However much the Other embodies the world's wisdom, much remains inchoate in his or her discernment of truth. For, according to the apologists, the culmination of wisdom can be reached only in the Word made flesh; all else is but a dim reflection of incarnation, the dwelling of God's wisdom with humanity. Christians are thus called to issue an invitation to the religious Other, welcoming others to recognize that the fructification of their own traditions and commitments is represented in the Christian faith. In Justin's approach, the Other exists as the Christian's pupil, the one to whom I must impart my own wisdom.[7]

The apologetic eye that views the Other as incomplete, as the one who stands in need of me, represents a departure from the biblical tradition that would grant privilege to the Other instead of ourselves. Apology pushes the Other away from the center to make room for the "I." Despite the obvious problems involved in this shift, the context in which the classic strands of this tradition were uttered helps explain how it occurred. The church was struggling in its first four centuries not just with issues of identity and unity, but with its own survival. As a small voice in a polyglot religious world, speaking in cities that were home

6. Justin Martyr, "The Second Apology of Justin for the Christians," in *The Ante-Nicene Fathers*, vol. 1, ed. Alexander Roberts and James Donaldson (Grand Rapids: Eerdmans, 1956), 193.

7. Tertullian offers another voice that assumes this apologetic tradition. For Tertullian, the logic of Christian apology is straightforward: just as Christ embodied the wisdom of God, those who follow Christ are called to embody the traditions Jesus inaugurated and to pass them on to all peoples of the world. "Christ Jesus our Lord...did, whilst He lived on earth, Himself declare what He was, what He had been, what the Father's will was which He was administering....He destined [twelve] to be the teachers of the nations....In like manner [they] founded churches in every city, from which all the other churches, one after another, derived the tradition of the faith." (Tertullian, "The Prescription against Heretics," in Robertson and Donaldson, eds., *The Ante-Nicene Fathers*, 3:252).

to synagogal Judaism, Hellenic mystery cults, various Gnostic spiritualities, and other Near Eastern religious traditions, the Christian community was forced to maintain its own distinctive voice (and at times to trumpet its own "superiority") if it was to avoid assimilation by its larger and more vocal religious neighbors. For the early Christians, the movement inaugurated by Jesus was indispensable; one "task" of the early apologists, then, was to demonstrate the uniqueness of the Word made flesh. Had it refused in this enterprise, the Jesus movement likely would have faded from the Mediterranean scene, absorbed by more established Hellenic traditions. In the era before Christianity's establishment, the early apologists maintained Christian identity and ensured the movement's future without closing itself to others who embodied different claims and traditions. They achieved this nonsectarian stance by issuing an invitation to the religious Other to recognize the full development of her own traditions in the Christian church. The unfortunate result of this invitation, however, was that it tended to diminish the distinctiveness of the Other in his or her own right; the Other existed only as a foreshadowing of the wisdom embodied in Christ.[8]

THE OTHER AS ENEMY

Once Christianity had established itself as a voice with considerable audience in the Mediterranean world, a different posture regarding the religious Other began to emerge. Although it would be simplistic to claim that Constantine's Edict of Milan, which in 313 gave the imprimatur to Christianity as the religion of empire, gestated this alternative posture, this official sanction

---

8. The apologetic stance that affirms the religious Other insofar as she or he points to Christ has continued into the present century. It enjoys widespread audience among several missionary groups who present the gospel not in antagonistic fashion (as a radical departure from "heathenism"), but as the fulfillment of the target culture's own traditions. The early Jesuit mission to China represents one example of this stance. See John Cobb's essay, "The Religions," in *Christian Theology: An Introduction to Its Traditions and Tasks*, ed. Peter C. Hodgson and Robert H. King (Minneapolis: Fortress, 1994), 359–60.

certainly abetted some disturbing trends.[9] For as soon as crown embraced church, anything that threatened the state could be dubbed as inimical toward orderly life in the Christian colony. The religious Other began to be viewed not only as a potential *convert*, as one who stood in need of the gospel, but as a potential *enemy* as well, as one whose commitments were antithetical to the way of life that Christian witness sought to unfold.

To be sure, this regard of the Other as enemy took centuries to take root in the minds of those who professed Christ. Even where its foothold was strongest, vocal minorities in the churches assiduously resisted its encroachment.[10] Nevertheless, virulent forms of this posture have occurred throughout the history of the church; too often has the pen of Christian apology been held in the fist of imperial aggression. Ghosts of the Conquistadors, Crusades, and Holocaust continue to haunt us with their damning logic: if the Other could not be made a convert to follow Christ, she or he was an enemy to be destroyed in the name of "truth." In the history of Christianity, there is scarcely a group—Jews, Muslims, Native Americans, African slaves—against whom this logic has not been leveled. The Other who threatens the powers-that-be and the Other who embodies different religious commitments are, for the imperial Christian, one and the same person.

Perhaps the most notorious theological chords in this troublesome tradition are the later writings of Martin Luther. Toward the end of his life, Luther appeared obsessed with what he perceived as Jewish intransigence in relation to the gospel. The Luther who was perceived by many to be a "threat" to the Roman Catholic church began to see a "threat" to Christ in the traditions of Judaism. His hatred and vituperation are transparent as he urges the Christian to "defend himself against the

---

9. Although the original scope of the Edict was more limited—namely, to extend freedom of worship and restitution to the Christian churches—its practical effect in subsequent years was to forge further ties between church and state.

10. The Anabaptist tradition—in its multiple forms—has been especially condemnatory of the church-empire alliance. The practice of pacifism among these groups documents their refusal to render the Other a faceless enemy. And, as their name implies, the Society of Friends offers an alternative embrace of persons of difference.

blind, venomous Jews..., to become the foe of the Jews' malice, lying, and cursing, and to understand not only that their belief is false, but that they are surely possessed by all devils."[11] Luther's recourse is as damning as it is twisted. Because Jews represent such a threat to the "truth" that Christian witness upholds, any and all means may be used to deal with the menace. Luther advises his readers to burn synagogues or schools, raze houses, steal prayer books, forbid rabbis to teach, abolish safe passage on highways for Jews, criminalize the practice of lending money, and force the younger Jewish population into manual labor.[12] The echoes of this hatred have continued into this century; indeed, Hitler was fond of citing the Luther we have laid bare. Although the Holocaust represents the most demonic application of the posture that considers the religious Other as enemy, its reverberations continue wherever religious difference becomes a thin mask for hatred.[13] Whenever the church becomes so wedded to imperial authority that it becomes synonymous with it (as among the Nazi *Deutsche Christen*), anyone who questions that authority can be twisted into an "enemy." The Other who "rejects" Christ then becomes the Other I am called to destroy. No more egregious distortion of the biblical tradition that privileges the Other exists than this reification of others as enemies. In an age of establishment Christianity, which we are only recently escaping, however, it has been an all-too-frequent stance.

THE OTHER AS ANONYMOUS CHRISTIAN

In response to the abuses of our burdensome imperialist past, another attitude toward the religious Other has emerged in this century. Witnessed most strongly among Roman Catholic theologians, particularly the documents of Vatican II and the

---

11. Martin Luther, "On the Jews and Their Lies," in *Luther's Works*, vol. 47, ed. Franklin Sherman (Philadelphia: Fortress, 1971), 306.

12. Ibid., 268–72.

13. Sadly, Christianity is not alone in its tendency to cast the Other in the role of enemy, as the recent ethnic/religious bloodletting in Sri Lanka, Algeria, and Rwanda serves to remind us.

writings of Karl Rahner, this position in some respects represents a return to Justin's tradition of Christian apology, albeit
with different emphases and a sensitivity to our contemporary
pluralistic context. This posture affirms the religious Other as
an "anonymous Christian," as one who is saved without explicit
confession of Christ. Although this posture maintains the intrinsic worth of the religious Other, and the need for Christians
to become *pupils of others*,[14] it nonetheless attempts to maintain
the *indispensability* of Christian witness in a religiously pluralistic world. In an era in which the gradual disestablishment of
Christianity is apparent,[15] this is a voice that is gaining wider
credence in the churches.

The documents of Vatican II have made this posture common
coin in many Catholic theological circles: "Those who, through
no fault of their own, do not know the Gospel of Christ or his
Church, but who nevertheless seek God with a sincere heart,
and, moved by grace, try in their actions to do his will as they
know it through the dictates of their conscience—those too may
achieve eternal salvation."[16] The religious Other, then, may be
implicitly affirming what Christians affirm explicitly. Those who
accept their lives in embrace of others are already saying yes to
God.[17]

Karl Rahner has been the leading theological exponent of
this posture. Confronted by the troublesome claim of Christian
orthodoxy on the church's unique status (*extra ecclesiam nulla
salus*) and the integrity of other religious traditions, Rahner

---

14. Notice how this coinage represents a reversal of the earlier apologetic model.

15. By "disestablishment of Christianity" I mean that Christianity has no longer
become self-evident or automatic for most North Americans, as it once was. The turn
to secularism and the influx of diverse ethnic groups who embody other religious
commitments have removed any sense of Christianity's "establishment" as *the* North
American religion. Rather than lamenting "Christendom's" passage, however, this
disestablishment may allow for the development of fresh voices within the tradition.
Douglas John Hall has written extensively on this theme. In his eyes, freed from
Christendom, we may yet become the *ekklesia*. See *Confessing the Faith* (Minneapolis:
Fortress, 1996), 1–30.

16. *Lumen Gentium*, in *Vatican Council II: The Conciliar and Post Conciliar Documents*,
ed. Austin Flannery (Northport, N.Y.: Costello, 1992), 367.

17. See Karl Rahner, "Thoughts on the Possibility of Belief Today," in *Later
Writings*, Theological Investigations 5, trans. Karl-H. Kruger (Baltimore: Helicon,
1966), 7.

affirms both. The lure of God, for Rahner, manifests itself in myriad forms. Insofar as each of the world's faiths—and the critiques of popular religion offered by atheism—affirm anonymously what Christianity affirms explicitly, they point toward salvation. Nonetheless, one can detect a supersessionism lurking beneath the surface of Rahner's writing: "The saving intercommunication of all justified men is the existential ontological precondition for the mediatorship of Christ. This saving intercommunion has its own history and *reaches its apogee in Christ*."[18] Christianity enjoys, from Rahner's perspective, a position of primacy even if other traditions are deemed salvific as well.

The difference between this posture and the earlier tradition of Christian apology is subtle. Whereas Justin claimed that the religious Other needs Christ to witness the flowering of his or her own wisdom and traditions, Rahner upholds that the religious Other already affirms Christ. Christian confession, in other words, makes explicit what is implicitly lived and spoken by the religious Other. The Other, then, becomes an "anonymous Christian," a person like me. According to this view, each of us needs the other to better respond to God's gracious offer of Godself that is whispered in all corners of the cosmos. Interreligious difference remains real, but at its core is also the summons to accept an offer that transcends difference. As we respond to that offer, Christians recognize in the face of the religious Other one who is very much like ourselves. In an age of Christianity's disestablishment, the "enemy" has disappeared and in its place emerges a friend. The question that remains, however, is whether this posture really does justice to difference or merely interprets it on my own terms.

THE OTHER AS STRANGER

A final attitude regarding the religious Other has recently surfaced on the theological scene. Suspicious of the commonality that Rahner's "anonymous Christianity" trumpets and attuned

---

18. Karl Rahner, "One Mediator and Many Mediations," in *Writings of 1965–67*, vol. 1, Theological Investigations 9, trans. Graham Harrison (New York: Herder & Herder, 1972), 84 (emphasis mine).

to postmodernity's celebration of difference, this approach glimpses the Other not as the one to whom I am drawn in a solidarity of similarity, but as *wholly other*. My interreligious neighbor, in other words, speaks an alien tongue, embodies foreign commitments, and unveils a world of difference. This alterity is heralded by voices as varied as the postmodern a/theologian Mark C. Taylor[19] and postliberals such as George Lindbeck. Though each of these voices offers a radically different program for the enterprise of Christian theology, they are one in suggesting that the Other presents the self to us as stranger, as one whose difference has too often been submerged by the tradition.

For Lindbeck, the difference of the religious Other is self-evident, since religions are self-enclosed linguistic systems. Like languages, they "can be understood only in their own terms, not by transposing them into an alien speech."[20] Where the apologetic tradition has erred is its suggestion that the Christian message can be comprehended in an alien context as the culmination of that culture's own traditions. Such an approach obliterates both the distinctiveness of Christian witness and the integrity of the host culture. For Lindbeck, in order to understand a religious tradition and affirm its propositional meaning, "one must be, so to speak, inside the relevant context; and in the case of a religion, this means that one must have some skill in *how* to use its language."[21] The apologetic tradition, in other words, has not taken *otherness* seriously enough, in regard both

---

19. See Mark C. Taylor, *Erring: A Postmodern A/theology* (Chicago: University of Chicago Press, 1984), for a fuller development of a postmodern anthropology and its deconstruction of the self. Taylor questions the individual self's autonomy, underscoring the primacy of relation between "self" and "other." "Since relations are constitutive, subjects are co-relative" (p. 137). Taylor heralds the "death" of the autonomous self. Citing Thomas J. J. Altizer, Taylor notes, "In losing its autonomy, [the 'I'] loses its own unique center and ground, and thereby it loses everything which had once appeared as an individual identity or 'face.' Facelessness and loss of identity now become the mark of everyone, as everyone becomes no one, and the 'I' is inseparable from the 'other' " (p. 142). For Taylor, the Other who is stranger is also the one with whom I am inextricably bound.

20. George Lindbeck, *The Nature of Doctrine: Religion and Theology in a Postliberal Age* (Philadelphia: Westminster, 1984), 129.

21. Ibid., 68.

to itself and to those others whom Christian mission has sought to engage.

One result of the sustained engagement of difference—contra Christian apologetics—is that the Other is often viewed as a stranger. As Kenneth Surin has noted, Hindu, Muslim, and Christian ways of thinking and acting are "imbricated in radically different *epistemes,* and are therefore registered in very diverse and maybe even incommensurable ways."[22] Facile attempts at dialogue that emphasize *translation,* therefore, are bound to fail. The Lutheran of North Dakota and the Therevada Buddhist of Laos cannot assume a common vocabulary, aims, commitments, or even assume that greater understanding will emerge when they encounter one other. Difference in some cases is so pervasive that conversation between the two parties is well-nigh impossible. The only hope, in such cases, is that each person encourage the other to become a better speaker of the language she or he possesses.[23]

In an era of the near-total disestablishment of Christianity as the "religion of culture," this recognition of alterity is a welcome advance. In contrast to the crusading triumphalism of much of the church's history, this stance enables Christians to embrace others as *different and real*—and as others with whom I am embedded in *relationship*—without claiming them as pupils, converts, enemies, or anonymous Christians. Despite its stress on interrelation, however, this postliberal (or postmodern) exclamation of difference can leave those who are radically "other" from each other trapped in their own cultural-linguistic backyards. Conversation becomes an intra-Christian (or intra-Buddhist) rather than an interreligious concern. The problem with this stance is that it may leave religious voices ill-equipped to address the pressing, common issues of survival and justice that beset life on this interrelated globe: the ecological poisoning of the planet, the ever-increasing gap between rich and poor, and the lack of adequate food and housing in

---

22. Kenneth Surin, "A 'Politics of Speech': Religious Pluralism in the Age of the McDonald's Hamburger," in *Christian Uniqueness Reconsidered,* ed. Gavin D'Costa (Maryknoll, N.Y.: Orbis, 1990), 206.

23. See Lindbeck, *Nature of Doctrine,* 61–62.

most corners of the world. Despite the ubiquity of cultural and religious difference, these are common concerns, momentous challenges that each person on this planet shares. My hope is that the alternative, kenotic approach that I will be presenting in the pages to follow may offer one avenue for both the exploration of religious *difference* and for the unification of disparate voices in the struggle with the life-and-death issues that face *all* persons today.

THE CHRISTOLOGICAL CONNECTION

Throughout the preceding typology of the religious Other in Christian thought, the christological question has been lurking in the background. For each of the models we have examined, the response to the question "Who is Jesus Christ?" has informed the attitude Christians have displayed toward their interreligious neighbors. The One professed as Lord has drawn Christians toward their vulnerable neighbors in compassion, as the Synoptic tradition urges, or toward them in benevolent instruction, as the early apologists suggest. Each of these two responses has perceived in the Other a *lack:* what the first response sees as a lack of basic necessity—food, clothing, shelter (cf. Matt. 25:35–36)—the second regards as an epistemological or religious lack. It is because many in the Gentile world lacked knowledge of Christ, according to Justin and Tertullian, that their wisdom was unfulfilled. Within the first two centuries of the Christian movement, then, Jesus Christ becomes not only the impetus for openness to the Other, but the *determinant* of what that Other needs. The Other who is different from me is the Other who needs Christ for fulfillment. This transition to a religious posture vis-à-vis the Other is something with which Christians have been struggling in the nearly two millennia since the apologists unleashed it.

As anyone who has surveyed the ambiguous history of the Christian church will notice, this apologetic turn has given birth to scandalous abuses. During the age of imperial Christianity, the Other who lacked Christ was often perceived as an enemy whose allegiance could be secured only by forcible conversion, as witnessed by several missionary movements in the Americas. If intransigence persisted among those who "lacked" Christ, they were either ignored as "heathen" or, in the worst cases, killed. Luther's polemics against the Jews are only one example of a horrific attitude that continues to haunt the contemporary church.[24]

In an age of Christianity's gradual disestablishment, more irenic responses to the religious Other have surfaced. Rahner's attitude of "anonymous Christianity" has perceived not so much a lack in the Other as an inchoate murmur of what the Christian already affirms. The Other already bears witness to Christ insofar as she or he accepts the mystery of human existence and its partnership with God.[25] The One whom Christians confess, Jesus Christ, calls us to recognize him in others. Incarnation, for Rahner, is writ large upon the variegated tapestry of creation.

The final response, that which views the Other as stranger, represents to some extent a departure from each of the previous strands. The Christ who is affirmed by Christians is not heralded as the One whom others lack, reject, or anonymously affirm. Rather, the communal confessions surrounding Jesus of Nazareth are part of what makes Christian witness utterly distinctive in a world of difference. Christ's centrality is resolutely affirmed *for Christians*, but is not imposed blatantly upon others. In response to this confession, the religious Other remains other in ways that are baffling and mysterious.

Our responses to the christological question "Who is Jesus Christ?," then, are not peripheral to the posture Christians adopt toward others. Indeed, these responses may provide the very foundation for that posture. What emerges as significant from our typology, moreover, is how often Christian profession of Christ has served to place the "I" at the center of our regard of the religious Other. It is this "I" who has possessed

---

24. From the Holocaust to the enslavement of Africans in the United States, from the obliteration of indigenous peoples on the American continents to the outbreak of ethnic war in all corners of the globe, "otherness" has often been perceived as a threat we are called to destroy.

25. See Karl Rahner, "On the Theology of the Incarnation," in *More Recent Writings,* Theological Investigations 4, trans. Kevin Smyth (Baltimore: Helicon, 1966), esp. 107–9, for a further development of this view.

Christ as the fulfillment of wisdom (Justin), who has wielded
Christ against others (Luther), who has assumed that others
profess him anonymously as I do by name (Rahner), or who
has claimed that others are so removed from this profession
that they are strangers to me (Lindbeck). Throughout much of
the history of Christian theology, it seems, christological confession has bolstered the "I" at the expense of the Other. This
history documents a surprising departure from the prophetic/
gospel tradition that privileges the Other more than the self.
In the chapters that follow, I will argue for a recovery of those
traditions, by drawing connections between christological confession and the encounter with the religious Other. The stage
is set, then, for an alternative approach.

An Alternative Model:
The Emptying Christ and Otherness

The scandals of the past and the obliteration of otherness that
have often been abetted by our confessions of Jesus as the Christ
demand that we reshape some contours of this central doctrine.
And yet, there are strands of the classic tradition that offer seeds
of hope, particularly those biblical themes that place the Other
at the center of our vision.

The alternative model that I will offer claims that the Other is
inherently unique, beautiful, and sacred, quite apart from any
perceived "need" the Other has for us or our particular religious commitments. Indeed, this Other emerges at the center
of both Christian confession and the life of discipleship. Difference, in other words, is not so much a "problem" of late
modernity, but intrinsic to the dynamic of Christian faith. One
way of recapturing this sacredness and beauty of the Other is
by a reexamination of what I am calling the "Emptying Christ."
My attempt in the following constructive theological chapters
will be to grapple with two specific claims Christians have made
about the person of Jesus Christ—he is both the *Incarnate One*
and the *Risen One*—and to examine how these claims affect
Christian discipleship in a world of religious difference. An
exploration of kenotic themes with regard to incarnation and

resurrection, as we will see, results in the de-centering of the autonomous, imperial self that views otherness as a problem. The Emptying Christ becomes, then, not the One who is proclaimed at the expense of others, but the One who unveils the beauty, detail, and difference of each concrete Other. Such confession, I will argue, amounts to a more faithful witness to the One who proclaimed much on behalf of others and little on behalf of himself.

CHAPTER II

THE INCARNATE, EMPTYING CHRIST

H AVING SURVEYED a historical spectrum of Christian responses to the question of otherness, it is time to offer an alternative christological approach. Two of Christianity's more shocking affirmations, it seems, are the proclamations of Jesus Christ as the Incarnate One and the Risen One. Traditionally, these claims have served at a minimum to distinguish Christianity from all other religions, and in certain cases even to demonstrate Christianity's "superiority" over others. The danger of triumphalism—the vaunting of the Christian self at the expense of the religious Other—lingers on the fringes of each of these convictions. My approach upholds the uniqueness of these core affirmations, but by bringing a much neglected aspect to the fore: a whispered presence of *emptying* surrounds these claims, at least as articulated in the New Testament. Jesus Christ, the Incarnate and Risen One, resists the all-encompassing and triumphal names we would heap on him precisely because he is the Emptying One. Two of the most significant articulations of this theme are present in the Christ-hymn of Philippians and in Mark's narration of the empty tomb.

In this chapter, I will advance an understanding of incarnation along the lines of kenosis (self-emptying), an argument that will reach its culmination in chapter 3. The image of kenosis is particularly relevant because it addresses the two relational issues central to Christology: the divine-human relation and the interhuman relation. Both relations, I would argue, are indispensable for making sense of any incarnational claim. Because this profession of the Emptying Christ hearkens to the invitation of the religious Other, moreover, it has the potential to fling Christians out of their own comfortable orbits and familiar categories.

The scope of this chapter is ambitious. In coming to grips with the question "What might it mean for Christians to proclaim the Incarnate One as the Emptying One?" I have posed two major tasks: (1) to examine the biblical roots and dangers of the kenotic image, because this examination will help guard against careless exploitation of such imagery; and (2) to assess two nineteenth-century understandings of this image (Gottfried Thomasius's and G. W. F. Hegel's), appreciating the strengths and the shortcomings of their differing appropriations of kenosis. We take up these tasks because a *historical* exploration of kenoticism will enable us to learn from our past, that we might better articulate the Emptying Christ with eyes and ears attuned to those others in our midst.

DANGERS OF KENOTIC IMAGERY

Because the image of emptying, or kenosis, is nothing less than a dangerous image, we must address these dangers from the outset. The theme of *self-emptying* has been used in our patriarchal context as fodder for the obliteration of the selfhood of women and marginalized men. Those suffering on the periphery have too often been encouraged in Christendom to give away all they have, until there is no self left to give. Certainly, appropriating this theme of kenosis in a responsible manner is a difficult task. If the present study were to suggest that self-sacrifice is the most important Christian "virtue" and offer it as normative for all people in all contexts, I would simply be perpetuating the image's sordid underside.[1] What is different about this project, I would venture, is that I will be using the image within a *relational* understanding of God, the world, and the interhuman. The problem with most traditional appropriations of kenotic

---

1. As Elisabeth Schüssler Fiorenza notes, "By ritualizing the suffering and death of Jesus and by calling the powerless in society and church to imitate Jesus' perfect obedience and self-sacrifice, Christian ministry and theology do not interrupt but continue to foster the circle of violence engendered by kyriarchal social and ecclesial structures as well as by cultural and political discourses" (*Jesus: Miriam's Child, Sophia's Prophet* [New York: Continuum, 1994], 106).

imagery is that they are not balanced by prophetic critique of those structures that engender meaningless suffering. Unless images of suffering, self-sacrifice, and emptying are accompanied by the denunciation of injustice, the image of emptying becomes simply a coping mechanism in contexts of oppression and not a prophetic critique of existing oppressions. Images of self-emptying, in other words, must be accompanied by images of *return*, whether one is talking about Christ, the world, or human beings in community.[2]

Our christological reflections, if they are to avoid this ominous legacy of abuse and overemphasis upon self-sacrifice, must take place within contexts that promote human flourishing, so that human beings might have life abundantly in God's world (cf. John 10:10). The approach of Paul Knitter's recent work becomes appropriate here. For it is not simply human flourishing that our contemporary context demands, but the vitality of the entire planet.[3] There is no better example of Martin Luther King Jr.'s dictum that injustice anywhere is a threat to justice everywhere than the biosphere itself, for the wounds of one thin strand invariably magnify themselves and scar all aspects of planetary life. One of our theological tasks, then, is to discern those strata in our tradition (and there are countless ones) that better enable the flourishing of all, that speak on behalf of life. We are called to study those traditions, know them well, and creatively reconfigure them in ways that might enhance our understanding of ecological and theological interrelationship today.

The following rearticulation of kenosis embraces reciprocity and self-affirmation. My approach, moreover, takes both *relationality* and *otherness* utterly seriously, having much in common with those voices (particularly process and feminist theologians) that advocate a wider, social understanding of the human being, the world, and God. Kenosis, in my articulation of it, is not a

---

2. I would also suggest that the imagery of kenosis is appropriate for Christians of the First World. Since the Western consumerist culture encourages its denizens to assert the self at the expense of others and the planet itself, is it not high time for Westerners to consider emptying that self, so that others may live?

3. Paul Knitter suggests "eco-human well-being" as a criterion for religious truth in *One Earth, Many Religions* (Maryknoll, N.Y.: Orbis, 1995), 118–35.

one-way street leading to self-abnegation, but a dynamic process of efflux and return, self-giving and self-affirmation.

One other item merits at least passing attention. I could have selected a more innocuous image for this christological study. Several other images, both scriptural and theological, might have trod upon fewer toes. But I suspect that these more innocuous images[4] have less "staying power," that they have less potential for the prophetic critique that our contemporary context demands. Times of crisis, times of challenge and injustice such as ours, require more than quiet, placid, unoffending images. They demand images that have the power to move and transform human understanding and practice. But I am also convinced that the most powerful images are the most dangerous; it is precisely for this reason that we need to be extremely careful with them. Whether the kenotic image is used on behalf of human flourishing, or instead becomes an oppressive tool of the powerful few, corresponds directly to the reflection and critique we bring to bear upon it.[5]

A BIBLICAL IMAGE OF KENOSIS

Let the same mind be in you that was in Christ Jesus,
who, though he was in the form of God,
did not regard equality with God
as something to be exploited,
but emptied himself,
taking the form of a slave,
being born in human likeness.
And being found in human form,
he humbled himself
and became obedient to the point of death—
even death on a cross.
Therefore God also highly exalted him

---

4. "Shepherd" might be one example.
5. Paul Tillich notes that one of the tasks of theology is to warn against the dangerous appropriation of religious symbols: "Theology can point out the religious dangers and the theological errors which follow from the use of certain symbols" (*Systematic Theology*, vol. 1 [Chicago: University of Chicago Press, 1951], 240). Certainly, this continues to be part of the theological task today.

and gave him the name
that is above every name,
so that at the name of Jesus
every knee should bend,
in heaven and on earth and under the earth,
and that every tongue should confess
that Jesus Christ is Lord,
to the glory of God the Father. (Phil. 2:5–11)[6]

Perhaps no other segment of Paul's correspondence has gar-
nered as much attention as this lofty and familiar Christ-hymn.
A rich and ambiguous passage, the hymn addresses the issue
of Jesus Christ's identity, but does so by multiplying questions
and by courting the danger of Christian triumphalism. What
does the verb "to empty" (*kenoun*) mean? Its use is rare in other
Pauline literature. Who does the hymn claim Jesus Christ is?
The divine and human imagery are fluid in reference to him.
Does the kenosis point to a preexistent Logos, divine Wisdom,
or to the humble pattern of Jesus of Nazareth, the "suffering
servant"?

The hymn itself may be one of the oldest liturgical formulations in the entire New Testament, antedating the ministry of
Paul and used in settings of early Christian worship.[7] If such dat-
ing is accurate, the familiar hymn represents some of the most
ancient christological material of the entire Christian tradition.
As we analyze this passage, then, we must recognize it as a *hymn,*
as language of praise, a language that is of a different order and
function than theological or homiletical language. Its purpose
is not primarily to express conceptual rigor and clarity, but to
give voice to praise and the conviction of God's presence in
Christ. The risk, then, in appropriating the hymn's image for
theological purposes is that we might shatter its evocative and
stirring poetry. Karl-Josef Kuschel's words serve as a persistent

---

6. This and all subsequent biblical quotations are taken from the New Revised
Standard Version, unless otherwise noted.
7. The indications that this Christ-hymn was used in liturgical settings are abundant. Note particularly the term "bend," which likely was a signal for participants
in worship to genuflect.

reminder of this danger: "For the poetic language of the text is not provisional theological language, nor a lower form of theological reflection. It has not arisen from the naive feelings of an enthusiastic poet which must now be brought down to the solid ground of theological sobriety by means of philosophical and conceptual reflection. Legitimate though conceptual theological and philosophical reflection may be, it must be relative to this poem, and not vice versa."[8] In short, to ignore the poetry is to do violence to the text.

Having issued this warning, however, we may appropriately ask theological questions of the hymn. The language of liturgy is by no means immune to examination and criticism, as recent controversies surrounding the use of gendered language with reference to God, Christ, and Spirit certainly suggest. The words we use to praise and proclaim God shape, for good or ill, our understanding of that God. It is therefore germane, if not indispensable, to examine the language of the Philippians hymn and make some tentative theological judgments of it.

One problem we encounter in the Philippians passage is that its central image is unique in the Pauline corpus. Only five times in the entire New Testament is the verb *kenoun* used; all of these uses occur in the undisputed letters of Paul, but in the other four instances the verb is used not in the sense of self-emptying, but in terms of something else (the cross, boasting, faith) being deprived of its effect. The word in these other instances is used to describe something other than a human or divine agent. What we have in the Philippians Christ-hymn, then, is a unique instance of an extremely rare New Testament expression. Indeed, as Kuschel notes, the use of self-emptying is unique in the entire body of contemporary Greek literature.[9]

Needless to say, our guideposts for interpretation here are relatively obscure, since we cannot summon a set of corresponding usages. Walter Bauer's concise entry gives two enigmatic phrases to define *kenoun*: to empty oneself, and to divest oneself of one's

8. Karl-Josef Kuschel, *Born before All Time? The Dispute over Christ's Origin*, trans. John Bowden (New York: Crossroad, 1992), 259–60.
9. Ibid., 253.

privileges.[10] The possibilities for how one ascribes this definition to Christ certainly are endless. As one surveys the wealth
of exegetical literature that grapples with the hymn, however,
four possibilities appear most prominent: the self-emptying describes (1) a mythical divine descent-ascent pattern that relies
heavily upon Gnostic redeemer myths; (2) the pattern of Jesus'
earthly ministry, leading up to his crucifixion and resurrection;
(3) the coming of divine Wisdom to creation; and (4) a loose
combination of these three themes, pivoting upon the image of
Christ crucified. Though each interpretation has held sway at
various periods in theological history, my conviction is that the
last option offers the best explanation of this puzzling and rich
liturgical hymn.

A "High" Christology of Descent and Ascent

Several strands of New Testament literature give much weight to
the theme of Christ's preexistence (John, Hebrews, First Peter,
and Ephesians—all of which appear chronologically after Paul),
but in terms of Paul's undisputed correspondence, no explicit
formulation of the preexistent Christ appears. Preexistence is
perhaps assumed by Paul, but in relation to his kerygmatic message, it appears unimportant in its own right. Regardless of
whether Paul explicitly emphasized it, the hymn does at least
suggest the question of preexistence and *divine* kenosis.
    The crux of the early formulation of Christ's preexistence is
straightforward: Jesus Christ is the Redeeming One sent directly
from God, whose existence antedates his appearance on earth.
This earthly appearance is described in terms of a descent,
a ministry of teaching, a humiliating execution, and a subsequent vindication through resurrection and return (ascent) to
the Father. Although it is obvious that such a prototheological
explanation of the "Christ-event" could occur only after the
community's "experience" of the Risen Lord, the rapidity with
which such formulation occurred is truly striking. If we accept
Martin Hengel's judgment that the Philippians hymn represents

---

10. Walter Bauer, *A Greek-English Lexicon of the New Testament*, trans. William F.
Arndt and F. Wilbur Gingrich (Chicago: University of Chicago Press, 1979), 428.

an early view of Christ's preexistence, then it appears that a rudimentary understanding of Christ's preexistence was in place within twenty years after Jesus' death.[11]

Those who would claim the Philippians text as evidence for an early belief in Christ's preexistence cite the puzzling phrases "he was in the form of God" and "being born in human likeness," which imply Christ's proximity to God and which might be understood in terms of a divine descent. Ernst Käsemann has noted the hymn's probable incorporation and modification of a Gnostic redeemer myth, which views the redeeming Christ as cosmocrator and inaugurator of a new eon.[12] Käsemann's and others' studies indicate that the hymn ties together the Christ-event and the inauguration of God's reign. Jesus Christ is the One sent by God, and this connection intimates a *divine* kenosis.

Although there is abundant evidence for interpreting the hymn's Christology in terms of a descending-ascending, preexistent redeemer figure, the hymn is not exhausted by such an approach. The hymn evokes the image of *divine* self-emptying, but also offers a depiction of human self-emptying. Although the hymn connects Christ's universal significance with the reign of God, it does not resemble the later, more developed formulations of preexistence found in John, Hebrews, and Ephesians. The weight of these contextual and chronological clues, in other words, suggests that the divine Redeemer or a "high Christology" is not the only implication of self-emptying.

A "Low" Christology of the Suffering Servant

A second interpretation of the Christ-hymn offers a departure from the redeemer myth we have just discussed. Instead of adopting the descent-ascent motif, this interpretation employs the figure of Adam as a foil to Christ and glimpses parallels between the kenosis pattern and the "suffering servant" images

---

11. Martin Hengel, *Studies in Early Christology* (Edinburgh: T. & T. Clark, 1995), 383. Even if we reject the widely accepted premise that the Philippians text represents a formulation of Christ's preexistence, the indisputable references to it in Hebrews, Ephesians, and John imply that such prototheological formulation was in place within the first fifty years of the first Christian century.

12. See Ernst Käsemann, "Kritische Analyse von Phil. 2,5–11," in *Exegetische Versuche und Besinningen*, vol. 1 (Göttingen: Vandenhoeck & Ruprecht, 1960), 51–95.

of second Isaiah.[13] Adam is the one who "grasped" for equality with God by reaching for the tree of knowledge; Christ is the one who refuses equality with God as a thing to be "grasped" (RSV). After Adam transgresses, his life is relegated to toiling as a slave, while Jesus of his own volition takes the "form of a slave." Adam is the man who is humbled before God after his transgression, while it is Christ who "humbles himself." While Adam remains disobedient unto the point of death, it is Christ who remains "obedient" even to death on a cross. At every step of the hymn's procession, then, there appears a deliberate contrast between Adam, the disobedient, grasping, humbled son, and Jesus, the obedient one who refuses to grasp and humbles *himself.* This foil reaches its climax at the hymn's conclusion: whereas Adam is the banished and humiliated one, God highly exalts Jesus Christ, who is given the "name that is above every name." Interpreting the hymn along these lines results in a distinct Christology: an anthropological emphasis or a "Christology from below" that highlights the pattern of Jesus' life and ministry.[14]

This "low" christological interpretation gains further credence when we compare the hymn with the "suffering servant" motif in Second Isaiah. The parallels between the "servant" of Second Isaiah and the kenotic hymn are certainly striking: Jesus takes the form of a slave, like the servant who "had no form or majesty that we should look at him" (Isa. 53:2). Both are described as "exalted" (Isa. 52:13, Phil. 2:9) and give cause for the nations to acknowledge them. Isaiah describes this wider significance as startling the nations, shutting kings' mouths (Isa. 52:15), while the Christ-hymn depicts this universal import with "every tongue" confessing Christ as Lord (Phil. 2:11). The most striking parallel, however, is their respective descriptions of death. The servant song notes that the servant "poured out himself to death" (Isa. 53:12), a phrase evocative of the

---

13. Some notable exponents of this view include J. Harvey, C. H. Talbert, and J. M. Furness. See an excellent bibliography in Kuschel, *Born before All Time?* 594–96.

14. Eugene TeSelle, after surveying several key passages in Paul's authentic correspondence, emerges with a similar conclusion: "The significance of Jesus lies principally in his renewed humanity." For Paul, at least, Jesus Christ is the "new man." See *Christ in Context* (Philadelphia: Fortress, 1975), 24.

Christ-hymn's self-emptying. For both songs, the focus on death is unmistakable, providing the pivot upon which the song turns for Paul ("even death on a cross") and the epitomization of the servant's suffering for Isaiah.

This alternative approach views the Christ-hymn as a liturgical interpretation of Jesus' earthly life: his service, ministry, and ultimate humiliation in death upon a cross. The hymnist, in other words, paints the significance of that life and the subsequent experience of Christ's resurrection by using the material that was closest at hand—the literature of the Hebrew Bible or the Septuagint. Although the hymn seems to focus chiefly upon the pattern of the earthly Jesus' ministry, some enigmatic phrases (such as "form of God") at the very least suggest preexistence as a possibility. To claim that the hymnist adopted the Gnostic redeemer myth is certainly overstating the case, but to claim that a nascent conception of *divine* emptying was operative within the hymn is certainly probable. Such is the judgment of Kuschel, who writes, "Regardless of the nuance of meaning that one decides for, *en morphe theou* cannot just refer to the earthly Jesus, but must imply some kind of pre-existent mode of being of Christ with God."[15] The hymn, indeed, highlights the tension between viewing Jesus Christ primarily as a divine redeemer or as a "renewed man" who humbles himself. Both are implied by its evocative poetry.

Jesus Christ: The Wisdom of God

A third and often overlooked interpretation of the Christ-hymn is particularly illuminating. Glimpsing the hymn more in continuity with the Jewish wisdom tradition than Gnostic formulations of a heavenly redeemer, this approach claims that the hymn portrays the incarnation, humiliation, and exaltation of Sophia. Jesus Christ, according to this tack, is the embodiment or incarnation of God's wisdom. Several prominent voices have suggested this avenue of interpretation, including Helmut Koester, who cites the Philippians hymn as the oldest extant

---

15. Kuschel, *Born before All Time?* 256.

Christian song to Sophia,[16] and Dieter Georgi, who claims that the Christ-hymn was grafted on to an earlier Jewish hymn, having parallels with Wisdom of Solomon 3–6.[17] The strengths and plausibility of this position are manifold: It glimpses the incarnation of Christ not only as an anthropological event, but also as a cosmic event. Some champions of this position note that the subject of the hymn is omitted and begins somewhat puzzlingly: "who, though he was in the form of God...." The omission is significant, because the hymn in its original form addressed Sophia. The Jewish Christian community came to identify the *figura* of Jesus with God's wisdom, and eventually the two began to be expressed in the same breath. The nascent church, in short, proclaimed Jesus Christ as the incarnation of the divine Wisdom, the coming of Sophia to creation.

If such an interpretation is correct, the hymn is remarkable in its interweaving of the interhuman and divine-human concerns. Jesus Christ, according to the hymn, is not only a renewed human being, but the One who exhibits conformity with God. The early Jewish Christians made sense of this intersection of the human and divine not by importing a Gnostic redeemer myth, but by drawing on the resonant chords within their own tradition. A "wisdom Christology" is a highly plausible background for the image of kenosis; nonetheless, its trajectories were rapidly suppressed and eclipsed, perhaps in the name of latent patriarchy,[18] perhaps in the name of the Gentile mission.[19] At the very least, the image of Sophia is submerged even by the

16. Helmut Koester, "The Structure and Criteria of Early Christian Beliefs," in *Trajectories through Early Christianity*, ed. James M. Robinson and Helmut Koester (Philadelphia: Fortress, 1971), 221.

17. Dieter Georgi, "Der Vorpaulinische Hymnus Phil 2,6–11," in *Zeit und Geschichte*, ed. Erich Dinkler (Tübingen: J. C. B. Mohr, 1964), 263–93, and the excellent summary by Jack Sanders, *The New Testament Christological Hymns* (Cambridge: Cambridge University Press, 1971), 70–74.

18. See the work of Elisabeth Schüssler Fiorenza in this regard, particularly *In Memory of Her* (New York: Crossroad, 1983), and *Jesus: Miriam's Child, Sophia's Prophet.* I will be drawing on Schüssler Fiorenza's work and articulation of wisdom in the subsequent chapter on Christ's resurrection.

19. See James M. Robinson, "Very Goddess and Very Man: Jesus' Better Self," in *Encountering Jesus*, ed. Stephen T. Davis (Atlanta: John Knox, 1988), 111–40. Robinson argues that early "Christology seems to have grown most rapidly in the exuberance (inspiration) of hymnic ecstasy and in this ecstasy to have flown on the wings of Wisdom mythology" (pp. 115–16).

time Paul pens his letter to the Philippians, at which point we
can only dimly discern Wisdom's traces.

The Divine-Human and the Interhuman

Though the anthropological strain is most dominant in the
kenosis hymn, questions of Christ's preexistence and the presence of Wisdom simply will not go away. In rudimentary, poetic
form, the hymn addresses the two central questions of Christology: the divine-human relation (the possibility of incarnation
and the divine wisdom) and the interhuman relation (the pattern of Jesus' life and ministry among us). If the hymn suggests
that both ways of glimpsing Christ are essential, then the pivot
upon which this suggestion turns is the crucified Christ. For
the crucifixion is what reveals both the extent of the earthly
Jesus' self-emptying and the cause of his subsequent exaltation.
The phrase "even death on a cross" appears at the center of
the Christ-hymn, the focus of its literary structure.[20] Here is
where the divine-human question and the interhuman question intersect.[21] The focal point is neither a speculative theory
of incarnation nor an exclusive recitation of Jesus' earthly ministry in correlation with familiar Hebrew biblical themes, but
the meeting of these two concerns precisely at the juncture of
the cross.

Luke Johnson views this focus upon the cross as fully consistent with the earlier theme of kenosis: "The cross is the ultimate
symbol of self-emptying and of the obedience that is faith. The
hymn has moved downward, in 'dispossession.'"[22] Christ's kenosis is nowhere more fully revealed and clarified than in his
crucifixion. The self-emptying of the hymn consists not primarily in a giving up of a divine mode of being, but in the radical

---

20. Some have argued that this phrase is likely the work of Paul's hand, reflecting
his own cruciform concern. If this assessment is correct, it adds further weight to the
idea that for Paul, the central answer to the question "Who is Christ?" was revealed
in the cross.

21. Kuschel has argued that the cross forms the perspective from which this
hymn is recited: "There can be no doubt that at the heart of this hymn lies the
experience of the crucified Jesus Christ, who has been exalted and thus is present
through God's Spirit as Kyrios" (*Born before All Time?* 260).

22. Luke T. Johnson, *The Writings of the New Testament* (Philadelphia: Fortress,
1986), 344.

event of the cross—the scandalous culmination of Jesus' life and ministry. The crucifixion is both the consequence of Christ's self-emptying and the most prominent example of that kenosis. It is because Christ is the crucified One that he is glimpsed as one who "empties himself" on behalf of others and who reveals himself as sent from God. If the hymn exposes one paradox in its proto-Christology, it is that no exaltation is possible without humbling; no fulfillment is possible without emptying.

Kenosis and Discipleship

The final critical aspect to note about Paul's use of the kenosis hymn is that it occurs embedded within much lengthier sections that address ethics and the Christian life. Paul quotes the hymn with the specific intent of informing the life of discipleship, not of exhaustively instructing his readers in matters of Christology. Before reciting the Christ-hymn, Paul urges the congregation at Philippi to "be of the same mind . . . [to] do nothing from selfish ambition or conceit, but in humility [to] regard others as better than yourselves" (2:2–3). Hardly an exhortation of abject self-denial, Paul's letter calls for the subordination of self-interest to the well-being of the wider community. Luke Johnson recognizes how Paul's exhortation has often been misinterpreted as the surrender of self: "This is a delicate statement easily corrupted. What does Paul mean? He does not call for a denial of self or personal projects. He calls for a functional 'reckoning' that relativizes individual interests for the sake of others."[23] Such is the unity that Paul advocates for the Philippian community: it should be of one mind in the consideration and service of one another.

The pattern of Christ's self-emptying, then, is not Paul's exercise in dogmatic theology. Though the question "Who is Jesus Christ?" certainly is lurking behind the hymn, it is not the sole question that the hymn addresses. The hymn also addresses the wider questions "How are we to live?" and "How are we to be a church?" These questions emerge once we recognize Paul's use of the hymn within the letter. Preceding the hymn with

---

23. Ibid., 343.

an exhortation on discipleship, Paul also follows it by noting exemplars of the faith (Timothy, Epaphroditus, and Paul himself) who embody the obedience that the hymn so eloquently expresses of Christ. Paul, in other words, moves from Christ to the community in the sections that follow the hymn: *his proto-Christology thus becomes a model for discipleship in the world.* As Martin Hengel notes, "The hymn occurs not in a context of dogmatic argumentation, but within ethical exhortations from the apostle.... The statements about humiliation and exaltation *have concrete application in life.*"[24] If one is to follow Christ, one must submit oneself to a circle wider than the self, relativize one's own privilege for the sake of others, live in community on behalf of others, and—for Paul at least—be willing to suffer precisely because one has emptied oneself of privilege.

Kenosis and Other New Testament Portrayals of Christ

Our exegesis of the Philippians Christ-hymn thus far has been carried out in comparative isolation from other New Testament depictions of Jesus Christ. We have begun our textual exploration narrowly, however, for specific reasons. Coming to grips with this most famous articulation of Christ's self-emptying requires that we isolate it from other theological currents, both current and ancient. To do justice to the text, we must discern as nearly as possible what it meant for Paul and his audience in their contexts. As our study has suggested so far, the profession of the Emptying Christ bound together both the christological question (who is Jesus Christ?) and the discipleship question (what does it mean to follow Christ?).

Our study, however, will not rest in this isolated consideration of Paul and his audience alone. We are exploring the imagery of kenosis not as a biblical artifact, but as a potential model for contemporary Christology. Because this broader application is part of our goal, we must also address, albeit briefly, other New Testament portrayals of Jesus. Is the kenotic theme a relatively minor chord in the New Testament witness, a strand that is dampened by the booming voices that proclaim Jesus

---

24. Hengel, *Studies*, 380 (emphasis mine).

Christ as king and cosmocrator? Indeed, many readers at this point may be wondering whether this treatment of the Emptying Christ has any consonance with the voices of the writers of the Synoptic Gospels, let alone other Pauline literature.

As we turn to these other witnesses, we should note that no singular New Testament "Christology" exists. What is apparent, rather, as one surveys its varied literature of Gospels, letters, and apocalypse is an abundance of Christologies, some complementary, some dissonant with one another. This prominent and at times bewildering juxtaposition of images and Christologies throughout the New Testament suggests that no single portrayal is able to offer an adequate description of the One from Nazareth. Rather, recognition of Jesus as the Christ evokes a multiplicity of voices and a constellation of images. Total harmonization between them all is neither possible nor desirable, for the words we use will never exhaust the images or meanings of the One whom we proclaim.

Despite this inability to harmonize the plethora of christological images, I would suggest that kenoticism is something more than an isolated, unique New Testament model. Indeed, as I mentioned at the outset of this chapter, a whispered presence of emptying surrounds several prominent biblical portrayals of Jesus, evident in the Synoptic Gospels, Johannine literature, and the Pauline letters. The Christ who empties himself on behalf of others is not a minor chord among several louder strains, but a resonant theme that echoes throughout several variations.

The Synoptic Gospels are nearly universal in their depiction of Jesus as the One who has emptied himself of any divine privilege. Jesus of Nazareth, for Mark, is not a *theios aner* (Godman) who travels the earth possessed of power and glory, but an itinerant who teaches in parables, proclaims the reign of God, and heals others. The narration of the "messianic secret," moreover, further underscores that for Mark, Jesus is the One who empties himself of privilege. Anything that would elevate Jesus above others is the very thing that Jesus rejects. Though the reader gains glimmerings of Jesus' identity as the Son of God, full recognition of this identity by another human being is evoked only at his crucifixion, where the consummate outsider, the centurion, recognizes Jesus as the Son of God (Mark 15:39). Throughout the rest of the Gospel, however, this is the very theme that is kept hidden. For Mark, the One who reveals himself as God's son is present not in clouds of glory, but as the One who exists with others, in a very human figure who relinquishes all pretensions of privilege, heals the sick, and teaches of God's imminent reign.

In a similar vein, the Gospel of Luke draws extensively upon themes of humiliation/exaltation and the relinquishing of privilege on behalf of others. Jesus of Nazareth is the One who pays particular attention to the outcasts, the scorned, and the oppressed. For Luke, this theme is announced even prior to Jesus' birth, in Mary's hymn of praise: "He has brought down the powerful from their thrones, and lifted up the lowly; he has filled the hungry with good things, and sent the rich away empty" (Luke 1:52–53). As Jesus embarks upon his ministry, this trajectory continues: "[The Lord] has sent me to proclaim release to the captives and recovery of sight to the blind, to let the oppressed go free" (Luke 4:18b). Throughout his narrative, Luke portrays Jesus' ministry in terms of the *inversion* of the accepted state of affairs. Those who have much will lose much, while those who lack will be fulfilled.[25] As the inaugurator of this scheme of redemption, Jesus is the One who has emptied himself of privilege "to bring good news to the poor" (Luke 4:18a).

The passion narratives of each Gospel reveal the extent to which Jesus of Nazareth has surrendered anything that would exalt him over others. For each of the Gospel writers, Jesus lives unto death his ministry of reconciliation and proclamation of release to the captives. The passion narratives do not depict the triumph of a God-man, but in somber and graphic detail describe the last days of a humiliated teacher. In the end, the One who has emptied himself on behalf of others is emptied of his

---

25. Luke's account Sermon on the Plain captures the heart of this theme of inversion and self-emptying. "Blessed are you who are poor, for yours is the kingdom of God. Blessed are you who are hungry now, for you will be filled.... But woe to you who are rich, for you have received your consolation. Woe to you who are full now, for you will be hungry"(6:20–21, 24–25).

own life on a cross. Even the Gospel of John, which is often resistant to the theme of Christ's self-emptying, bears witness to this humiliation.[26] Indeed, John offers perhaps the most compelling image of Jesus as servant in the entire Gospel literature: Jesus washing his disciples' feet as they share their last meal together (John 13:1–20). During his final hours, Jesus is not the master who is served, but the servant who reaches out to others. This inversion of roles reaches its culmination as John records Jesus' last words from the cross. By claiming, "It is finished" (John 19:30), the Johannine Jesus gasps the final breath of a servant's life.[27]

The theme of Christ's self-emptying is also unmistakable throughout the Pauline correspondence. Though the details of Jesus' life and ministry seem of little significance to Paul (especially when compared with the Gospels), he highlights the theme of emptying or inversion of privilege as central to the lordship of Jesus Christ. In the second letter to the Corinthians he notes, "For you know the generous act of our Lord Jesus Christ, that though he was rich, yet for your sakes he became poor, so that by his poverty you might become rich" (2 Cor. 8:9). For Paul, the abiding and sustaining power of the Risen Lord is connected precisely to Christ's setting aside of privilege, so that all might participate in the new life in him. It is because Christ has emptied himself that all are saved through him.[28]

---

26. John's Gospel verges on a *theios aner* depiction of Jesus. Portrayed less as a humble servant and more as the incarnate Logos, the Johannine Jesus refers at least as often to himself (the famous "I am" sayings) as to others. The focus of the narrative has shifted from the Synoptists' thematization of God's reign to John's depiction of Jesus' person, the One who was in the beginning with God. In many instances the Johannine Jesus appears less as a self-emptying servant and more as a triumphal, all-knowing divine man.

27. Notice that, for John, the image of Jesus as servant does not amount to masochistic sacrifice. It is precisely because Jesus has much as the incarnate Logos that he is able to "empty himself" on behalf of others. The One who serves, in John's narrative, is not the One who has obliterated himself, but the One who is infinitely rich as the wisdom of God.

28. The self-emptying pattern of the Risen Lord, for Paul, is significant not only in terms of soteriology and Christology, but also in terms of the life of discipleship. Descriptions and images of Christ are thus connected invariably to Paul's exhortations on behalf of the Christian life. Christological imagery has practical consequences in the most mundane of human events. We have already made this connection clear in our exposition of the Philippians Christ-hymn, and it is present in Romans and

As this brief survey has suggested, the theme of self-emptying is hardly unique to the Philippians Christ-hymn. Broadly apparent throughout the Synoptic Gospels, it is evident in John's narration of Jesus' last days, interwoven throughout Paul's letters, and present to a lesser extent in First Peter and Hebrews,[29] the Emptying Christ presents himself as both One who saves and One who unveils a distinct pattern of life on behalf of others. The Philippians Christ-hymn, then, offers in vivid poetry a christological theme that wends its way throughout the New Testament witness. The Emptying Christ is present not simply in an isolated expression of praise, but presents itself in whispered form wherever Christ's servanthood and being on behalf of the Other are stressed.

The Emerging Image of Christ

Most prominent in this proto-Christology are the following: First, the hymn claims that both the divine-human and the inter-human relations are fundamental to asking the question "Who is Jesus Christ?" It addresses the former by proclaiming Christ as being "in the form of God," and addresses the latter by noting Christ's obedience, his being-on-behalf-of-others, which is continued even to his ignominious death upon the cross. Christ is the locus, the prime example, of God's intimate relation to the world and our own intimate relation to each other.

Galatians as well: "Each of us must please our neighbor for the good purpose of building up the neighbor. For Christ did not please himself" (Rom. 15:2–3); "Bear one another's burdens, and in this way you will fulfill the law of Christ" (Gal. 6:2). For Paul, Jesus Christ is not a triumphal figure who "founds" the church, but a servant who saves precisely because he has emptied himself, a servant who presents a new way of being in the world on behalf of both the neighbor and the stranger.

29. The letter to the Hebrews stresses the *mediatorship* of Christ, with particular emphasis upon the efficaciousness of the "priest's" sacrifice (Hebrews 10) and the *humanity* of Jesus, who suffers even unto death (Heb. 2:9). In First Peter, however, this theme of humiliation takes on some more scandalous hues, as slaves are urged, "Accept the authority of your masters with deference, not only those who are kind and gentle but also those who are harsh. For it is a credit to you if, being aware of God, you endure pain while suffering unjustly...because Christ also suffered for you, leaving you an example, so that you should follow in his steps" (1 Pet. 2:18–19, 21). In this instance the example of Christ's sacrifice is extended to those who possess no privilege whatsoever. Those who possess nothing are encouraged to submit themselves to further humiliation. Certainly, this is the kind of abuse against which our contemporary articulation of kenosis must speak.

Second, the question "Who is Jesus Christ?" is asked not within an abstract sphere of contemplation about Christ's relationship to God apart from the world, but in direct involvement with concrete others. Paul approaches the question of Christology in continuity with the life of discipleship, so that *confessing* Christ as the One sent from God becomes inextricably bound to *following* Christ. In making this confession, moreover, Christians encounter the Other not as stranger, convert, or adversary, but as a neighbor who invites us to listen, pay attention, and respect. Throughout the New Testament witness, the Other emerges at the center of the christological question. Recently, it has become somewhat in vogue to privilege the "practical" questions of theology over the "speculative" ones. Countless voices have called for a reordering of theological priorities, from revisionists to liberationists, from feminist theologians to African American theologians, from narrativists to those interested in interreligious dialogue.

The priority of "praxis" has emerged as a dominant concern in the late twentieth century. Gordon Kaufman summarizes these concerns in his recent constructive work: "The central question for theology is not merely, or even preeminently, who or what God is . . . and what the central problems of human existence are. It is not primarily a speculative question, a problem of knowledge, at all. Most fundamentally it is a *practical* question: How are we to live?"[30] I would suggest that this brief exegetical study of the kenosis hymn implies that the questions of knowledge and praxis are more deeply interrelated than even revisionists such as Kaufman would have us believe. The issue is not, I would venture, that of giving priority to praxis over knowledge, but that of exposing their multifarious connections. If this exegetical study of the Emptying Christ has shown us anything, it has surely shown that the speculative question "Who is Christ?" and the practical question "How are we to be disciples?" are profoundly intertwined.

What this study has unveiled, in other words, is the *primacy of*

---

30. Gordon Kaufman, *In Face of Mystery* (Cambridge: Harvard University Press, 1993), 15.

relation in Christian confession and the life of discipleship. The biblical witness claims in loud voice that interrelation—between God, Christ, and human beings—is writ large upon the cosmic tapestry. None of these relationships, moreover, can be proclaimed as if they were divorced from the interhuman sphere. The confession of Jesus as the Christ is bound up with Christian recognition (or in its distortion, rejection) of the Other. The Philippians Christ-hymn is helpful in highlighting these interrelationships, although it is lacking in its specification of them. Obviously, this second-order task is not its primary purpose, for the hymn seeks to give voice to praise. One task of theology is to spell out these relationships, to paint in broader terms what the New Testament imagery suggests. What characterizes the relationships of the incarnational claim of God in Christ? How does this recognition of relation affect those who proclaim it? We now turn our attention to these questions.

THEOLOGICAL UNDERSTANDINGS OF KENOSIS

Throughout the life of the church, exegetical studies rarely rest in themselves. The primary movement of the biblical text, in this sense, is its extension to the world. One task of theology, then, is to demonstrate appropriate application of biblical texts and the ways in which they might offer lenses of description for the world we inhabit. Our task now is to move from an analysis of the biblical text to a more specifically theological vision of the kenotic Christ. Before I offer my own version of a kenotic theology of incarnation, however, we must listen briefly to some prominent voices of the nineteenth-century church, Gottfried Thomasius and G. W. F. Hegel. We hearken to their work not solely out of antiquarian interest, or simply because they both employed the theme of kenosis, but because we acknowledge that contemporary reflection, like exegesis, cannot rest in itself. Theology can never begin de novo, but continually draws upon the wisdom of previous voices, learning from their mistakes and acknowledging their shortcomings. In order to contribute our own voices to the theological conversation, we must also listen to others. With this centuries-old conversation

in mind, then, we turn to Thomasius's incarnational kenoticism
and Hegel's image of God's self-divestment. For Thomasius,
the resolution of the christological question results in rigid
adherence to Chalcedon, while for Hegel, it amounts to a radical reformulation of the relational God. Though the writings
of both men have their limitations for present-day theological
reflection, they both provide germs of thought for a contemporary articulation of kenosis. We read them in the hope that their
work might help us move from a poetic description of Christ (a
New Testament hymn) to a more comprehensive theological
exposition.

Thomasius's Attempt to Uphold Chalcedon

To plunge oneself into the writings of Gottfried Thomasius is
a fascinating and frustrating journey. By adopting a kenotic
view of Christ, Thomasius gave impetus to a short-lived movement in German Lutheran orthodoxy that sought to uphold
classical creedal statements about Christ in the face of contemporary crises of belief and coherence. The strengths of his
incarnational perspective are the depths in which it describes
the identification of God with humanity and vice versa. Christ,
for Thomasius, becomes the very image of this divine-human relationship. The beauty with which he paints this interrelation,
however, is rapidly eclipsed by his steadfast allegiance to the
metaphysics of the classical Christian creeds. In seeking to uphold classical orthodoxy, Thomasius offers us an arcane and
outmoded worldview, with the result that his Christology is
somewhat wooden in its slavish adherence to the categories of
Chalcedon.

A Relational, Kenotic Approach

Over the course of a hundred years Thomasius's work has almost become a forgotten strand in Christian history. If his
theology is read at all, it is usually as a historical artifact remote
from contemporary concerns. Nonetheless, Thomasius argues
persuasively for a *comprehensive* theory of incarnation in the second part of his seminal *Dogmatik*, which involves all of humanity.
His theory, moreover, is a provocative portrayal of a *relational*

God. For Thomasius, incarnation is not only the coming of God
to humanity, but the subsuming of humanity in God, an act that
affects and even changes God.

If there is a central drive to Thomasius's approach, it is to
uphold the classic creedal affirmation that Jesus Christ is "at
once complete in Godhead and complete in humanity, truly
God and truly human . . . recognized in two natures without con-
fusion, without change, without division, without separation."[31]
In explicating his position, Thomasius rejected the theory of
Schleiermacher and Bauer that the "human" Jesus was subject
to a gradual penetration of the divine. Jesus thus would be
viewed as a "deified man," but not as Emmanuel, "God with
us." Neither could Christ be viewed, according to Thomasius,
as an omniscient and omnipotent man. The incarnation was
not a Docetic disguise, for in proclaiming Christ as the Incarnate One, Thomasius claimed that one had to subject Christ
to all the limitations and restrictions of the human condition.
The pious picture of Jesus as God walking around on earth,
perfect in all respects, all-knowing and all-powerful, actually
dispelled Christian hope because it rendered Christ inhuman.
"The Christian's hope in faith is nothing if Christ is not man just
as much as he is God—divine-human person."[32] Christ cannot
redeem what he does not assume; if our depiction of incarnation undercuts Christ's authentic humanity, the very ground of
redemption washes away.

Thomasius thus sought to avoid the danger of Docetism by
weaving together three themes: deity, humanity, and unity. Only
when these three chords are given equal accent can the confu-
sion of attributes and the bifurcation of Christ be avoided. From
the outset, however, Thomasius's approach is beset with difficulty. His writings trumpet the unequivocal affirmations of "true
God, true humanity," and delight in the paradoxes he seeks to
explain. He writes, "Christ is the personal unity of divine being

---

31. The Chalcedonian "definition," quoted in Peter C. Hodgson and Robert H.
King, eds., *Readings in Christian Theology* (Minneapolis: Fortress, 1985), 210.
32. Gottfried Thomasius, *God and Incarnation in Mid-Nineteenth Century German
Theology*, ed. Claude Welch (New York: Oxford University Press, 1965), 36.

and human kind, the man who is God."[33] There is little room for
nuance here. Either one affirms unambiguously Christ's deity,
humanity, and their intrinsic unity, or—in Thomasius's view—
one is piled onto a rather large heap of heretics.[34] Though such
statements gain nuance in his theoretical kenoticism, their very
simplicity seems to invite misunderstanding, Christomonism,
and even triumphalism. Jesus, in brief, becomes God, an un-
speakably "higher" Christology than even the orthodoxy of
Chalcedon.

Despite his shortcomings, Thomasius was able to offer a
powerful relational understanding of God and humanity. For
Thomasius, God and humanity do not stand against one another as strangers, but as capable of communion. "Man as
personal creature is related to God, receptive to divine communication, structured for living intercourse with God.... [This]
offers no hindrance even to the most intimate communion."[35]
Humanity, in other words, is continually open to the mystery of
God. Enacting the very best of the "Catholic analogical imagi-
nation,"[36] Thomasius portrays the profound interconnections,
the innate addressability of humanity with God. From the beginning, human beings are invited to be in communion with
God, which is none other than the *possibility* of incarnation.
God's communion with humankind, according to Thomasius,
reaches its apogee in the incarnation. God's desire and love for
the creature are so strong that God chooses to become one with
the creature, subject to all its limitations and conditions.

The Self-Limitation of God?

For Thomasius, the only way for the possibility of incarnation
to become *actual*, the only means by which the infinite can
be contained within the finite, is through the voluntary self-

---

33. Ibid., 59.
34. Thomasius writes, "Every representation which does not allow the confession,
'The man Jesus Christ is God,' contradicts our Christian consciousness" (ibid., 37).
A "higher" christological statement is scarcely imaginable!
35. Ibid., 40.
36. The phrase is from David Tracy. See his presidential address in *Proceedings of
the Catholic Theological Society of America* 32 (1977): 234–44.

limitation of the infinite. Here is where Thomasius's approach departs most dramatically from the classical theology of divine attributes. For in claiming that God limits Godself, Thomasius appears to question the theological position that upholds God as immutable and omnipotent.

The crux of Thomasius's kenotic approach is easily summarized: becoming incarnate in the person of Jesus of Nazareth, the Second Person of the Trinity, the "Son," voluntarily divests himself in order to be subject to the limitations and structures of human existence. In Thomasius's words, the incarnation "is certainly not a divesting of that which is essential to deity in order to be God, but it is a divesting of the *divine mode of being in favor of the humanly creaturely form of existence,* and *eo ipso* a renunciation of the divine glory."[37] The Son, in other words, "empties" himself of his glory to exist in and with humanity. As a result, humanity becomes part of the fiber of God's existence. The claim "God with us" is nothing less than the profoundest interpenetration of humanity by divinity, God's participation in the life and limitations of the creature.[38]

The Son's divestment of his glory, his voluntary self-limitation in becoming incarnate, is echoed by the Incarnate One's humiliation during his earthly life. Thomasius proposes a twofold understanding of the divine kenosis: first, the self-limitation of the *discarnate Logos;* second, the kenosis of the *incarnate Logos,* the continuation of this self-limitation in the life of Jesus, his voluntary association with the "least" of society, his humiliation, and—most centrally—his crucifixion.

In becoming human, then, the Son submits himself to all the world's malevolence and calumny. Such are the depths to which God identifies Godself with humanity, that the Son will humble himself even to death by becoming incarnate in the world. This final step of crucifixion, Thomasius claims, "is in view even from

---

37. Thomasius, *God and Incarnation,* 48 (emphasis mine).
38. Incarnation is "appropriation and penetration of the human by the divine, and therefore also impartation and participation of the divine in the human—one in the other. . . . The eternal Logos makes the human nature . . . truly his own precisely by placing himself in its innermost depths" (ibid., 45–46).

the beginning.... His whole course of life on earth is a going to death, one great act of suffering obedience."[39] It is not suffering for suffering's own sake, however, that motivates the Son to undergo crucifixion. The crucifixion is not simply the logical unfolding of a self-limiting deity, or a necessity imposed by the pattern of kenosis. Rather, the crucifixion points to the "deepest mystery of self-denying love, a deed of love in which the eternal Son of the Father becomes like unto us, in order in suffering and dying to reconcile us with God."[40] The Son's identification with humanity is so strong in the person of Jesus Christ that he is willing to die along with humanity on the cross.[41]

Making the claim, as Thomasius does, that the Son voluntarily limits himself is not tantamount to claiming that God relinquishes being God in the incarnation. Thomasius is aware of this potential misunderstanding, which some exponents of kenotic theology actually embraced.[42] In fact, Thomasius is rather cautious in his assigning of kenosis to the divine attributes. In this sense, he does not depart dramatically from the classical attribute tradition, or even submit it to much criticism; rather, he reconfigures this tradition by using a heretofore little-employed distinction between the *immanent* and *relative* attributes of God. According to Thomasius, the divine attributes can be divided into two types: the immanent, which are God's freedom, eternity, holiness, truth, and love; and the relative, which are God's omnipotence, omnipresence, and omniscience. The first category describes who God is in

---

39. Ibid., 67.

40. Ibid., 49.

41. Thomasius's conception of self-denying love is certainly vulnerable to devastating critique. At times his description of Christ's "love" runs perilously close to masochism, so that the greatest love one can show is to obliterate the self in the name of the other. Clearly, this is a theme that has been appropriated and abused in our own time. At this point it is worth asking whether Thomasius's vision and valorization of suffering is too damaging to be worth retrieving. At the very least his approach demands the correctives of feminist and liberationist approaches.

42. The most radical exponent of kenotic doctrine in the nineteenth century was Wolfgang Gess, who held that the Logos actually changed itself into a man by laying aside its divinity. For a concise portrayal of the kenotic movement as a whole, see Claude Welch, *Protestant Thought in the Nineteenth Century*, vol. 1 (New Haven: Yale University Press, 1972), 233–40.

Godself, while the second describes who God is in relation to the world. According to Thomasius, God can relinquish God's relative attributes and *not cease being God*. The immanent attributes, however, "God cannot give up because he would thereby give himself up."[43] Thus God—or more precisely, the Son—surrenders God's relative attributes in order to accommodate Godself to the constraints and confines of humanity, but in surrendering them God remains absolutely free, holy, and eternal. Because the Son has surrendered his relative attributes, however, the person of Jesus Christ is not viewed as an omnipotent, all-knowing superman bearing little resemblance to the human race. Thomasius thus makes a distinction *within God* that is not echoed until the emergence of process thought in the twentieth century.[44]

Although Thomasius also stresses Christ's exaltation—the return of the self-limiting Son to his prior glory—he does not suggest that God remains unchanged and unaffected by the kenotic dynamic. The "divine life," according to Thomasius, does not proceed identically before and after the Christ-event. Indeed, the incarnate whisper of God with humanity changes forever both God and humankind. Here is where Thomasius makes the most stunning suggestions: the event of incarnation, the complete identification between God and humanity, means that humanity, "in the person of Christ [is] taken into the inner circle of the Trinity—and surely not in a transitory mode, but for ever."[45] This incorporation of humanity in the divine life amounts to nothing less than a supplementation of the inner-Trinitarian relationship. Thomasius is claiming not only that the incarnation affects God's relationship with the world, but also that it changes forever the immanent Trinity. To proclaim Jesus Christ as the Incarnate One is to claim simultaneously "God with us" and humanity with God.

---

43. Thomasius, *God and Incarnation*, 94.
44. A further parallel with process theology is Thomasius's suggestion that the event of incarnation *affects God*, a tentative precursor to process theologians' questioning of the immutability of God. We will explore this suggestion shortly.
45. Thomasius, *God and Incarnation*, 83.

An Assessment of Thomasius

Thomasius's Christology is guided, in large part, by the twin
prongs of the Chalcedonian formula: Jesus Christ is "at once
complete in Godhead and complete in humanity, truly God and
truly human."[46] In answer to the creeping Docetism of some
contemporary orthodox Lutheran circles and the newfound
Ebionitism of nascent Reformed liberalism, Thomasius affirmed
unequivocally, and with equal emphases, Jesus Christ as the
God-man. The novelty in his approach appears in the way he re-
solves the seemingly indecipherable conundrum of such creedal
affirmation. In the face of ever-mounting difficulties standing in
the way of Chalcedonian orthodoxy (historical-critical studies
of the Gospels, Kant's critique of theology, and the near abandonment of the metaphysics of Chalcedon in terms of defining
"God" and "human"), Thomasius offers an innovative interpretation and appropriation of a classic biblical image: the kenotic
Christ. If there is a strength to Thomasius's kenoticism, it is that
it takes the *humanity* of Christ with the utmost seriousness.

One problem with Thomasius's approach is that he views incarnation as a puzzle that demands deciphering: "How can the
infinite inhabit the finite?" His answer to the problem, though
creative in its articulation of the intimate relation between God
and humanity, resurrects the age-old distinction between the
divine and human "natures," a distinction that had already become problematic in the Enlightenment. The problem is not
so much that Thomasius maintains this distinction (most Christologies do), but that he articulates it solely within the wooden
confines of Chalcedonian orthodoxy. The net effect is that these
puzzling categories of "nature" and the conundrum created by
the One who embodies both natures, Jesus Christ, eventually
override Thomasius's concern with the relationship between
God and humanity. Thomasius, in short, does not offer an
alternative philosophical conceptuality for glimpsing this relationship, and his reliance on a widely discredited one is what
makes his thought somewhat obscurantist.

---

46. The Chalcedonian "definition," quoted in Hodgson and King, eds., *Readings
in Christian Theology*, 210.

A second problem with Thomasius's incarnational approach is that it is forthrightly triumphalist, a trait that eventually eclipses some of the Christ-hymn's poetry. Though he is quick to affirm the humiliation of Christ, this humiliation is eventually eclipsed by the glorious strands of Christ's exaltation. Indeed, Thomasius inaugurates his Christology with the assertion that the "appearance of Christ in the world is the great fact that . . . is the center of the whole salvation-history . . . the inner ground of the entire saving revelation."[47] At the center, it seems, there is no room for an other. Either one assents to the universal lordship and triumph of Christ or one is beyond the pale of salvation. Every conviction, we are reminded, that does not allow the simultaneous confession of the man Jesus as God is a departure from Thomasius's forthright Christocentrism.[48] At this point Thomasius's rigid dogmatism has smothered any poetry of praise. His exposition of the Philippians Christ-hymn is primarily the articulation of a "high" Christology, a definitive triumph of the God-man that has lost sight of the hymn's purpose: to give praise.

Thomasius's approach also dampens any concern with discipleship. His high Christology focuses exclusive attention on the paradox of the God-man without turning our attention to the neighbor. In the end, the relationship that seems of ultimate significance is the inhabitation of God in Christ. The "difference" the incarnation makes in the interhuman sphere appears negligible. Such omission of discipleship certainly runs contrary to Paul's use of kenosis, in which nearly every christological statement is connected to practical, face-to-face encounters with others. Thomasius's concern with upholding the categories of Chalcedon, in short, obscures the face of the Other.

In light of these several difficulties with Thomasius's kenotic approach,[49] it makes sense to examine a near-contemporary

---

47. Thomasius, *God and Incarnation*, 31.
48. Ibid., 37.
49. We might also cite a fourth difficulty with Thomasius's incarnational approach: it bases an entire Christology on a relatively thin strand of biblical material. Thomasius's kenoticism is rarely juxtaposed with Gospel accounts of the Incarnate One. Though my suggestions also make extensive use of this "thin strand," I hope to show more resonance with other biblical portrayals of Christ.

approach that bears similar resonance, namely, the thought of
G. W. F. Hegel. Before we attempt a constructive appropriation
of kenoticism, we need to see how a similar approach—God's
self-divestment—is offered in the mind of a more thoroughly
relational thinker. For Hegel, the exposition of the Emptying
Christ results not in the saving of the classical, Chalcedonian
tradition, but in the radical reformulation of God's being and
activity in the relational cosmos.

Hegel's Incarnational Approach

Although the bulk of Hegel's work antedates Thomasius's
kenoticism by some thirty years, Hegel's Christology seems more
"modern" from our perspective. Far less prone than Thomasius to upholding the two prongs of Chalcedon at all costs,
Hegel offers an unapologetically Trinitarian account of the
incarnation that is attuned to current relational sensibilities.
Hegel's central image for incarnation is God's self-divestment
or diremption (*Entäusserung*), which has some parallels with
Thomasius's idea of kenosis, albeit with different emphases. His
account, moreover, frees both God and humanity from somewhat static conceptions of "being" or "nature," and glimpses
them more within relational categories of becoming. The result is an account of incarnation that appears less woodenly
dogmatic and more resonant with contemporary dialogical
concerns.

The Possibility of Incarnation

Undergirding Hegel's worldview is the somewhat benign recognition that our encounter with and understanding of others is
always mediated. Knowledge and understanding arise out of the
inescapability of interhuman relationship. We exist and understand through concrete encounters with others. "Everything
which exists *is*, to be sure, but only is as something mediated....
But it *is mediated*, is relative, is essentially a relationship; some
other is necessary to its being."[50] To know an other, to encounter

---

50. G. W. F. Hegel, *Lectures on the Philosophy of Religion*, vol. 1, ed. Peter C. Hodgson
(Berkeley: University of California Press, 1984), 410.

an other, is to recognize that something happens between that other and myself. Mediation—what happens between myself and an other—is not my totalizing engulfment of that other, but the recognition that the other is different from myself. Mediation, in other words, points to the authentic difference between entities but also to our need for others and the possibility for understanding others.

The human encounter with the divine is no exception to the inescapability of mediation. Contrary to some schools of mysticism—and even Schleiermacher's "immediate feeling of absolute dependence"—Hegel claims that our knowledge of God is always conditioned by the "between" that separates and distinguishes God from ourselves. Accordingly, our "knowledge" of the divine is continually mediated by an other: God is revealed in creation, in the community of the church, and in the person of Jesus Christ:

> When I represent God to myself, then I have God immediately before me. Yet mediation is also contained in this simple, immediate relation. First, I am the knower, and second, there is an object, which is God. My knowing God is in general a relationship, and therefore is something mediated. I am a knower and a religious believer only through the mediation of this content, through this object. We cannot point to anything at all that does not contain mediation within itself.[51]

This stress on mediation might be called Hegel's "speculative theory of incarnation." As one of the distinguishing hallmarks of "revelatory religion,"[52] the incarnation represents the intersection, the "between space" that represents the di-

---

51. Ibid., 413.
52. The terms that Hegel employs for Christianity are fluid, and often occur interchangeably. The two most common designations are the "revelatory" (*offenbar*) religion and the "consummate" (*vollendet*) religion. This usage, however, does exhibit change throughout the course of Hegel's work. Generally speaking, Hegel's preferred usage in *Phenomenology of Spirit* and the 1824 *Lectures on the Philosophy of Religion* is the "revelatory" religion, whereas in the 1827 *Lectures* "consummate" religion appears more prominently. Neither title is for Hegel mutually exclusive, although the latter occurs with greater frequency in the later stages of his work.

vine to humanity. Yet it is also the mutual "be-coming," as it were, of both humanity and divinity. As Peter Hodgson notes in his recent anthology of Hegel's religious writings, "Such a theory has two sides: the first side is the divine becoming human (substance divests or empties itself of itself and becomes self-consciousness); the second is the human becoming divine (self-consciousness divests itself of itself and makes itself into a universal self)."[53] Incarnation is possible both because humanity is oriented toward the divine and because God is concerned with humanity. Both represent possibilities for the other.

Whereas the God-man, the strange combination of divinity and humanity, represents a problem for Thomasius, for Hegel this combination points to the essential affinity between God and the human race. Rather than swallowing the formula of Chalcedon without question, Hegel gives the classical formulation his own distinctive spin by glimpsing divinity and humanity together.[54]

Self-Divestment as Being-for-an-Other

All of creation, for Hegel, points to the *possibility* of incarnation. Hegel describes this aspect of the divine activity—this will to be made manifest in an other—as Logos or Sophia, names that are often associated with the Second Person of the Trinity.[55] But for Hegel, unlike Thomasius, the Second Person is connected with far more than the person of Jesus Christ. Thomasius's extreme Christocentrism verges on an exclusive identification between the Logos and Jesus Christ, whereas for Hegel, the Logos names something wider: God's ever-present activity with and for an other, which can be glimpsed throughout creation. In his 1831 *Lectures* Hegel writes most eloquently of this pervasive incarnational sensibility and of the communion that is possible between humanity and God:

---

53. G. W. F. *Hegel: Theologian of the Spirit*, ed. Peter C. Hodgson (Minneapolis: Fortress, 1997), 20.

54. In his 1824 *Lectures* Hegel writes, "What [the incarnation] posits is that divine and human nature are not intrinsically different—God [is] in human shape" (*Lectures on the Philosophy of Religion*, vol. 3, ed. Peter C. Hodgson [Berkeley: University of California Press, 1985], 214).

55. See Hegel, *Lectures*, 3:288.

God should be known as being for other, for humanity. . . . The possibility of reconciliation is present only when the implicitly subsisting unity of divine and human nature is known. Human beings can know themselves to be taken up into God only when God is not something alien to them, only when they are not merely an extrinsic accident upon God's nature, but rather when they are taken up into God in accordance with their essence and freedom. The implicitly subsisting unity of divine and human nature must be revealed to humanity in an objective way; this is what happened through the incarnation of God.[56]

The incarnation, thus, is not a violation of Christ's "human nature," or a puzzle that must be solved by resorting to kenotic formulation, but the fulfillment of the "subsisting unity" between divine and human nature, the coming together of those made for communion with each other.

Another way of describing the incarnation, for Hegel, is with the term "divestment" (*Entäusserung*).[57] God's drive to be-for-an-other, to reveal Godself, reaches its apogee in Christ. When God wills to be with humanity, God does not remain enclosed upon Godself, but divests or "empties" Godself for others. For Hegel, the content of revelation in Christ is "nothing else than the history of spirit, the history of God . . . , the divine history as that of a single self-consciousness which has united divine and human nature within itself—the divine nature in this [human] element. The first [aspect] of this history is the *single, immediate human being* in all his contingency, in the whole range of temporal relationships and conditions. To this extent this is a divestment of the divine."[58] Both humanity and God *need* a concrete other for their own self-development. Humanity and God are only implicitly self-related until there is an other for each.[59]

---

56. Ibid., 314.
57. This term is rich and laden with legal and religious overtones. It might also be translated as "renunciation," "giving up," or as "alienation." Note that Karl Marx used the term to describe the "alienation" between worker and labor inherent in capitalism.
58. Hegel, *Lectures*, 3:239.
59. This reading of Hegel has been gained in large part through conversations with Peter Hodgson and Eugene TeSelle.

The genuine difference between humanity and God necessi-
tates God's "divestment" of Godself in the incarnation. Unlike
Thomasius, however, Hegel does not view this divestment primarily in terms of God's accommodation to a human form;
Entäusserung, for Hegel, points more directly to the full enflowerment of the implicit unity between God and humanity
and their genuine need for one another.

Hegel's use of the imagery of emptying, in other words,
is always co-constituted by imagery of fulfillment. God's self-
emptying in Christ also involves a *return* to Godself as the full
development of Godself. The return, in Cyril O'Regan's words,
is never a return to the same, but to the *more*.[60] The kenotic
movement, accordingly, corresponds not simply to humanity's
need for God and God's concern with humanity, but to the
consummation of the divine-human relation. "The real logic of
emptying appears to be that of the covert filling of presence and
the healing of its lack. The movement of *kenosis* of presence is
in consequence an agent of *plerosis* [fullness]."[61]

As the intersection of the divine and human trajectories, and
the revelation of their underlying unity, the Christ-event also
represents the confluence of the divine and human "stories."
For this reason, the story of Jesus can be viewed in two ways:
"The story of Jesus is something twofold.... Not only [is there]
this outward history, which should only be taken as the ordinary
story of a human being, but also it has the divine as its content: a
divine happening, a divine deed, an absolutely divine action."[62]
Those who glimpse the life of Jesus as only a human phenomenon miss the confluence of these two stories. This merging of
stories, or the realization of the implicit unity and communion
between God and humanity, is Hegel's way of grappling with
the "two natures" question, a solution that moves far beyond
the wooden categories of Thomasius.

---

60. Cyril O'Regan, *The Heterodox Hegel* (Albany: State University of New York Press, 1994), 169.

61. Ibid., 200. Unlike Thomasius, however, Hegel involves more than the "Son" in this kenotic movement. Kenosis, for Hegel, is primarily constitutive of the dynamic of God as *Spirit*. Again, Hegel has significantly broadened the incarnational trajectory.

62. Hegel, *Lectures*, 1:399.

From Death to Life

Contrary to Thomasius's view of the crucifixion, which represents a necessary, salvific prelude to the triumph of Christ's glorious exaltation, Hegel grapples more intensely with the negativity of Christ's crucifixion. For Hegel, God's will to be-for-an-other is so strong that God goes to the depths of the human condition, resolutely facing the specter of death. Directly opposed to those who would deny that the crucifixion affects the "Father," Hegel resurrects the patripassian position and claims that in the crucifixion "*God has died, God is dead*— this is the most frightful of thoughts, that everything eternal and true *is not*, that negation itself is found in God."[63] The negative, the tragic, and death itself are incorporated as moments *within* God. God thus is not removed from or unaffected by suffering, but experiences it *as God's own*. As a consequence, Hegel's view of incarnation does not have the triumphal ring of Thomasius's. Rather, Christ's incarnation represents the "confluence of stories—divine and human" that delves into the depths of tragedy, a tragedy never forgotten, but absorbed into the life of God.

Remarkably, the incorporation of the negative within the fabric of the divine is what presents possibilities for the continuation of life. For Hegel, this continuation occurs primarily in the ecclesia, the community of the faithful who remember and witness the "death of God" in Christ. In his *Phenomenology of Spirit*, Hegel writes powerfully, "The *death* of the divine Man, *qua death*, is *abstract* negativity, the immediate result of the process that comes to an end only in the universality of *nature*. In spiritual self-consciousness, death loses its natural signification. . . . Death is transfigured from what it immediately signifies, the non-being of *this individual*, into the *universality* of the spirit, which lives in its community, dies there daily and daily rises again."[64] The ecclesia is thus promised a new life, nourished through the continual remembrance of a particular death in Jesus Christ and

63. Ibid., 3:323.
64. Cited in Hodgson, *Theologian of the Spirit*, 133–34.

God's embodiment of negativity, fragility, and suffering in that event.[65]

Here we begin to sense the full range of Hegel's incarnational sensibility. By extending the promise of life to believing communities who faithfully remember the suffering and death of Christ, Hegel broadens the incarnational trajectory to include the church. Unlike Thomasius, who severely restricts the incarnational lens to include only the person of Jesus Christ as specified in the Chalcedonian definition, Hegel displays a much wider purview. In Hegel's conception, the incarnation appears less as a puzzle or surd and more as the full enfleshment of God's activity of being-for-an-other, an activity that includes the splendor of creation, the concrete embodiment of Jesus of Nazareth, the agony of his suffering and death, and the continued remembrance of that suffering in "belief-ful" communities. The story of incarnation, then, does not begin in Bethlehem and end with Christ's resurrection; rather, it is inaugurated in the vulnerable God who extends Godself to the world and continues to live and grow wherever the church remembers God's embodiment in creation.

An Assessment of Hegel

For Hegel, the incarnation suggests God's concern with humanity and humanity's orientation toward God. The strengths of this position are manifold. First, Hegel offers a more comprehensive sense of the meaning of incarnation. By describing God's incarnation in Christ within a wider vision of creation and church, Hegel's approach is more inclusive than Thomasius's christocentric exclusivism. Far more than the historical figure of Jesus of Nazareth is included in this cosmic sensibility; indeed, we might claim that for Hegel, the entire cosmos is filled with traces of God's being-for-an-other. God gives of Godself throughout the entire creative process, because God needs an Other and we need God. Jesus Christ becomes no less

---

65. An excerpt from Hegel's 1827 *Lectures* is particularly illustrative here: "The human, the finite, the fragile, the weak, the negative are themselves a moment of the divine, . . . they are within God himself, . . . finitude, negativity, otherness are not outside of God and do not, as otherness, hinder unity with God" (*Lectures*, 3:326).

central in this approach, but this centrality is discerned at the center of a cosmic whole. As it is for Paul in his Philippian correspondence, the Other emerges not on the periphery of the christólogical question but at its very core.

The second strength of Hegel's approach is its thoroughly relational character. With words that seem at times to be attuned to present-day sensibilities, Hegel paints a vivid portrait of the relationship between God and humanity. Because humanity and divinity are, for Hegel, intrinsically related, the incarnation appears less as a cosmic surd and more as the apogee of the entire creative process.

Finally, Hegel's incarnational perspective is suggestive because of his novel treatment of the crucifixion. His interpretation of the cross neither echoes the sacrificial strains of Thomasius nor valorizes suffering of its own accord. The crucifixion, rather, represents the full extent of God's will to be-for-an-other. Indeed, for Hegel, when Jesus Christ suffers and dies on Golgotha, God incorporates that death into Godself and suffers along with the world. The significance of the incarnation is not captured in a repristination of Chalcedon (à la Thomasius), but in a stark description of the vulnerable God who is the ground of relation throughout the cosmos, the One who is affected by all.

The most substantial criticism I would venture against Hegel's wider incarnational sensibility is that a creeping totalizing vision at times undercuts some of the strengths I have just highlighted. Such is the case particularly when faced with the challenge of religious Other. Both the religion of Christianity (at least in its ideal form) and the *figura* of Christ are consummate figures. Christianity is the "consummate religion,"[66] and Christ is the fullest possible enflowerment of the implicit unity between God and humanity. At best, Hegel is an inclusivist, a theologian open to the wisdom of other religious traditions, but only if it falls into the comprehensive sweep of his understanding of Spirit. Though we surely cannot fault Hegel for not recognizing

---

66. "Consummate religion" is Hegel's preferred moniker for Christianity after the *Lectures* of 1824. In *Phenomenology of Spirit* and the 1824 *Lectures* he employs the more irenic "revelatory religion." See note 52.

the need for dialogue in his own time (his own knowledge of Buddhism was severely limited and his milieu was largely a Christian one), we might question his up-front endorsement of Christianity as the consummate religion. If nothing else, our contemporary context demands that we question the grand in-clusivism of Hegel's incarnational claims, both in the name of genuine religious *difference* and in the name of a critical Re-formed principle: the church, theology, and our conceptions of God and Christ are in continual need of reform. With this context in mind, we turn to a tradition that embodies a gen-uine world of difference, Buddhism, and to the difference the Christian-Buddhist encounter makes in our articulation of the God who reveals Godself in Christ.

CHAPTER III

PROFESSING CHRIST AND ENCOUNTERING BUDDHISM

O UR HISTORICAL SURVEY of the kenotic tradition has proven helpful as we now turn our attention to the issue of incarnational Christology in a context of religious pluralism. The exploration of the biblical material, with particular focus on the Philippians Christ-hymn, has suggested that the speculative question of Jesus Christ's *identity* cannot be asked apart from the practical question of Christian *discipleship* in the company of others. This survey, furthermore, has suggested that both the divine-human and the interhuman dimensions are fundamental to any approach to the question "Who is Jesus Christ?" Finally, our work has uncovered resources in which these relationships might be described more fully: Thomasius's kenoticism and Hegel's conception of God's self-divestment are two examples of the second-order specification of the biblical text's poetic and evocative imagery. Our preference, as we have seen, has been for the latter example: a rearticulation of the relational God is preferable to an approach that seeks to uphold the definition of Chalcedon at all costs, particularly when we recognize that one of the chief intentions of the authors of Chalcedon was to describe the *relation* of God in Christ.

Our task now is to articulate these relationships in a vocabulary that is more germane to our context. Here is where the "payoff" of our historical survey emerges, here that the religious Other appears at the forefront of incarnational claims. In addressing the question "What does it mean to proclaim Jesus Christ as the Incarnate One in an age of religious pluralism?" this chapter will take up two tasks: first, to suggest how a profession of the Emptying Christ leads Christians into encounter with the Zen Buddhist articulation of *sunyata* (emptiness); and second, to offer the glimmerings of my own constructive, kenotic understanding of incarnation that perceives the religious Other at its very core.

CHRISTIANITY AND BUDDHISM IN DIALOGUE

Does the Christian profession of the kenotic Christ have any resonance with the Zen Buddhist articulation of *sunyata* (emptiness)? I would be hesitant to explore this question if we suggested from the outset that Buddhists and Christians were making the same general claims about emptiness in parallel vocabularies.[1] Such adoption of a "harmonizing hypothesis" would eclipse the many possibilities for authentic religious encounter and change when faith meets faith. Authentic dialogue, by contrast, admits from the outset that one does not know the religious Other, that one cannot speak on behalf of his or her claims, even when they sound strikingly familiar.

With this admonition against making facile claims for the religious Other in mind, I approach the topic of Buddhist-Christian dialogue with some trepidation. As a Christian, I can only suggest an impoverished view of some core Buddhist convictions about cosmic emptiness. Yet I offer this study convinced that the Christian claim of the kenotic Christ might offer an avenue for the exploration of consonance and dissonance between the two traditions. One has to begin the conversation somewhere, and it makes sense to begin where the traditions' language is somewhat similar. Once inaugurated, however, there is no retreat to one's private religious backyard. The interreligious conversation is liable to launch an internal Christian theological critique in direct response to Buddhist claims. The logic of interreligious dialogue, then, is not to convert the Buddhist to

---

1. The approach of John Hick, though far more nuanced than this generalized sentiment, might represent the closest theological parallel to this benign wish for harmonization. Hick's approach hypothesizes that all the world's religious paths represent varied approaches of turning from "self-centeredness" to "Reality-centeredness." See *A Christian Theology of Religions* (Louisville: Westminster John Knox, 1995), 11–30.

Christianity or vice versa, but to encourage the deeper development of each religious tradition, a deepening that can occur only in the encounter with radically different others.[2] The result of such dialogue, for Christians, is a fascinating exploration of the underside of our totalizing claims about God and Christ. Masao Abe and Raimundo Panikkar, as we will see, are key exemplars of such an approach.

Core Buddhist Concepts of Emptiness, Compassion, Interrelationship

Attempting to summarize the core convictions of Buddhism may be as futile as it is ludicrous. Surely, we should be leery of any endeavor to distill a living faith into a tidy set of propositional formulae, whether that faith be our own or that of another. My intent certainly is not to condense the wisdom of the Buddha, and the multiple schools of thought that arose in his wake, in a few pages. Rather, the goal is to suggest three themes that emerge in Buddhist literature that have resonance with our preceding christological reflections. Such an approach certainly runs the risk of smothering the great richness and diversity of the Buddhist tradition, yet it is the only approach that I feel qualified to offer. As a relative novice in the field of Buddhist literature, I will certainly fall short of the rigor that Buddhist scholars would seek to uphold. I am conscious also of the danger in applying the generic title of "Buddhist" to an entire corpus of literature. Buddhism has many faces with multiple schools (Therevada, Mahayana, and Tantric) and an immense proliferation of doctrine and teachings. There is no easily discerned "Buddhist worldview," just as there is no readily depicted, monolithic Christian outlook. Instead, multiple outlooks abound in both traditions. In what follows, I attempt to isolate three themes that have broad resonance with all the Buddhist schools, none of which, I would venture, is

---

2. This vision is shared by John Cobb, who writes that one goal of dialogue is that we thereby deepen our understanding of our own tradition. "Dialogue with [others] would be first and foremost for our own sake as Christians. We would hope to enrich our lives and purify our faith by learning from them" (*Beyond Dialogue: Toward a Mutual Transformation of Christianity and Buddhism* [Philadelphia: Fortress, 1982], 47).

the subject of broad disagreement across schools.[3] The three
that I have chosen are intentionally evocative of some of the
themes we have already discussed: emptiness, compassion, and
interrelationship.

Perhaps the most familiar teaching of Buddhism is its articulation of *emptiness* (or in the Japanese Zen tradition, *sunyata*)
as a cosmic theme. Buddhist wisdom teaches that all existence
is suffering, that this suffering is caused by attachment to fleeting, illusory "things," and that the way to free oneself from the
monstrous hold of "things" is to recognize their emptiness and
evanescence. Anything, for the Buddhist, can be the source
of attachment: the self, one's possessions, one's relationships,
one's family, even one's belief in "God." Regardless of the source
of attachment, each will engender suffering. Liberation, thus,
can be achieved only by breaking the idolatrous barnacles of
attachment and accepting the emptiness of all. The Heart Sutra, one of the most familiar and cited Buddhist texts, expresses
this cosmic emptiness paradoxically: "Here, O Sariputra, form is
emptiness, and the very emptiness is form; emptiness does not
differ from form, form does not differ from emptiness; whatever is form, that is emptiness; whatever is emptiness, that is
form. The same is true of feelings, perceptions, impulses, and
consciousness."[4] Regarding anything in the universe as permanent or immortal is ultimately an illusion, because emptiness
pervades even those things to which we cling most strongly.

Masao Abe offers a concise formulation of *sunyata* in a recent
work: "Sunyata is entirely unobjectifiable, unconceptualizable,
and unattainable by reason and will. It also indicates the absence
of enduring self-being and the non-substantiality of everything
in the universe. It is beyond all dualities and yet includes them."[5]
Here is where the differences between Buddhism and Christian-

3. Several excellent anthologies of Buddhist literature are readily available.
Among them are the compendium of Edward Conze, *Buddhist Scriptures* (London:
Penguin, 1959); Sarvepalli Radhakrishnan and Charles A. Moore, *A Sourcebook in In-
dian Philosophy* (Princeton, N.J.: Princeton University Press, 1957); and Henry Clarke
Warren, *Buddhism in Translations* (Cambridge: Harvard University Press, 1953).

4. Conze, *Buddhist Scriptures,* 162–63.

5. Masao Abe, *Buddhism and Interfaith Dialogue,* ed. Steven Heine (Honolulu:
University of Hawaii Press, 1995), 7.

ity begin to display some of their stronger hues. For despite the similarities in vocabulary, Buddhist *sunyata* is hardly evocative of the Christian profession of Christ's kenosis. While "emptying" in the Christian context points to the distinct pattern in which God's love is revealed, for the Buddhist, *sunyata* touches the emptiness at the heart of the universe. From the Buddhist perspective, even love can become an object of attachment and the cause of suffering. Clearly, the dynamic of Christ's kenosis and the phenomenon of cosmic *sunyata* do not point to the same reality, for the claim of *sunyata* is far more radical.

It is the nature of *sunyata* to "de-thingify" everything, for as soon as one substantializes any entity, feeling, or passion, attachment has already gained the upper hand. The razor of *sunyata* is so sharp that it cuts through *all* conceptualities, even itself. It displays such a comprehensive, negative sweep that it is impossible even to write about it. Even the written word, *"sunyata,"* amounts to unwarranted substantialization. Emptiness, in short, is emptied of any specific content, but is not thereby rendered a nihilistic or timeless void. We need only recall the Heart Sutra to recognize that emptiness is always accompanied and co-penetrated by form.

The second core Buddhist conviction that will sound familiar to Christian ears is its teaching of *compassion*. The ubiquitous presence of suffering in the Buddhist worldview does not evoke cosmic indifference; rather, the more acutely one is aware of the suffering of all sentient beings, the greater one's compassion is kindled. We sense this compassion most strongly in the figure of the Bodhisattva, who postpones enlightenment so that others may be enlightened through him. Though songs and strains of compassion are prevalent in all schools of Buddhism, one from the Tantric school (Saraha's "Treasury of Songs") is particularly evocative:

> The fair tree of thought that knows no duality, spreads through the triple world. It bears the flower and fruit of compassion, and its name is service of others. The fair tree of the Void abounds with flowers, acts of compassion of many kinds, and fruit for others appearing spontaneously,

for this joy has no actual thought of another.... He who
clings to the Void and neglects Compassion, does not
reach the highest stage. But he who practises only Compassion does not gain release from toils of existence. He,
however, who is strong in practice of both, remains neither
in Samsara nor in Nirvana.[6]

Certainly, for Buddhists, the demand of the Other is felt with
much gravity. One cannot recognize emptiness without expe-
riencing compassion for fellow human beings. Yet Buddhist
compassion is markedly less attentive to *particularity* than its
counterpart, Christian love. Acts of compassion are to arise
"spontaneously" with little attention to the situation of the re-
cipient. For the Buddhist, every human being, regardless of
situation, requires the same elixir: enlightenment. One result of
this universal diagnosis of humankind is that vastly divergent social, economic, and political situations rarely are acknowledged
as contexts in which compassion is extended.[7] The reason for
this perceived lack is that these particular contexts become objects of attachment as well. An undifferentiated compassion,
extended to all sentient beings, is the fruit of enlightenment,
whereas the scandalously particular love of an Other, from the
Buddhist perspective, is often an abiding source of suffering.

The third resonant chord concerns the Buddhist intuition of
interrelation or dependent co-origination, or in Sanskrit, *pratityasamutpada*. Basically, the core Buddhist conviction is that
nothing in the cosmos happens independently from anything
else; indeed, each event, thing, or idea that arises affects everything else, whether past, present, or future. The cosmos is, in
short, a vast, interrelated web of dependent co-arising, or as
the Visuddhi-Magga notes, "It is dependently on each other
and in unison and simultaneously that the factors which consti-

6. Conze, *Buddhist Scriptures*, 179–80.
7. This difference has also been acknowledged as one reason why the Buddhist
understanding of history and its strand of social and political ethics are less developed than their Christian counterparts. See Masao Abe, *The Emptying God*, ed. John
Cobb and Christopher Ives (Maryknoll, N.Y.: Orbis, 1990), 59–61, and John Cobb's
response (pp. 91–101).

tute dependence originate the elements of being."[8] Raimundo Panikkar offers another summary of this intuition: "What the Buddha intuits is the permanence of impermanence, so to speak. That is, he intuits the entire cosmos in its becoming and in the interrelationship of all its parts, he sees the dependence of one thing on another, he discovers the absence of any independence whatever."[9] The trumpeting of independence is yet another illusion human persons are prone to adopt. What the Buddha offers instead of the illusion of the isolated monad is the most ecological worldview of all: even the flutter of a dragonfly's wings has bearing upon everything else in the universe.

Although this articulation of interrelation exhibits some similarity with recent Christian relational theologies, the Buddhist intuition is far more radical. Whereas Christian relational theologies are focused chiefly on divine-human or interhuman concerns, the Buddhist vision probes the interconnectedness of the entire cosmos. Despite Buddhism's lack of attention to the particular entities that constitute relationships, it is vastly attentive to the pervasiveness of relationality within the universe.

Clearly, there is resonance between such core Buddhist convictions as *sunyata,* compassion, and *pratityasamutpada* and their Christian correlates: kenosis, love, and interrelation. Yet it is precisely in their similarities that the divergence between them is most strikingly discerned. What for the Christian amounts to the "emptying revelation of God's love" is for the Buddhist yet another example of excessive attachment to an evanescent phenomenon. Perhaps Masao Abe expresses this utter difference best: "In Christianity only God is good and there is none that does good. All human beings have sinned in Adam, and the whole creation is subject to vanity. By contrast, in Buddhism, there is nothing permanent, self-existing and absolutely good, for everything without exception is co-arising and co-

---

8. Warren, *Buddhism in Translations,* 168.
9. Raimundo Panikkar, *The Silence of God: The Answer of the Buddha,* trans. Robert R. Barr (Maryknoll, N.Y.: Orbis, 1989), 54.

ceasing, impermanent, without 'own-being,' empty."[10] Given
their unambiguous divergence, might there be ways of engaging the differences of Christianity and Buddhism in ways
that enhance both traditions? Might the kenotic conception of
incarnation be informed by the Zen Buddhist notion of *sunyata*?

Abe's Theology of Incarnation

Masao Abe has offered a coherent theology of incarnation
along specifically kenotic lines, with admirable dialogical results. I am narrowing the focus to Abe at this point not because
he is representative of Buddhism per se, but because he offers one example of the fruit of Buddhist-Christian encounter.
Broadly representative of the Japanese Zen tradition, yet also
conversant with the major Catholic and Protestant strands of
Christian theology, Abe is a remarkably well-qualified dialogical voice. He understands the traditional Christian claim of
incarnation while offering his own Zen interpretation of the
same event. Such work has proven provocative and controver-
sial, and undoubtedly has done much to further the imperative
of Buddhist-Christian encounter. For these reasons alone, Abe's
work merits close attention.

For Abe, God's "incarnation" in Christ points most centrally
to the aspect of self-negation within God: "Christ's kenosis signifies a transformation not only in appearance but in substance,
and implies a radical and total self-negation of the Son of
God."[11] Abe's take is essentially a Christology "from above" that
views incarnation not merely as divestment of a divine mode
of being (à la Thomasius) but as the total divestment of divinity itself. Abe's interpretation takes Hegel's conception of
God's being-for-an-other one step farther: God's being-for-an-
other amounts to a completely negative moment—the total and
radical surrender of God's own subjectivity. It is not simply the
incorporation of the negative as a moment within God, but the
suggestion that the negative is the defining moment of the di-

---

10. Abe, *The Emptying God*, 48.
11. Ibid., 10.

vine life. The incarnation is revelatory of God precisely because it unveils the "nothingness" of God.[12]

This complex read of the incarnation is at times difficult to decipher. Abe's interpretation issues forth in characteristically dialectical statements that are reminiscent of Buddhist koans. His reformulation of the doctrine of Christ's kenosis is typical of this deeply paradoxical sensibility: "The Son of God is not the Son of God (for he is essentially and fundamentally self-emptying): precisely because he *is not* the Son of God he *is* truly the Son of God (for he originally and always works as Christ, the Messiah, in his salvational function of self-emptying)."[13] Kenosis is the orchestration of the eternally negative movement that is the essence of God and the heart of the cosmos. For Abe, the incarnation represents not chiefly the descent of God in the person of Christ, but the relative emptiness of God's "Godness." The God who is revealed in Jesus Christ is not presented as an entity to which one might cling, but as the eternal subject of self-negation.

The dynamic of the kenotic God in the "person" of the "Son" (Abe retains the traditional names designating the Trinity) does not display a purely negative sweep. Indeed, Abe suggests that the self-emptying movement is revelatory of a positive content, that is, God's love. The God of incarnation is not the genesis of nihilism but the source of unbounded love for creation. Yet this specification of God as love is characteristically dialectical: "God is not God (for God is love and completely self-emptying); precisely because God is not a self-affirmative God, God is truly a God of love (for through complete self-abnegation God is totally identical with everything including sinful humans)."[14] God reveals the divine self as love precisely because God does not remain closed in upon Godself in self-affirmation, but strips the divine self of "Godness" to be for humans.

The effect of Abe's kenotic exposition of incarnation is to

---

12. Abe's interpretation of incarnation resounds with the echoes of the left-wing Hegelians, the God poured out into the world without return. I am indebted to Eugene TeSelle for drawing this comparison.

13. Abe, *The Emptying God*, 11.

14. Ibid., 16.

stand nearly all Christian conceptions of divinity on their heads. God is God, for Abe, precisely because God is *not* God. All of our characterizations, descriptions, and attributes of God are thereby shattered: "The completely kenotic God, in my view, is neither immanent nor transcendent, but thoroughly immanent and thoroughly transcendent at one and the same time. The completely kenotic God is not merely impersonal but deeply personal, in the sense that this God is self-emptying and fulfills God's unconditional love to save everything without exception, including the unjust and sinful."[15] As soon as we describe God as transcendent, we eclipse the specific content of God's reconciling love; if we describe God as immanent, we "thingify" the God who is revealed only in emptiness.[16]

Incarnation as kenosis, for Abe, does not mean the disposal of Christian categories of revelation, fulfillment, or love. Indeed, as we have already seen, Abe's incorporation of the negative within these categories deepens and confirms their meaning. Christ's kenosis and fulfillment, in short, go hand-in-glove. In response to a critique raised by Hans Küng, Abe writes of *pleroma* (fullness) as occupying as central a position as kenosis. Yet for Abe, unlike some Christian theologians, Christ's fulfillment is not the result of a prior condition of self-emptying (Christ's exaltation is not *caused* by his humiliation); rather, Christ's fulfillment *is* his humiliation, his exaltation *is* his kenosis. Kenosis does not engender *pleroma*, but both are found intertwined in the same, eternal, self-negating event. "The state of humiliation and the state of exaltation are not two different states but a single, dynamic one; that is, humiliation as it is is exaltation, and exaltation as it is is humiliation; kenosis as it is is pleroma, and pleroma as it is is kenosis."[17] The cross thus occupies a

---

15. Ibid., 18.
16. Abe's portraiture of God here is strikingly evocative of Robert Scharlemann's. Indeed Scharlemann's poignant phrase, "the being of God when God is not being God," has parallels with what Abe is attempting to articulate. See Scharlemann, *Inscriptions and Reflections* (Charlottesville: University Press of Virginia, 1989), 30–53. I know of no comparative studies of these two thinkers, but such work would be immensely helpful in furthering the cause of Buddhist-Christian dialogue.
17. Masao Abe, *Divine Emptiness and Historical Fullness*, ed. Christopher Ives (Valley Forge, Pa.: Trinity Press International, 1995), 229–30.

prominent space in Abe's depiction of the self-negating and self-relativizing Son of God.

In response to any critique that would characterize his project as a chiefly negative interpretation of the incarnation, Abe affirms the positive direction of his incarnational spin. The brilliance of his project, moreover, is that he sees the positive as continually bound up in the negative. Emptiness and fulfillment, kenosis and *pleroma*, self-affirmation and self-negation, always occur simultaneously for Abe, and there is no better example of this than the fulfilling/emptying Son of God. Abe writes, "God's total kenosis is neither God's self-sacrifice for something else nor God's self-negation for nihilistic nothingness. Rather, God's total kenosis is God's self-emptying for absolutely 'nothing' other than God's own fulfillment as love."[18] Abe's incarnational, dialogical approach thus is a critique of both the Nietzschean embrace of nihilism and the reified Christian interpretation of incarnation as triumphal fulfillment. The incarnation is the most lucid instantiation of the emptying/fulfilling God, the revealing/concealing Other, the affirming/negating embrace of love. To glimpse these possibilities in simultaneity is to approach an understanding of Abe's incarnational vision.

Toward a Transformation of Buddhism and Christianity

For Christianity, the thematization of kenosis has been a relatively lost chord in theological history, often disappearing under a dark cloud of monotheistic totalization or outright christocentric triumphalism. Buddhists, on the other hand, have often underscored the doctrine of *sunyata* and the idea of the impermanence of all things so strongly that the conception of history and justice quickly subsides into the background. One aim of Buddhist-Christian dialogue, given these respective lacunae, is the mutual enrichment of each tradition: an external critique that exposes the lacuna, followed by internal transformation and the fuller development of each tradition's respective vision. The Christian tendency toward monotheistic

---

18. Ibid., 258.

absolutization might thus be tempered, while the comparative paucity of Buddhist ethical reflection and attention to the
particular Other might be expanded.

Abe recognizes the relatively slim conception of ethics within
Buddhism: "In contrast to the Buddhist pair of 'wisdom and
compassion,' the Christian pair is 'love and justice....' Accordingly, in Christianity, love without justice is not true love and
justice without love is not true justice.... The Buddhist equivalent to the Christian notion of love is the notion of compassion,
but there is no Buddhist equivalent to the Christian notion of
justice."[19] Abe's assessment does not claim that the Christian
conceptions of justice are sufficient in themselves. Nor is it to
say that what the Buddhist "needs" is the mere insertion of justice into his or her worldview. Indeed, Christian formulations
of justice are equally problematic to Buddhists, since they are
often accompanied by rather sharp distinctions between "right"
and "wrong," and by at least the implicit adoption of the idea of
struggle on behalf of the "good," both of which are antithetical
to the Buddhist conception of interrelationship and the emptiness of all distinctions. Yet, this lack of a correlate of justice can
at times lead to an ethical indifference that runs counter to the
Buddhist ideal of compassion. The task, then, for Buddhists,
is to develop an adequate Buddhist response to the problem
of social evil and injustice, informed by its own articulation of
compassion. The task, from the Buddhist perspective, is simply
to make such praxis and ethical reflection more explicit, if only
to underscore the primacy of interrelationship and compassion.

Christianity's propensity toward absolutization appears frequently in reference to God's "activity" in the incarnation. For
even when perceived as the subject of kenosis, God is generally acknowledged as ultimately enduring and permanent,
even immutable. The "emptying God" is thus prone to idolatrous reification. It is precisely through conversation with the
Buddhist that such conceptions of God begin to totter. For in
considering the kenotic God (an image from the Christian scriptures), Christians must at least entertain the possibility of God's

---

19. Abe, *The Emptying God*, 179.

total kenosis, an image of God for which all definitions and conceptualities appear as empty. Because the Buddhist ideal of emptying is so total, it might help Christians better affirm along with the mystics in our tradition the "God beyond God."[20]

Through conversation with Buddhists, Christians begin to recognize the poverty of all conceptualities of God. Likewise, through conversation with Christians, Buddhists might recognize trajectories toward social ethics within their own tradition. Only when *sunyata* is perceived dynamically is it rendered something other than static indifference. In Abe's words, "True Sunyata is not static but dynamic—it is a pure and unceasing function of self-emptying, making self and others manifest their suchness.... When we clearly realize the notion of the kenotic God in Christianity and the notion of dynamic Sunyata in Buddhism—deepening their respective unique characters— we find a significant common basis at a deeper dimension."[21] Such conversation moves Buddhist-Christian dialogue beyond concerns with superficial similarities to a more serious consideration of the difference between traditions and transformation among them.

The Surprising Fruit of Kenotic Dialogue: Apophaticism and the "Otherness" of God

Despite the dissonance between Buddhist and Christian worldviews, adherents of each tradition can learn much from each other. The deeper recognition of the ethical trajectory within Buddhism and the heightened sensitivity toward idolatry within Christianity are but two examples of the fruit of interreligious conversation. Yet the most groundbreaking result of Buddhist-Christian dialogue, at least from the Christian perspective, is the challenge it presents to the doctrine of God. Two possibilities

---

20. Paul Tillich's reflections on the doctrine of God might prove helpful here, for Tillich astutely recognized the theological propensity to render God (or at least our conception of God) an idol. See *Systematic Theology*, vol. 1 (Chicago: University of Chicago Press, 1951), 235–89. Note also that Tillich's attention toward the end of his life turned with pressing concern toward dialogue with Buddhists. See *Christianity and the Encounter of World Religions* (1963; reprint, Minneapolis: Fortress, 1994), 33–47.

21. Abe, *The Emptying God*, 61.

emerge from this challenge as Christians come to grips with
their articulation of the One who creates, sustains, and re-
deems: (1) the encounter with Buddhists pushes to the fore
the apophatic tradition, in which God is addressed as much
in negation as in affirmation; or (2) this encounter enables
Christians to conceive a more adequate conception of the *relational God,* the One who requires otherness and difference for
God's very "be-coming." In most contemporary treatments of
Buddhist-Christian dialogue, the first option appears most frequently.[22] Despite the importance of this recognition, I would
suggest that the second option is the more significant today.
Despite the apophatic strands of our own tradition, and the
iconoclasm of Christian monotheism, Christianity remains a
fundamentally affirmative tradition. It can never be as deeply
apophatic as Buddhism, for at the heart of the Christian message is not the God who empties Godself without return (Abe's
God who is not God), but a God who is revealed in Christ.
The Christian God is not an empty cipher, but the "Yes" woven throughout the universe. Although this affirmation is not
an "anything goes" position (and in this case Christians need
the apophaticism proffered by Buddhism), it can be articulated
more adequately if we take seriously the *relations* between God,
the world, and the human being. The wisdom of the Buddha,
from the Christian perspective, is that it allows us to glimpse
these relations in greater detail. The God who empties Godself
in Christ requires otherness for God's very being; difference, in
other words, is intrinsic to incarnation.

The importance of the apophatic strand, however, need not
be neglected in this incarnational perspective. And here is
where Buddhists might help Christians to reclaim the iconoclasm of their own tradition. This reclamation becomes even
more critical once Christians in the West acknowledge their
own secular and demythologized context. For those attuned
to the secular milieu, there soon appears to be *nothing* that
one can utter about "God" that does not run the risk of in-

---

22. John Cobb's *Beyond Dialogue* and Raimundo Panikkar's *The Silence of God* are
two recent treatments that privilege the apophatic strand.

coherence or reification. Raimundo Panikkar has diagnosed this environment with more acuity than perhaps any other religious thinker, and for him, it is precisely through dialogue with Buddhists that Christians might yet have something to say in a modern, secular age. Dialogue with Buddhists, simply put, might allow Christians to glimpse their own cherished doctrines and conceptualities more dialectically. If the Buddhist intuition is internalized, there is no statement about God that does not at the same time reflect what God is *not*. Even the most simple, straightforward statement about God, "God is," must be viewed in this dialectical manner.[23] The Buddhist intuition of "nothingness," in other words, might correct absolutizing tendencies within the Christian tradition. Panikkar writes, "God is at once ever-present absence and ever-absent presence, God 'is' never what is thought, or what 'is'; and in turn God is always what is thought, as indeed underlying all that in any way 'is.' "[24] The wisdom of Panikkar's perspective is that it grasps both horns of the God-dilemma: on the one hand, the Christian God is the One who must be affirmed as the ground and lure of all, but on the other hand, any articulation of this affirmative One is bound to fall short of the reality it seeks to express. Christians, in other words, *must* speak about God precisely because we *cannot* speak about God. By conceiving God dialectically, however, Christian theologians might bespeak the mystery (in apophaticism) revealed in the incarnation (by affirmation). Both perspectives are necessary to avoid the ubiquitous danger of idolatry and yet acknowledge the gracious "yes" uttered by the self-emptying God.

The brilliance and creativity of Panikkar's expression of both Buddhist and Christian sensibilities is that by taking to heart both the claims of "God" and "emptiness," Panikkar frees God from the strictures of "being," and views God also in terms of

---

23. The approach here bears some resemblance to Thomas Aquinas's notion of *analogy* in portraying the divine, and Sallie McFague's suggestion that all statements about God are metaphorical. See Thomas Aquinas, *Summa Theologica*, vol. 3, 1a. 13 (London: Eyre & Spottiswoode, 1964), 47–97; Sallie McFague, *Metaphorical Theology* (Philadelphia: Fortress, 1982), chs. 1, 2, 4, and *Models of God* (Philadelphia: Fortress, 1987), part 1.

24. Panikkar, *The Silence of God*, 132.

"non-being." Making explicit reference to the resurrection, an
event that "reveals" God precisely in the "absence" of the empty
tomb, Panikkar writes, "God is always the one risen from the
dead and absent among the living.... God is not an *esse-ad*—a
being present and facing things—but an *esse-ab*, a 'being' from
which beings draw their origin. Strictly speaking, God neither
has nor is *esse*, but 'is' *esse-ab*, an absence, a nonbeing from which
beings take their origin."[25] Here Panikkar's direct engagement
with both Christian and Buddhist texts has brought his conception of God quite close to the classical apophatic sensibility: God
is revealed as much in the "is not" (non-being) as in the "is" (being). As a result, God is freed from the wooden confinements of
being and viewed more appropriately in *relational* terms. God is
not sufficient in Godself, but becomes God in interconnection
with the entire cosmos. Yet even relationality cannot exhaust or
enclose God. It is the wisdom of the apophatic sensibility (particularly when drawn out through conversation with Buddhists)
that God cannot be contained by any description, category, or
definition, including our description of relation or even the
name, "God." Yet because "God" refuses to be contained, God
is the One who "ex-ists" (lives out) in relation with others. One
result of the Christian-Buddhist conversation is that our conceptualities of God might thus be pushed away from "being"
and more toward relational "be-coming."[26] God is not primarily
self-sufficient, *a se*, but open to what is other than God.[27]

As important as a recovery of the apophatic strand is to the
business of Christian theology, we sell ourselves short if it is the
only strand we gain from the Buddhist-Christian conversation.
In our secularized age, most Christians—particularly theolo-

---

25. Ibid., 131. Panikkar's thematization of resurrection as "absence" is suggestive
of my own, which will be developed in the following chapter.

26. In subsequent sections of this work, I will often hyphenate the words "be-
coming" and "being." This aberrant spelling is intended to free theological,
christological, and anthropological statements from static conceptualities. God,
Christ, and human beings are best understood as *relational* entities; by describing their "be-coming" and "be-ing," I offer a linguistic reminder of their profound
interrelationship.

27. The echoes of deconstruction are particularly prevalent here. Mark C. Taylor's recent work explores the limits of traditional God-talk by first addressing how
not to think God. See *Nots* (Chicago: University of Chicago Press, 1993), 11–27.

gians—are well-attuned to the complexity and nonreferentiality of God-talk. Indeed, in this context, the problem is not a reckless profusion of language about God, but a certain "crisis of confidence" in speaking of the divine.[28] As a deeply affirmative tradition, Christianity must continue to say *something* about the nature of God, however provisional that affirmation may be. For without it, incarnation soon vanishes in the smoke of divine mystery and apophatic negation. Here is where the conversation with Buddhists again may help. One kernel of the Buddha's wisdom is that which is conceived as static, perduring, and unchangeable is illusory and empty. Anything that is "thingified" is subject to radical negation. Certainly, in many instances throughout Christian theology, God has been rendered a Supreme Being, as the grandest "thing" of all. Whether one describes this perduring nature as God's aseity, immutability, or perfection, what is suggested is that God is wholly sufficient in Godself. Otherness is peripheral to the "being" of God. It is precisely this depiction, however, that a Buddhist sensibility strips away. By taking to heart both the Zen Buddhist intuition of *sunyata* and the Christian affirmation of God's creativity, Christian theologians may yet have something to say about the relational God. The "God" who is empty, the "God" who is an idol, is precisely the God who exists sufficiently in Godself; the God of incarnation, however, is the God who is revealed in *otherness.*

One way of salvaging this recognition of the relational God in an age attuned to the complexity of God-talk is by combining the apophatic sensibility of Abe and Panikkar with Hegel's conception of the God who is emptied in an Other. From a Christian perspective, otherness and particularity are not illusions, but writ large upon the tapestry of creation. In Hegel's words, "Otherness is requisite in order that there may be

---

28. The movement away from larger, systematic theologies to more focused, contextual concerns, though sorely needed in our pluralistic age, has rendered some theologians incapable of making even tentative claims about the nature of God. I owe thanks to Peter Hodgson for pointing out this "crisis of confidence" on the contemporary scene.

difference."[29] Difference, moreover, is both real and fundamental to authentic relation. The God who is utterly self-sufficient is not capable of relation; neither is the God who empties Godself without return into the world. The God of incarnation, however, implies something else: taking a cue from Hegel, this God is the one who "releases the other to exist as a free and independent being."[30] Different, yet related, this other, the world, becomes the locus for God's revelation. The world, in other words, is *where we meet God*. Without this other, God cannot be known; God needs the world for God's very be-coming. The result of this combination of Buddhist apophaticism and Christian affirmation is twofold. On the one hand, Christianity, as an incarnational tradition, cannot ingest the totality of Buddhist emptiness; God is not the One who empties Godself into creation without return. Rather, the "yes" of God is a "yes" to both God and the Other—indeed, to all aspects of creation—and the relationship between God and the beloved Other. On the other hand, Christian theology cannot claim that relationality represents all there is to say about God. Though incarnation echoes as a resounding "yes" throughout the cosmos, it does not exhaust the be-coming of God. At the heart of the incarnation remains the God who is wholly Other than that to which God is related. God is both *related* and *transcendent;* revealed in an emptying that fulfills both creation and God, God is also the inexpressible One who transcends any particular instance of relation.

Stated alternatively, the be-coming of God is rendered explicit in relation to the world; God relentlessly and creatively seeks an Other. Relationality is not the ancillary spillover of an internally fulfilled divine Trinity, but constitutive of God's very otherness. The God of incarnation neither swallows those with whom God relates nor becomes submerged in relation, but preserves the difference and detail of each related Other.

Resuming our earlier theme, this God of incarnation can be construed as the kenotic God: God's emptying in the world

29. G. W. F. Hegel, *Lectures on the Philosophy of Religion*, vol. 3, ed. Peter C. Hodgson (Berkeley: University of California Press, 1985), 292.
30. Ibid.

(God's capacity for relation) is not without return, but for the fulfillment of divine relatedness. As the One who empties Godself in the world, God makes Godself vulnerable to the world's tragedy, suffering, and scorn. Because God is affected by the world's negativity, each moment of that world is preserved within God. Jesus Christ, the kenotic One, becomes the symbol of God's relationship, openness, and vulnerability to the world. In Christ, this relationship approaches fulfillment—a fulfillment that does not rest either in a God emptied utterly in the world or in a God who subsumes all into Godself, but in a vibrant movement between God and the related Other.

Idolatry manifests itself, however, when we attribute *everything* to this symbol of relatedness, Jesus Christ. The reason that the *figura* of Jesus Christ has become such a barrier to the religious Other is that he is rendered the *exhaustion* rather than the *revelation* of God.[31] To look to Christ alone for the emptying of God in the world is to obscure the focus on relationship at the heart of an incarnational perspective. It is to render a relational tradition an ossified one. One result of Christianity's engagement with Buddhism is to reclaim that relational core, to recognize that at the center of the Christian worldview is not God *a se,* but the One who ex-ists with others.

The Buddhist-Christian encounter has direct consequences for the deepening of each tradition's own convictions. The challenge of Buddhism yields wisdom for Christian incarnational reflections and imaginative portraiture of God. The Emptying Christ unveils an immensely wider world in which voices heretofore ignored in Christian theology—the voices of Buddhists—begin to be heard. Having surveyed our exegetical, historical, and dialogical material, we can now turn to a constructive expression of the Incarnate Christ. How might we express the claim of Christ Incarnate in a way that takes our biblical and confessional heritage seriously while at the same time paying attention to voices of others in our midst?

---

31. As Paul Knitter has noted, "The Mystery has been *revealed* in Jesus, *not removed* or resolved" (*Jesus and the Other Names* [Maryknoll, N.Y.: Orbis, 1996], 37).

TOWARD A CONSTRUCTIVE THEOLOGY
OF INCARNATION

The word "incarnate" incorporates the Latin root *carn-*, designating "flesh" or "body." According to the *Oxford English
Dictionary*, the adjective has the primary definition of "clothed
or invested with flesh; embodied in flesh; in a human bodily form...of a person, soul, or spirit." Its primary meaning,
in other words, corresponds with *embodiment*.[32] In reference to
Christ, then, our interpretation of incarnation should claim that
Jesus Christ "embodies" something. But what is it, precisely, that
Christ embodies? I would suggest that Christ's embodiment encompasses the historical life of a particular body—a history that
reveals its distinctive shape in Jesus of Nazareth's relationships
with the "least" of society. Whether Jesus breaks bread with those
whom the world scorns, or whether he heals those whose bodies are diseased and bruised, he *embodies* the proclamation of
the reign of God. This "en-acted" proclamation and surrendering of privilege (kenosis) points to the *interhuman* dimension of
incarnation, yet it also suggests something more. Christ's being-
for-the-other renders explicit God's love in the world, or the
divine-human dimension of incarnation.

Incarnation as Embodiment

We begin this consideration of Christ's embodiment by recalling the specific life of a Palestinian Jew in the first century. As
soon as we commence, however, we run into difficulties. We
have no direct access to the "life of Jesus," either in the form
of firsthand biographies or extensive historical record. Our only
access to his life is through the witness of the Gospels, which are
distinct products of communal confession in the two or three
generations after Jesus of Nazareth's death. The concern of the
Gospels, in other words, is not biographical, but to proclaim
the sustaining power of the Risen Lord. The "facts" of Jesus'
life are difficult—perhaps even impossible—to separate from

---

32. Indeed, the explicit theological reference to Christ's incarnation is minimized
in the *OED*. It is one example among many of the embodiment that incarnation
suggests.

the memory and continuing influence of the Risen One among the nascent Christian communities. Yet this recognition is significant in itself. The recollection of Jesus Christ's life is very much informed by the influence his life had upon those communities that gathered in his name. Indeed, Christ's life is not exhausted by the bare facts of biography, but is brought into more distinct configuration when we consider the influence, memory, and interpretation of that life. Human life, in short, is not exhausted by the accumulation of facts and data about particular persons, but is more wholly constituted by human relationships—how we influence others and how others influence us. For the life of Jesus, then, it is important from the outset to acknowledge that this particular life (even though many distinct "facts" about that life are irretrievable) is thoroughly constituted by relationships with others and with the communities that bear his name.

Irretrievable as several details of this life may be, there are some things we can claim about Jesus of Nazareth with relative assurance. First, there was such a person as Jesus, who partook in a fully embodied, flesh-and-bones existence. Second, much of his ministry centered on the practices of shared meals and healing the sick. Third, his preaching focused chiefly on one image: the reign of God, a rule approximated in those acts of reconciliation and healing initiated by his ministry. Although there is no universal consensus on even this much about the person of Jesus of Nazareth, these three claims are widely shared by most New Testament scholars.

As obvious as the first claim sounds, it is one that is summarily overlooked by countless Christians. To proclaim Christ as embodied is to take his human body utterly seriously, a body with all the passion, strength, limitations, and beauty of our own.[33] To claim Christ as incarnate is to claim that the distinctive shape of Jesus' life was colored in *all* its aspects by his distinctly human body. His was a body blessed with strength, for to work as a

---

33. The bodily aspect of Christology is often overlooked. If you doubt this, try asking a Sunday school class about Jesus' sexuality, and you will likely get a panicked look in response. Indeed, the failure to take Christ's body with utter seriousness seems at times to suggest that many Christians are "closet Docetists." (This example comes from a lecture given by Sallie McFague in the contemporary theology course at Vanderbilt Divinity School in the spring of 1997.)

carpenter in the first century required long hours of physical labor. Unlike the hands of the scribes and the priestly classes, his hands bore the rough traces of the sun, the calluses of hand tools, and eventually the scars of the cross.[34] His was not only a body that possessed strength and beauty, but also a body that bore the lashing of whips, the agony of thorns, and a gruesome execution.

Perhaps no aspect of Christianity has sustained this focus upon the body more prominently than the sacramental tradition. The sacrament of eucharist, in particular, privileges the body more than any other aspect of Christian worship. This focus upon the body is reflected in the Synoptic Gospels' remembrance of Jesus' words at the last supper. In his final meal with his disciples, Jesus offers bread and wine as tokens of his life: "While they were eating, Jesus took a loaf of bread, and after blessing it he broke it, gave it to the disciples, and said, 'Take, eat; this is my body' " (Matt. 26:26). This same sequence of verbs, "take," "bless," "break," and "give," occurs identically in Mark's Gospel and in almost identical form in Luke's (where "gave thanks" is used instead of "blessed"). Part of what the Synoptists are suggesting here is that this supper should serve as a summary of Christ's life, that those reading the Gospel emerge with a greater understanding Christ's embodied ministry. The Synoptists, in other words, echo the kenotic theme of the Philippians Christ-hymn. Just as Jesus takes, blesses, breaks, and gives the bread, he performs these gestures in his own life: a life taken, not solely for himself, but on behalf of others; a body blessed to proclaim the reign of God and to do the will of the One who sent him; a body broken by misunderstanding,

---

34. John Dominic Crossan notes that a carpenter in first-century Palestine was not a "skilled, well-paid and respected member of the middle class," but a member of the lowest classes. "In general, the great divide in the Greco-Roman world was between those who had to work with their hands and those who did not" (*Jesus: A Revolutionary Biography* [San Francisco: HarperCollins, 1994], 24). Crossan's brief class analysis of first-century Palestine places Jesus in the "artisan class, that group pushed into the dangerous space between Peasants [that majority of the population whose agricultural labor supported the upper classes] and Degradeds or Expendables [castaways such as beggars and slaves]" (p. 24). Jesus of Nazareth's embodied life was in many instances vulnerable, both in terms of his inauspicious background and in terms of the destabilizing message he preached.

mockery, scorn, and eventual crucifixion; a life given on behalf of others, not in self-abnegation, but in order to fulfill both others' lives and his own.[35]

It is striking how much of Jesus' practice, as remembered in the Gospels, stresses food—that which is necessary to sustain bodies. The Gospels recall Jesus as the One who feeds those who gather to hear his message (feeding the five thousand), who dines with sinners and outcasts (Mary Magdalene and Zacchaeus), who celebrates at wedding feasts, and who breaks bread with his disciples during his final days. Jesus is the One with bread in his hands and wine in his cup, feeding those who are hungry and associating with persons both scurrilous and scorned. Indeed, it seems as if Jesus would share a meal with anyone who invited him. By eating with anyone, Jesus demonstrates his relationship with everyone who would ask.[36] Inasmuch as Jesus embodies this undiscriminating practice of shared meals, he lives out "his own parable" of "open commensality," the disregard of all conventional rules of association.[37] The bread that Jesus holds in his hands he extends to *all* bodies.

Christ's embodiment, furthermore, privileges those "bodies" whom society despises. Each of the Gospels records Jesus' association with lepers, whose bodies have been disfigured and mangled by disease, and prostitutes, whose bodies have been

---

35. These reflections on the connections between Christ's body and the words of institution are inspired most directly by a sermon, "Four Gestures of Grace," preached by Rev. Stephen Hancock at Second Presbyterian Church, Nashville, on September 7, 1997. Hancock's sermon offers a vivid and suggestive portrait of the embodiment of Christ's body and how we remember that embodiment each time the church celebrates the eucharist: "[Mark 6:34–44] is the first written account ever made, we think, of Jesus with bread in his hands. And it gives a clue as to what was so powerfully characteristic about what he did with it; what he always does with what's in his hands. Mark uses four verbs to tell the story of what Jesus did and what he always does, not just with bread but with everything he touches, including every life he's touched, including his own life. The four verbs? The four gestures of Christ: He took, he blessed, he broke, he gave." Crossan remarks that the first two verbs correspond to the master, while the last two are representative of servanthood. "Jesus, as master and host, performs the role of servant, and all share the same food of equals" (*Revolutionary Biography*, 181). Jesus' disregard for conventional distinctions in the serving and sharing of food is striking.

36. A shared meal is one of the chief practices cross-culturally by which persons sustain relationships with each other. See Crossan, *Revolutionary Biography*, 68.

37. Ibid., 69.

reduced to sexual objects. Sallie McFague has suggested that Jesus' practice of radical inclusivism in relation to the body implies a preferential option for those on the margins: "*The story of Jesus suggests that the shape of God's body includes all, especially the needy and outcast....* The distinctive character of Christian embodiment is its focus on oppressed, vulnerable, suffering *bodies,* those who are in pain due to the indifference or greed of the more powerful."[38] The body that Jesus embodies finds its closest parallel in those bodies that are rejected and despised, for his is the body broken and given for others. Yet this brokenness and rejection is not the last word. Jesus' embodiment, in other words, offers immense hope to those who suffer, because his is an *empathetic* body; he is the One who heals others.[39]

The sheer number of times that the Gospels record Jesus as a

---

38. McFague, *The Body of God* (Minneapolis: Fortress, 1993), 164.

39. It would be a careless consideration of Christ's body that did not mention how Christ's suffering and crucifixion have been glorified in large portions of Christian theology and preaching. For some strands of the tradition, suffering appears an end in and of itself, something to be sought after by all Christians. A few early apologists, for example, long for their own torture See Ignatius of Antioch's letters in *Ancient Christian Writers,* vol. 1, trans. James A. Kleist (Westminster, Md.: Newman, 1949), 60–99. Indeed, in the worst cases, the suffering of Jesus appears as legitimization for any and all forms of societal violence and abuse. Countless are the experiences of women who as victims of domestic abuse seek counseling from a minister only to be urged to "endure patiently" the battering and rape and to serve as an example of suffering endurance for their husbands or partners. See Marie Marshall Fortune, *Sexual Violence: The Unmentionable Sin* (New York: Pilgrim, 1983). The turning of a blind eye to violence in our midst perpetrated under the name of the "suffering Christ" is nothing less than the perpetuation of our society's own cycle of sexual and domestic abuse. The foisting of Christ's "body" upon this sordid cycle of abuse is inexcusable and is diametrically opposed to the empathetic embodiment I am suggesting.

An approach that parallels my own reflection on the sufferings of the embodied Christ is found most with powerful strains of hope in the writings of several womanist theologians. Jacquelyn Grant writes of the belief "in Jesus as the divine co-sufferer, who empowers [black people] in situations of oppression" (*White Women's Christ and Black Women's Jesus* [Atlanta: Scholars Press, 1989], 212). Grant mines the resources of American slave narratives and prayers, finding in them suggestive images for how the suffering Jesus served not to legitimate oppression, but as a subversive image that empowered black slaves to work against oppression and offered hope in the midst of even the most ruthless abuse. "[The] slave woman did not hesitate to identify her struggles and pain with those of Jesus. In fact, the common struggle made her know that Jesus would respond to her beck and call" (p. 213.) See also the examples of slave songs and spirituals in Milton C. Sernett, *Afro-American Religious History: A Documentary Witness* (Durham, N.C.: Duke University Press, 1985), 111–32. These songs offer powerful examples of how the image of the suffering Jesus was a source of strength for those in the most abominable of situations.

healer is remarkable. In this regard, Jesus is likewise undiscriminating, bringing wholeness to the blind, lepers, paralytics, and the possessed. To claim Jesus as a healer, however, is not to place him at the same level as the thaumaturgist or hawker of elixirs. His was not the instantaneous healing of miraculous touch that has become customary in charismatic revivals. Rather, Jesus' practice of healing extended to a much deeper level, affecting not simply the symptoms of physical ailment, but the embodied life of the one stricken by disease. Jesus, in Crossan's words, addressed the illness and the ostracism it caused.[40]

The example of Jesus' healing of lepers is particularly illustrative. Since the disease of leprosy resulted in the banishment of those afflicted by it, leprosy represented a rupture of social relatedness. Lepers were the ones excised from their homes, no longer connected to others because of fear and loathing.[41] The healing of Jesus addresses this entire situation of ostracism, and not simply the physical manifestations of disease. Jesus refuses to "accept the disease's ritual uncleanness. . . . By healing the illness without curing the disease, Jesus acted as an alternative boundary keeper in a way subversive to the established procedures of his society."[42] Jesus, in short, refuses to reduce lepers to their illness, and regards each one as a whole person. In actuality, it is those others who have excluded the leper who are sick, and it is only Jesus who recognizes this. Jesus disregards those self-imposed boundaries that would separate "the sick" from others, and thus enacts a healing more comprehensive than the workings of any miracle drug.

Jesus' table fellowship and ministry of healing are the practical fruits of the central theme of his preaching: the reign of God. The proclamation, as witnessed in healed and nourished bodies, does not so much describe a holy place or elevated truth as it does a reconciling praxis. Jesus message, furthermore, does not center on himself, but reaches out to a reenvisioned and renewed world. In Crossan's words, "The Kingdom of God was

---

40. Crossan, *Revolutionary Biography*, 82.
41. The parallels with the contemporary AIDS epidemic are striking, where those with HIV are effectively expelled from mainstream society.
42. Crossan, *Revolutionary Biography*, 82.

not, for Jesus, a divine monopoly exclusively bound to his own person. It began on the level of the body and appeared as a shared community of healing and eating.... One entered the Kingdom as a way of life, and anyone who could live it could bring it to others."[43] As Jesus preached it, the reign of God amounted to a radical reordering of priorities and distinctions, and the relinquishing of privilege: away from the structures of power and exclusion that set clean against unclean, Gentile against Jew, man against woman, master against slave, and toward a reconceived community in which persons formerly at odds with each other would sit at table and break bread together.

Jesus of Nazareth inaugurates in his person an embodied ministry of "open commensality"[44] and healing, whose theme is broadly characterized as the reign of God. Both the *person* and the *work* of Christ thus begin with fleshy, vulnerable human bodies. We might describe this work of Christ—the trajectory beginning with his person—as kenosis, or the being of the Incarnate One on behalf of the Other.

Incarnation as Kenotic Relationality

Beginning with the body, or adopting a "Christology from below," I would offer the following proposal: To claim Christ as incarnate is to claim that the man Jesus embodies in the flesh the closest possible identification with the human Other, without the surrender of his own self-identity. To view this incarnation as kenosis, moreover, is to claim that Christ's relation with the beloved Other is so intimate that he empties himself on behalf of the Other. One example of this relation depicted in the Gospels is Jesus' practice of table fellowship (e.g., Matt. 9:10–13; Luke 19:1–10).[45] Jesus of Nazareth breaks bread with

---

43. Ibid., 113.

44. The term is from Crossan, *Revolutionary Biography*, ch. 3.

45. The theme of Jesus' table fellowship is a familiar one in liberation theologies, since it is here that Jesus' identification with the poor is offered in a shared meal. Aloysius Pieris effectively summarizes this practice: "(1) Jesus' *renunciation* of biological, emotional, and physical ties that bind him to the 'world' (Jesus' *struggle to be poor*), and (2) his open *denunciation* of mammon, which organizes itself into principalities and powers by dividing humankind into the class of Dives and the

and heals those tax collectors, prostitutes, and sinners whom society scorns. He views these outcasts, in short, as *having a claim upon him.* Whether evidenced in his table fellowship, his feeding of those who are hungry, his healing of the sick, his openness to children, his love for the one who would betray him, or his willingness to endure crucifixion, Jesus "empties" himself of supposed self-privilege and turns toward the Other, to those near at hand in need. His life is marked by a relinquishing of supposed self-privilege in relation to marginalized human Others.

This type of interhuman identification is echoed in the work of Emmanuel Lévinas, who thematizes what I suggest Christ embodies in this incarnational approach. Lévinas employs the concept of *divestment* of the individual self in relation to the Other, a theme that bears some resemblance to the image of kenosis. Lévinas writes, "The more I return to myself, the more I divest myself... of my freedom as a constituted, wilful, imperialist subject, the more I discover myself to be responsible.... I am 'in myself' through the others."[46] Such divestment does not imply the surrender of the self or the abject debasement of one's subjectivity, but the relinquishing of any claims to privilege and superiority by the individual self. Only by "emptying" the imperialized, individual subject, can one take seriously the reality and subjecthood of the Other, only then is the door to mutual relation with another opened.

Part of the nuance of Paul's use of kenosis in the Christ-hymn is precisely this aspect that Lévinas is uplifting—the divestment of one's own privileges.[47] To surrender one's privileges is to suggest that the Other has a claim upon oneself, to bespeak interrelationship at its deepest level. This claim of the Other, moreover, takes seriously the radical differences between human beings; it renders impossible the subsuming of the "you" by a totalizing "I." The call of responsibility for another, in other

class of Lazarus (Jesus' *struggle for the poor*)" (*Love Meets Wisdom* [Maryknoll, N.Y.: Orbis, 1988], 134).

46. Emmanuel Lévinas, *Otherwise Than Being*, trans. Alphonso Lingis (Boston: Martinus Nijhoff, 1981), 112.

47. See Walter Bauer, *A Greek-English Lexicon of the New Testament*, trans. William F. Arndt and F. Wilbur Gingrich (Chicago: University of Chicago Press, 1979), 428.

words, brings into configuration the irreducible detail and difference of that concrete Other, an alterity that, for Lévinas, occurs in the mysterious and compelling signification of the face. The Other's face thematizes the sheer difference of the Other, the refusal to be encapsulated by my own conception of that person, the inviting and haunting reminder of *difference*. Only to the careless observer, we should note, do two faces look the same. In Lévinas's words, "The face to face is a final and irreducible relation. . . . It makes possible the pluralism of society."[48] The face, in its nakedness and vulnerability, issues forth in ethical imperatives, by summoning us to uphold the integrity of each embodied, dazzlingly different individual.

Lévinas's relational anthropology calls us to recognize the authenticity and subjecthood of each person, even to the extent of surrendering our own supposed privileges vis-à-vis that human Other. Human beings thus become more human in situations of radical openness to other human beings, through giving to one another. The kenotic self, in short, does not represent the troubling reemergence of self-abnegation, but the recovery of what many feminist and process theologians call the *relational self*. To suggest the kenotic dynamic as one aspect of a relational theory of incarnation is to offer the following proposal: Kenosis implies a dynamic of efflux and return, a recognition of the concrete Other without the surrender of one's self-identity. Jesus Christ is the Human One insofar as he "incarnates" this dynamic in his life, even unto his death upon a cross. For Christians, Jesus Christ is the embodiment of authentic humanity,[49] a humanness that emerges in and with distinct human Others. Jesus Christ's selfhood, in other words, becomes more fully delineated the more he identifies himself with others, the more he recognizes the claims of others upon him. Viewed through this relational lens, the "humanity" of Christ emerges not as a proposition—à

---

48. Emmanuel Lévinas, *Totality and Infinity*, trans. Alphonso Lingis (Pittsburgh: Duquesne University Press, 1969), 194.

49. Or, as Karl Barth writes of Jesus as the "true man": "To be a man is to be with Jesus, to be like Him. To be a man is thus to be with the One who is the true and primary Elect of God" (*Church Dogmatics*, vol. 3, part 2, ed. G. W. Bromiley and T. F. Torrance [Edinburgh: T. & T. Clark, 1960], 145).

la Chalcedon—but as a consequence of Christ's absolute identification with and responsibility for the Other. Kenosis thus conveys the most intimate level of interhuman relation, the full humanity of Christ's incarnation.

The Divine-Human Dimension of Incarnation

The Christian claim of incarnation, however, has always suggested something more than the assertion of Christ's full humanity. For Christians, the incarnation has as much to say about God and God's relation to the world as it does about human persons. Particularly when explicated along kenotic lines, the idea of incarnation becomes a virtual fountainhead of speculation on God's involvement with the world. The approach I would offer, however, is a moderate one. My intention is to glimpse the continuities between Christian claims of creation and incarnation, and to give some specificity to the claim of God's involvement with both. The reverberations here will sound familiar, having much in common with those theologians who advocate a wider incarnational sensibility.[50] We would do well to heed the words of Karl Rahner on this matter: "We can understand creation and Incarnation as two moments and two phases of the *one* process of God's self-giving and self-expression."[51] I am privileging this focus on creation because it represents the widest possible scope of God's activity in the world; indeed, for Christians, creation might represent the totality of the divine activity, *creatio continua*. Creation is the context of God's revelation; or, conversely, the world is where we meet God. The result of such privileging of creation is not the relegating of Christology to a secondary or derivative status, but the glimpsing of the Christ-event within a broader perspective, viewing it as something that has resonance with all of creation. Incarnation thus becomes something more than a cosmic surd or an aberration upon the stage of creation, and

50. Hegel's Christology, as we have seen, offers a helpful approach for understanding incarnation within a larger cosmic context.
51. Karl Rahner, *Foundations of Christian Faith*, trans. William Dych (New York: Crossroad, 1978), 197.

becomes instead the enflowerment of God's creative intent for the cosmos.

To describe the cosmos under the banner of "creation" is to claim that the universe itself is a gift. The world, according to the Christian claim, is not the necessary emanation of a remote deity, but the place of God's self-manifestation. The world, in short, *matters* to God. God and creation are thus from the beginning enmeshed in relationship, so that the destiny of creation is bound up with the history of God. Furthermore, the Christian tradition has also made a clear distinction between God and creation. This claim is hardly surprising, since only between entities that recognize and preserve difference is authentic relationship possible: God and creation, in other words, are related yet other. The engagement with Buddhism that we have just highlighted only serves to confirm this recognition. Both the God who is "un-related" and the God who empties Godself into the world without return must be resisted with an apophatic "no." To claim God as creator is profoundly iconoclastic: the creative God abhors idolatrous reification by underscoring both the otherness of God and the reality of the world's relation with God.

One way of expressing the originative and sustaining dynamic of creation is with the language of kenosis: God's close identification with the Other (the world) without subsuming the beloved Other. To be-for-an-other, as we have seen, is to give of oneself. The most intimate identification would be the emptying or aspiration of Godself in the world, a creative kenosis that would not deplete God, but fulfill the relationship between creation and creator. God would become more fully God, and the world would become more fully itself through this kind of intimate identification and kenosis. Thus understood, creation depicts the emptying of God into the world, God's gift of be-coming to the Other. This creative God is revealed most expressly in the incarnation: the God who reveals Godself in love to an Other and who thus becomes vulnerable to all the world's pain, injustice, suffering, and tragedy.

Because creation underscores the intimate identification of God with the world, humanity—as part of that world—is from the beginning made for relationship with God. This is yet another resonance with the classical incarnational sensibility of Irenaeus and Augustine: humanity and God are not strangers, but capable of communion with each other.[52] God does not remain remote from the world, but whispers God's presence to the world. The heart of God's intention for creation, in other words, is love, the giving of God's self to a genuine Other.

Incarnation represents the segment of creation where God's relationality is most fully glimpsed. For Christians, this relationality is embodied most distinctively in the person of Jesus Christ. Christians appropriately affirm God's presence in Christ, because he incarnates, makes real in the flesh, the genuine openness of interhuman relation. The One who represents the fulfillment of human relationship—Jesus Christ—offers a fleeting glimpse of God's relationship to us. God's gift on behalf of the Other (creation) is rendered concrete in Christ's openness to the human Other. Christ's kenosis thus represents not only the enflowerment of authentic humanity, but also God's identification and concern with what is other than God. It is precisely because Christ embodies the human condition so completely that he is said to intimate God with us.

Stated in more traditional terms, the incarnation represents the *reconciliation* of God and humanity, the full expression of Emmanuel, God with us. As the One who incorporates the world's fragility, suffering, and loss into Godself, God lures the cosmos toward healing and redemption. Hegel has expressed this aspect as well as anyone in the tradition: in Christ, "God has shown himself to be reconciled with the world, that even the human is not something alien to him, but rather that this otherness, this self-distinguishing, finitude as it is expressed, is a moment in God himself, although, to be sure, it is a disappearing moment."[53] The "story" of incarnation suggests that otherness is intrinsic to the be-coming of God, that the long and rocky path of estrangement, suffering, and tragedy—symbolized

---

52. A recognition that even Karl Barth, in his later years, embraced! See *The Humanity of God*, trans. John Newton Thomas (Atlanta: John Knox, 1974), 37–65.
53. Hegel, *Lectures*, 3:327.

in the cross—are gathered together and taken up as moments within God.

What is most intriguing about Hegel's conception—and here is where our reflections echo a Buddhist sensibility—is that each instance of incarnate relatedness is a *disappearing moment*. The God who is expressed in the incarnation, in other words, cannot be contained by any relationship with the world. Though Christians look to Christ for the fullest expression of Emmanuel, the symbol of Christ can enclose neither the otherness of God nor the relationship between God and creation. For redemption is more a promise than an actuality. Jesus Christ points to the possibility of redemption, but he does not exhaust it. Only a privileged Westerner could make this mistake: only those insulated in creature comforts, inured to the groaning of the planet and with faces turned away from the massive suffering in their midst, could proclaim so glibly that in Jesus Christ everything is "already redeemed." Though the actuality of redemption disappears into the future, it is nonetheless promised in the midst of concrete relationships, symbolized most distinctly in a vulnerable God who extends Godself to creation. An incarnational theology, as a relational theology, affirms that in the beginning is the relation, but also recognizes that each moment of relation is evanescent. To suggest anything else is to claim that the living relationship that incarnation symbolizes can be neatly contained. As the apophatic tradition would remind us, any relationship thus restricted, any redemption proclaimed as fully present with us, is bound to disappear.

SUMMARY:
KENOSIS AND THE RELIGIOUS OTHER

Having traversed a wide range of biblical and theological reflection, we have explored the suggestiveness, power, nuance, and even the dangers of kenotic imagery. Though the image is burdened with an ambiguous history, I believe it offers a credible portrait of incarnation in a (post)modern, religiously pluralistic age. The image is coherent because of its focus on relationality rather than anachronisms of "nature."[54] Jesus Christ, in other words, is the kenotic One as he "empties" himself on behalf of others, as he renders concrete the relationship between God and creation. Incarnation, according to the interpretation I have proffered, is *embodiment,* Jesus Christ's embodiment of a distinct human body (a body like ours), his enfleshment of authentic human relationship in which the self is not constituted in isolation but in relation to others, and his relativizing of self-interest in regard to the well-being of others. More significantly, the human be-ing that Jesus Christ embodies is also the concretization of God's relationship to creation. It is in Christ that the divine relationality is most clearly discerned, through Christ that one is offered an intimation of God who empties Godself in love. Because Christ epitomizes the interhuman relation par excellence, he also offers a window to the divine-human relation.

For Christians, on one level there can be no question about the kenotic Christ's uniqueness. Christ's embodiment of being-on-behalf-of-others, or in Douglas Ottati's words, "Jesus Christ ... as authentic humanity appropriately directed toward God,"[55] is the heart of what it means to claim human beings and God as made for relationship. This concretization of the divine and human trajectories in the person of Jesus Christ renders him unique and, for Christians, indispensable. Nevertheless, a thoroughly kenotic understanding of incarnation points to something broader than Christian exclusivism. The kenotic Christ's uniqueness manifests itself in a way that stubbornly resists imperialistic or triumphalistic appropriation. The confession of the kenotic Christ cannot rest in pointing to the *figura* of Jesus Christ alone, above all others. To advocate such a narrow Christocentrism is tantamount to truncating the kenotic dynamic that Jesus Christ embodies. Christ's being-for-others would thus disappear under the distortion of triumphal appropriation.

---

54. That is, Christ's "divine" and "human" nature, and the conundrums this division invariably creates.

55. Douglas F. Ottati, *Jesus Christ and Christian Vision* (Louisville: Westminster John Knox, 1996), 95.

Christ's kenosis, in other words, points to something larger than the claims that Christians make about a man in first-century Palestine who claimed relatively little for himself. The dynamic of kenosis depicts the relationality between God and the world and between concrete human beings, relations that undergird Christian claims about reality itself. Kenosis points to God's intimate identification with the world, and the demand of our own identification with the whispered summons of the Other (particularly the religious Other) in interhuman encounter.[56]

The confession of the kenotic Christ, I would argue, issues forth in a distinct praxis of Christian discipleship: openness to the Other. Certainly, such is the intent of Paul in his exhortation to the Philippians, that his audience be of "the same mind" as the kenotic Christ, that they look to others as well as themselves, that they grow in understanding and service to one another. To experience the Other, to break the bonds of the totalizing "I" and to recognize the subjecthood of the "you," is nothing less than a gift. For Christians, such claims about recognition coalesce around claims made about the person of Jesus Christ and the demands of following the Incarnate One. Yet in confessing a kenotic Christ, the One who empties himself on behalf of others, any triumphalistic claims about Christ are emptied as well. For triumphing over another is hardly existing on behalf of the Other. My conviction is that in confessing the One who embodies being-with-others so completely, Christians open themselves as well to the utter gift of the Other, to the endless mystery and bedazzling surprise of interhuman relationship. Such christological confession may indeed issue forth in a renewed call for interfaith dialogue and in genuine openness to the religious Other. Confession of the kenotic Christ, in other words, draws Christians back into encounter with traditions different from their own. The appearance of Jesus as the

---

56. One of the most memorable of Jesus' parables, that of the good Samaritan (Luke 10:25–37), portrays at its center a "religious Other," one who was considered neither Jew nor Gentile, a stranger generally viewed with scorn. A "good" Samaritan, for Jesus' audience, was an oxymoron. Undoubtedly, it is significant that Jesus' openness to the Other included even this cultural and religious stranger.

Christ and the face of the religious Other are two aspects of the same living, incarnational trajectory. Neither is ever exhausted, and Christians return to both again and again. But what of that other "scandal" of Christian uniqueness? Do Christian claims about the Risen One have any relevance in the dialogical arena? It is to these questions that we now turn.

CHAPTER IV

THE ABSENT PRESENCE OF THE RISEN CHRIST

THE RESURRECTION has often been heralded as the quintessence of Christian triumph. In affirming Jesus Christ as the Risen One, Christians proclaim that death has lost its painful sting and that the life and ministry of this obscure carpenter from Nazareth have been vindicated forever. "Still he lives today," sounds the proclamation, a chord that has nourished and grounded Christian hope for well-nigh two millennia. At times this emphasis upon Christ's triumph over the grave has seeped into the soil of religious triumphalism. The resurrection then becomes not only the locus of Christian hope and remembrance, but one of the hallmarks of Christianity's "uniqueness," a definitive manifestation of God's mighty act, against which all other religious traditions pale. This unfortunate coupling of Christian triumphalism with the profession of Jesus Christ as the Risen One has wended its way into countless theological treatises throughout the centuries. Often is the resurrection interpreted as the triumph of Christian truth; rarely is it glimpsed as a possible avenue for interreligious encounter.

What I will explore in this chapter is precisely this aspect—the invitation of encounter—that so many treatments of resurrection have missed. The proclamation of Jesus Christ as risen, as I see it, is nothing short of a shocking and evocative affirmation: powerful not only because of its puzzling suggestion of the emergence of life out of death, but also because it suggests a continuation of the kenotic dynamic that we explored in the previous chapters. The claim that I will advance throughout this chapter is that Christ's "self-emptying" pattern of incarnation does not disappear with his death but emerges renewed in the nascent church's collective experience of the Risen One, a conviction that continues today wherever that Risen One is proclaimed. A helpful image that we will employ in interpreting the resurrection is Mark's narration of the empty tomb. As we will soon see, the jarring conclusion to Mark's Gospel serves as a summons for his readers to take up the story again from its beginning. Remarkably, the open-endedness of Mark's narrative and the empty tomb itself allows for the possibility of a new story to begin at the threshold of death. The inconclusiveness of the story, in other words, invites us to encounter Christ again among the living. We encounter the Risen Christ not in the frozen absolutes of the past but in the imaginative and mysterious possibilities of today. One possibility, indeed, is the arena of interfaith dialogue. This connection of kenotic imagery with the empty tomb offers a long-overdue alternative to the Gordian knot of resurrection triumphalism and the familiar obstacles it presents to interreligious encounter.

The task of this chapter is ambitious. First, I will explore the biblical roots of this suggestive image by examining the Markan Easter narrative in detail. Second, I will offer some literary/theological observations and proposals about the inconclusiveness of Mark's Gospel and the ambiguity of the empty tomb itself. The absence of an ending, in short, might offer a new beginning for christological reflection. Finally, I will offer some brief, constructive proposals for a theology of resurrection in our pluralistic age. The hope of this chapter, in other words, is to offer an image of the Risen Christ that launches Christians out of their own comfortable confines, upon the threshold of an immeasurably wider world.

A BIBLICAL IMAGE OF THE EMPTY TOMB

When the sabbath was over, Mary Magdalene, and Mary the mother of James, and Salome brought spices, so that they might go and anoint him. And very early on the first day of the week, when the sun had risen, they went to the tomb. They had been saying to one another, "Who will roll away the stone for us from the entrance to the tomb?"

When they looked up, they saw that the stone, which was
very large, had already been rolled back. As they entered
the tomb, they saw a young man, dressed in a white robe,
sitting on the right side; and they were alarmed. But he
said to them, "Do not be alarmed; you are looking for Jesus
of Nazareth, who was crucified. He has been raised; he is
not here. Look, there is the place they laid him. But go,
tell his disciples and Peter that he is going ahead of you to
Galilee; there you will see him, just as he told you." So they
went out and fled from the tomb, for terror and amazement had seized them; and they said nothing to anyone,
for they were afraid. (Mark 16:1–8)

As the earliest extant Gospel, Mark gives us some of the best
access to the Jesus-traditions of the early Christian communities. Saturated with jarring and cumbersome prose, the text has
puzzled interpreters for centuries. In what is perhaps a fitting
Markan conclusion, the author(s) multiply questions instead of
answering them: Who is the unnamed man in the white robe?
Why do Mary Magdalene, Mary the mother of James, and Salome run away from the tomb in fear? Why do they remain silent
and tell nothing to anyone? The perplexing ending has clearly
baffled copyists as well, as is evident by at least two different
addenda that give the story a tidier resolution.

The man in white offers a stunning word: Jesus has already
gone ahead of the women, along the road to Galilee. They
are to seek him there, at the birthplace of his public ministry,
not at its tragic end. The ending of Mark's Gospel, in other
words, compels readers to pick up the story again from its beginning, calling them back to the inauguration of the Nazarene's
ministry. Neither a triumphalist resurrection narrative nor a
somber demise on the cross, Mark's perplexing ending yields
numerous possibilities for further encounter rather than a tidy
denouement.

Mark's Portrayal of Jesus and the Role of Proclamation

Mark's portrayal of the empty tomb is the recapitulation and
culmination of his narrative of Jesus as the Anointed One of

God—a narrative that offers two responses to Jesus. On the one hand, Mark documents the abysmal failure of those who would follow Jesus. If there is a recurrent theme in this Gospel, surely it is the disciples' consistent ineptitude in interpreting the Nazarene, their hapless stumbling over any path he would show them. Part of Mark's intention is to demonstrate that even those who were closest to Jesus were unable to comprehend the significance of the One in their midst. This blindness to the presence among them is documented consistently until the time of the crucifixion, at which time Jesus is utterly alone: rejected by the authorities, scorned by the crowds, abandoned by his disciples. In Robert Smith's words, "The call to faith and discipleship, echoing and resounding through the entire gospel, is met time and again with misunderstanding, inadequate confession, and dismal rejection, with the result that Jesus in his passion is totally alone, forsaken, without disciples, without any human possibilities."[1]

On the other hand, Mark narrates the remarkable influence Jesus has upon "outsiders." Nowhere is this more evident than in the Markan portrayal of the crucifixion. In his final hour, the only persons with Jesus are two criminals in agony beside him, a few mocking bystanders, and a Roman soldier at the crosses' feet. If ever there were outsiders to the Gospel narrative, surely these scoundrels are they. Yet at the moment of Jesus' death, in his cry of lament, it is only the consummate outsider, Jesus' executioner, who becomes "the only human character in the narrative to identify Jesus properly: 'Truly this was God's son' (15:39)."[2] The frank affirmation of the one who drove nails into Jesus' hands stands in direct contrast to his abandonment by those who would follow him.[3]

---

1. Robert Smith, *Easter Gospels: The Resurrection of Jesus According to the Four Evangelists* (Minneapolis: Augsburg, 1983), 52.
2. Luke T. Johnson, *The Writings of the New Testament* (Philadelphia: Fortress, 1986), 168.
3. The exception, of course, is the three women whom we encounter both at the crucifixion and upon the threshold of the empty tomb. Mary Magdalene, Mary, and Salome have not yet abandoned their teacher at Golgotha. But even these three, we should note, look at the cross "from a distance" (Mark 15:40), unable to partake in this agonizing drama.

For Mark, the story of Jesus is marked by a compassionate
ministry to outcasts, a proclamation of the reign of God, and the
disciples' incomprehension of the "messianic secret." Throughout his ministry, Jesus of Nazareth attracts followers, in the form
of both large crowds and a more intimate circle of close associates. These followers, however, wind up misinterpreting the
life and message of the Nazarene and abandon him. At the
Gospel's conclusion Jesus Christ is utterly alone and forsaken,
so that no follower is present at his burial (although the two
Marys see "where the body was laid" [Mark 15:47]), and none
is present to witness the resurrection. Even the message that he
is risen appears to fall on deaf ears, for those gathered at the
tomb on Easter morning run away in fear. If Jesus Christ is proclaimed as the Risen One in Mark, this proclamation does not
depend upon the faithfulness of the community, but upon the
mysterious and gracious power of God.

The pivot upon which the whole pericope hinges, then, is
not the discovery of the empty tomb, but the proclamation of
Jesus as risen, spoken by the young man in the white robe: "Do
not be alarmed; you are looking for Jesus of Nazareth, who was
crucified. He has been raised; he is not here. Look, there is the
place they laid him. But go, tell his disciples and Peter that he is
going ahead of you to Galilee; there you will see him, just as he
told you" (Mark 16:6–7).[4] The young man's proclamation has
such force that it leaps out of the context in which it is uttered.
The good news that Jesus of Nazareth has been raised is directed
not just to Mary Magdalene, Mary, and Salome, but to Mark's
audience, which includes the contemporary reader. Mark does
not narrate the resurrection as a past event, but proclaims that
Jesus Christ is alive to those who would encounter him now.[5] At

---

4. Pheme Perkins equates the man's message with the kerygma: "The words
of the angel in v. 7 clearly represent the preaching of the early church and are
not an interpretation of the tomb itself" (*Resurrection: New Testament Witness and
Contemporary Reflection* [Garden City, N.Y.: Doubleday, 1984], 115). Note that Perkins
views the appearance of the man in the white robe as an angelophany.

5. This conviction that Jesus Christ was "alive" or "exalted" arose within a remarkably short span of time for those gathered in his name. Undoubtedly, this
conviction provided much of the "staying power" for the early Christian communities. Within a relatively brief span of time (fifty years at most), this acknowledgment
of the "presence" of the Risen Christ grew, spawning multiple layers of Easter tra-

the center of Mark's Easter narrative, then, is not an exhaustive account of the hows and whys of resurrection but the stubborn proclamation of Jesus Christ as the Anointed and Risen One.

Fear and Silence as a Response to the Mystery of God

Mark's proclamation ends on a perplexing and fearful note: "So they went out and fled from the tomb, for terror and amazement had seized them; and they said nothing to anyone, for they were afraid" (Mark 16:8). In the Greek text, this fear strikes an even more haunting chord, closing oddly with a conjunction (*gar*). The effect is that the reader is left hanging over a gulf of the unknown. We neither read of the women's fear dissipating the farther they run from the tomb, nor do we witness their recounting of the resurrection news. On these issues, the text is remarkably silent. Does such fear and silence represent yet another inept response to the person of Jesus Christ? Or is it rather in reverence to the proclamation of Christ as risen?

The most common interpretation is that Mark stresses the women's fear and silence as another instance of failure in discipleship. Pheme Perkins is one exponent of this view: "Mark consistently uses 'they were afraid' for the disciples' failure to understand or react appropriately to Jesus' words.... The ending of the gospel also carries a warning in its incompleteness. One must not repeat the pattern established by the disciples and the women."[6] Though Perkins's reading pays attention to Mark's consistent use of dramatic irony in his Gospel (we recognize the disciples' inadequate responses when we see them and are hence admonished not to follow in their steps), it glimpses silence and fear as wholly negative responses. An alternative view, however, is equally possible: because the women, for Mark, more closely approximate the call of discipleship than do the Twelve, their silence might be glimpsed in a positive light.[7]

---

ditions, of which the appearance narratives and the empty tomb tradition are the main strands. See Johnson, *Writings*, 101–10.

6. Perkins, *Resurrection*, 122. Perkins's interpretation is shared by R. H. Lightfoot. See *The Gospel Message of St. Mark* (Oxford: Clarendon Press, 1950), 91–93.

7. Only Mary Magdalene, Mary, and Salome are present at Jesus' crucifixion and burial; only they are entrusted with the good news of the Risen Lord.

In an intriguing work that explores the ambiguity of Mark's ending, J. Lee Magness offers another interpretation of the women's fear. Although the common interpretation suggests that what the women should have done is proclaim the "good news" immediately to anyone who would listen, Magness suggests that "indiscriminate proclamation is discouraged by Jesus. ... Silence is not necessarily a result of ignorance or misunderstanding; it is a function of knowledge.... Fear is an appropriate response to the display or the report of the display of divine power."[8] Indeed, there are instances in the Markan narrative where Jesus specifically commands those who witness his healings *not* to tell others what they have seen.[9]

Nevertheless, in the empty tomb narrative, the women have been commanded to tell the good news to an appropriate audience—the disciples and Peter—a command that we do not see carried out in the Gospel itself. In retrospect, however, it is clear that the narration of the women's experience at the tomb *has been told.* For independently of any consideration of the historicity of this pericope, it has been recounted for well-nigh two millennia since its composition. Silence, in other words, does not have the last word in this passage. Rather, Mark's refusal to establish a tidy ending to his jarring narrative, along with the women's silence itself, offer suggestive possibilities for the retelling of the story generations hence, wherever two or three are gathered in remembrance of the Risen One. The women's fear engenders a silence that gives birth to subsequently appropriate speech. Magness has a similar read on the Gospel's conclusion: "The functions of fear and silence [are] in a basically positive light; they imply a proclamation which is actualized outside of the text but in the story by the participation of the reader."[10] The reader imaginatively reads the ending to the story

---

8. J. Lee Magness, *Sense and Absence: Structure and Suspension in the Ending of Mark's Gospel* (Atlanta: Scholars Press, 1986), 98–99.

9. One prominent example is Jesus' restoration of a young girl to life (Mark 5:35–43), where those who witness the event are told that "no one should know this." Even in instances where those who behold Jesus' miracles are ordered to tell others, what is encouraged is discriminate proclamation—telling the appropriate people, not simply anyone who would listen. See Mark 5:1–20.

10. Magness, *Sense and Absence*, 105. "Silence and speech are two equally appro-

in the ending that *is not there.* The absent ending thus enables the resurrection story to be actualized anew with each fresh reading.

The absence of a formulaic conclusion to Mark's Gospel is also suggestive of the theme these christological reflections have consistently emphasized: emptiness. Jesus of Nazareth, the One who empties himself on behalf of others, is affirmed as the Risen One of the empty tomb. Sought by Mary Magdalene, Mary, and Salome in a stone sepulcher (where we would expect him to be), he is present in this context only in emptiness and absence. Where we would seek him, there he *is not.* Mark's narration of the resurrection is not primarily about Christ's miraculous triumph over death and the grave,[11] but his absence from the haunting chambers of an empty tomb and the proclamation that he is elsewhere. It is in this situation of Christ's *absence* that his presence is affirmed. The dynamic of kenosis, in other words, has continued even unto death. Jesus Christ, the One who relinquishes all privilege and empties himself on behalf of others, resists even the triumph of resurrection victory. Mark's proclamation thus empties the Risen One from a particular, narrow locale (the tomb where he might be worshiped) and depicts Christ as going on ahead of his disciples. The Risen One, in short, cannot be contained even by those who would worship him. Resisting all attempts at enclosure, the Risen Christ treads the road to Galilee, in the promise that he will there encounter others.

From Galilee to the World

It is significant that the women who have come to embalm Jesus will see him again not at the center of religious authority, Jerusalem, but in Galilee, on the border of the Gentile world. With this message, Mark draws the reader back to the land where Jesus' ministry began, to the comparative backwater of a far-flung region of Palestine. What is the significance of placing

---

priate responses to the phenomenon of miracle. They are not mutually exclusive even in the same setting" (p. 99).

11. These imaginative descriptions are connected with the later, apocryphal Gospels.

the Risen Christ in this somewhat obscure land, away from the
locales that played such a prominent role at the end of Jesus'
life? Smith offers an illuminating interpretation: "As Jerusalem
was for Mark the place of rejection and death, the city of opposition, so Galilee was the place of Jesus' ministry of teaching
and healing, and it was the land where that mission was to be
resumed."[12] Mark's location of the Risen Christ in Galilee suggests both the "fringe nature" of the followers of Jesus,[13] and
that the movement itself will take them farther away from the
presumed "center."

For first-century Jewish-Christians, Galilee stood on the edge
of the Gentile world. Mark's location of the Risen One at
this border likely stands as a sign for the church's mission to
the Gentiles: "In a post-resurrection situation a symbolic reference...may be taken to be references to Jesus leading his
disciples into the Gentile world. It is in the Gentile world of
the church's mission that they will see him."[14] Indeed, if it is
the case that Mark's Gospel was composed for a community
within the Gentile world, this reference to Galilee would be
all the more poignant.[15] Norman Perrin also notes that Galilee
"in Jewish thinking...[was] itself a district of marked ethnic
mixing...[and] was a symbol for the work of God in the whole
world."[16] If this characterization is accurate, the risen Christ is
not to be present in the homogenized setting of the familiar,
but upon the threshold of a world of difference. The empty
tomb's reference to Galilee thus becomes an open invitation to
that world.

One of the literary devices that Mark employs so effectively is

---

12. Smith, *Easter Gospels*, 38.
13. "Can anything good come out of Nazareth?" (John 1:46) also reflects this
regional bias.
14. Norman Perrin, *The Resurrection According to Matthew, Mark, and Luke* (Philadelphia: Fortress, 1977), 27.
15. Most scholars surmise that the community for whom Mark wrote was predom-
inantly Gentile, located outside Palestine, perhaps in Rome. See Michel Clevenot,
Materialist Approaches to the Bible, trans. William J. Nottingham (Maryknoll, N.Y.:
Orbis, 1985), 62. Smith claims that Mark's audience has suffered persecution in
Nero's Rome. See *Easter Gospels*, 22.
16. Norman Perrin and Dennis C. Duling, *The New Testament: An Introduction*, 2nd
ed. (San Diego: Harcourt Brace Jovanovich, 1982), 243.

dramatic irony, so that the reader sits in a position of privilege in relation to the complex series of events and proclamations in which the Gospel characters participate. The irony mounts and achieves its climax in the Gospel's puzzling conclusion. For here is where the Gospel presents itself as a forward-looking story, a future of which the characters within the story have few inklings, but of which the reader has already partially partaken. Mark offers in the perplexing conclusion not a backward-looking "history" of resurrection, but a present- and future-oriented narrative that achieves its greatest resonance in the reader's own context. Whereas the women run away from the tomb in fear and silence, the reader knows that the proclamation entrusted to them has been announced time and again. Whereas they are to progress along the road to Galilee to encounter the Risen Christ, the reader knows that this road to Galilee continues to be walked. The openness of the empty tomb, in this sense, encourages openness to the future. At the same time, however, the Gospel's openness strikes the contemporary reader as unsatisfactory. The absence of a tidy resolution leaves us hanging with an absent and empty denouement. Does this "emptiness" have anything to say in our context? It is to this issue that we turn next.

THE OPENNESS OF LANGUAGE AND THE PROVISIONALITY OF ENDINGS

Mark's conclusion is jarring and perplexing, cumbersome and abrupt yet strangely suggestive. It multiplies questions as much as it seeks to answer them. Yet these frustrating elements are what make the story accessible and open to our pluralistic age. Strangely enough, it is the puzzling note upon which the Gospel closes that renders it perhaps the most appropriate rendition of any of the resurrection narratives, marked as it is by provisionality and ambiguity, absence and presence, conclusion and beginning. Suggestive of a story beyond the text, Mark's ending is most helpful in its remarkable openness to other possibilities and a world of difference.

J. Lee Magness writes, "One of the more intriguing of the

many ironies of language is that 'words do not signify the presence of things but their absence.' "[17] Language attempts to render present that which cannot be grasped. We speak and write about what is not immediately accessible or visible. Evocative distance and absence are more characteristic of language than a simple one-to-one correspondence between "words" and "things." This absent quality is what makes language open to infinite forms and ever novel articulations. In short, no phrase uttered is ever the same.

Narrative endings, moreover, are as provisional as the language that constitutes them. It is hard to imagine a text that offers complete closure, that signals the point upon which the reader turns his or her back upon it. For if a book or an article is a good one, we return to it again and again. The endings of those stories and articles that seize our attention are provisional because they invite us to revisit their plots and arguments. What emerges with each return, then, is something utterly new, something that is reducible neither to the reader's subjective experiences nor to the author's own intentions and constructions. Conclusions, in other words, invite new interpretive beginnings; they release a text to an immeasurably wider world.

Few literary works manifest this juxtaposition of ending and beginning more forcefully than Mark. For Mark's conclusion resists any attempt at closure. The "final word" is supplied neither by the text nor by the reader's own appropriation of the text. The Gospel's central question, "Who is Jesus?," becomes all the more pressing because it is not answered specifically within the text. It can be answered only by the reader's continual engagement of that text in specific contexts. The "ending" of the Gospel, in short, is not actualized until it becomes a beginning *for me*, within an interpretive community. Mark's Gospel strenuously resists any facile attempt at a final word, and thus invites the reader to begin again. This absent ending, moreover, is not easy news for the reader; rather than offering a hurried resolution, it suggests that extensive interpretive work remains to be done.

---

17. Magness, *Sense and Absence*, 15 (quoting Tzvetan Todorov).

Attempting to Close the Story

For many, this openness to the new and the provisionality of the ending is unsettling. An "open ending" causes discomfort because it is ambiguous rather than definitive, because it questions rather than confirms. Because of this discomfort, perhaps, we search for authorities that would close what is open. This temptation toward closure is particularly strong with the Markan narrative. Mark's unwillingness to describe the resurrection or to delineate the resurrected body of Christ is constantly accompanied by the church's (and theologian's) attempts to "fill in the gap"[18] and supply a definition, to specify some content to the puzzling empty tomb.[19] Our longing, in short, is for closure, although Mark indirectly warns against it. As we should recall, Mark's resurrection narrative contains an event that seeks to close the story—the rolling of a stone in front of Jesus' tomb.[20] Mark thus notes the most definitive attempt to close the story of Jesus—his own burial—and the anticipated "end" to what was practiced and embodied in his name.

What the Christian claim of resurrection implies, however, is precisely the opposite of narrative closure. For to claim Jesus Christ as the Risen One is to claim that he is in some way "alive," that is, present within the community that "re-members" him. "The belief that Jesus is alive...amounts to claiming that his 'story' is not over; the narrative of what Jesus did is not a completed thing, as the author of the fourth gospel characteristically reminds us in saying that the whole world could not contain the

---

18. The phrase is from Rowan Williams, "Between the Cherubim: The Empty Tomb and the Empty Throne," in *Resurrection Reconsidered*, ed. Gavin D'Costa (Oxford: Oneworld Publications, 1996), 99. The church in its ambiguous history has often attempted to transform this literary inconclusiveness into a resolution, as evidenced by at least two canonical addenda to Mark.

19. Elisabeth Schüssler Fiorenza argues that this ambiguity is what subsequent Easter traditions sought to remove. The "appearance traditions," according to her study, invested those in the church's nascent authority structures with a certain power. Those who saw the Risen Lord were closest to the foundational, authoritative events of the church. Eventually, the ambiguity and openness of the empty tomb tradition became trampled underfoot by the "tidier" appearance traditions, which reinforced the hierarchies already emerging. Mark appears anomalous because its openness was less amenable to "kyriarchal" appropriation. See *Jesus: Miriam's Child, Sophia's Prophet* (New York: Continuum, 1994), chs. 4–5.

20. Clevenot, *Materialist Approaches*, 110.

full record of the acts of Jesus."[21] Though it is tempting to offer
an authoritative conclusion to the story of Jesus, to establish
some exhaustive claims about Jesus' resurrection, it is imperative that we not yield to this temptation. The Gospel of Mark is
strangely unsatisfying in supplying full closure, starkly unyield-
ing in its paucity of resurrection data, hauntingly suggestive in
its narrative and resurrection absence. Might the suggestiveness
of absence, this remarkable openness, be enough? For the resurrection is something that cannot be enclosed, just as the story
of Jesus cannot be slammed shut. This inviting openness, the
plain refusal to be neatly contained, is what gives the resurrection its continual resonance. The story of Jesus, simply stated,
begins again.

The Empty Tomb: Absence or Presence?

Our exposition thus far has suggested that Mark's narration of
the empty tomb is evocative of *presence,* the continuing influence
of Jesus within the community of faith. Though this undoubtedly is the strain most familiar to the majority of Christians,
I would suggest that the empty tomb is as equally suggestive
of *absence*—the resurrection itself is not reducible to a present
content. In this sense, the empty tomb remains empty and is
not simply a necessary precursor to the "happy ending" of the
Risen Christ's appearance. The empty tomb, in other words, reveals both presence and absence, and in this manner stubbornly
resists any triumphalistic appropriation.

In her resurrection reflections, Elisabeth Schüssler Fiorenza
stresses the theme of Christ's presence. The presence of the
Risen One manifests itself in the struggle to affirm life in the
face of death-dealing odds. Such affirmation of the Risen One's
presence is essential if Christian reflection is not to cave in to
those who would roll the stone in front of the tomb, thus closing
the story of Jesus indefinitely. "The empty tomb does not signify
absence but presence: it announces the Resurrected One's presence on the road ahead, in a particular space of struggle and
recognition such as Galilee. The Resurrected One is present in

---

21. Williams, "Between the Cherubim," 94.

the 'little ones,' in the struggles for survival of those impover-ished, hungry, imprisoned, tortured, and killed, in the wretched of the earth."[22]

Familiar as this chord of presence is to most Christians, we must recognize the haunting absence of the empty tomb narra-tive as well. For the looming note of absence in the Markan text will not go away, no matter how assiduously we seek to bury it. This absence, moreover, is what connects the kenotic, incarnate Christ to the proclamation of the Incarnate One as risen.

The more we uncover the cultural-political milieu of the Easter stories, the less naively we can view them. The writers of the Gospels are painfully reminiscent of us, seeking to validate their own particular communities in ways that often ignore the absence of Christ from parochial interests. As Rowan Williams writes,

> [The Easter narratives] are painfully untidy stories, reflect-ing sometimes all too plainly the various political interests at work in the formulation of the tradition, yet contain-ing more than those interests can manage. The central image of the gospel narratives is not any one apparition but the image of an absence, an image of the failure of images, which is also an absence that confirms the reality of a creative liberty, an agency not sealed and closed, but still obstinately engaged with a material environment and an historical process.[23]

Despite their lack of innocence, however, the Gospel narratives are nearly uniform in their documentation of the failure of any single image or interpretation of the Risen Christ. If there is one recognition toward which this failure of imagery points, it is the inability of language to enclose the kerygma. Indeed, what is most appropriate in the face of this language-exhausting mystery is not the establishment of a single, authorized voice or interpretation of the resurrection, but the acknowledgment of

---

22. Schüssler Fiorenza, *Miriam's Child, Sophia's Prophet,* 126.
23. Williams, "Between the Cherubim," 100.

many voices.[24] The Gospels, then, are hardly unsullied windows through which we glimpse the resurrection, but unapologetically partisan attempts at articulating that in the face of which all language falls short. If there is a universal quality to the Gospels, it is their documentation of the failure of any one voice, any one image, in bespeaking incarnation and resurrection. The absence of an authorized imagery, in this sense, is universal.

The Risen Christ, accordingly, is the One who empties himself of any parochial, localized context. His is not a presence to be sought at our own convenience or for our own justification. For where we would seek him, there he is not. The presence of the Risen One is not a securing idol; it cannot be made to conform to the particular programs, desires, and aims of any one person or group. Rather, his absence is a lure, drawing us into the future and toward others, so that we might encounter him in others. Emptying himself of the familiar, comforting status quo, the Risen Christ goes on ahead of us, challenging us to follow him. As Mark's absent ending refuses to succumb to definitive conclusion, the Emptying Christ abhors exclusive identification and exhaustive definition. The Risen One manifests himself in absence and openness to God's reign.[25]

The literary effect of the empty tomb, in other words, is to empty the conclusion of the "Christ story" of any neat, triumphal, ready-made appropriation. As soon as we locate the risen Christ, this location will continue to elude us. Mark articulates an *absence of presence* in which the risen Christ manifests himself not as an idol, but only as Christians open themselves to the continual influx of the new. The only way to encounter the Risen Christ is to be open to others, the future, and the unexpected. The "road to Galilee" may put us back upon the path to a familiar locale, but what we will encounter there is far from conclusive. Along this path the Emptying Christ presents

---

24. Indeed, the multiplicity of voices is symbolically enshrined in the Christian canon. Why do Christians acknowledge four Gospels? Apparently, one of the reasons is that no single voice can do justice to the good news that it speaks.

25. Peter Hodgson emphasizes that the authority of Jesus "pointed away from himself; it was not a self-referential quality. His authority was really the authority of God on behalf of the basilea" (*Winds of the Spirit* [Louisville: Westminster John Knox, 1994], 263).

himself again with renewed vigor. In the absence of triumph, the Risen One's presence cannot be restricted, particularly to those who claim to "know the story." The resurrection story, in other words, cannot be closed in upon itself.

Other New Testament Portrayals of the Risen Christ

Mark's Gospel, as we have seen, narrates an absence of the Risen Christ. But is this portrayal simply an aberration from the otherwise consistent articulation of Christ's presence in the other Gospels and in Paul's letters? If there is an underlying theme to the Christ's resurrection in the New Testament, that theme seems to be captured in the *appearance traditions,* where the Risen Christ manifests himself to his followers, and not in the perplexing absence of the empty tomb. Is absence, then, an anomaly, scandalous to the proclamation of Christ as risen? For some, no doubt, Mark's narration was troubling, as witnessed by the two canonical addenda to his Gospel. Nevertheless, as we examine the New Testament appearance traditions, what emerges is not a triumphal chord, antithetical to the absence we have uncovered, but rather a *presence of absence.* The Risen Christ who presents himself to his followers is not One who can be apprehended as definitively and fully present to them. Rather, something different is implied: a mysterious, even dangerous presence that even his closest followers do not recognize.

This presence of absence is perhaps best documented in the Gospel of John. Like Mark, John narrates a discovery of the empty tomb (John 20:1–18),[26] but expands this narration by including Mary Magdalene's vision of the Risen Christ. This appearance, however, is likewise mysterious. Face to face with the Risen Christ, Mary Magdalene does not recognize Jesus until he calls her by name. After Mary exclaims her recognition, Jesus gives a perplexing admonition: "Do not hold on to [*haptou*][27] me, because I have not yet ascended to the Father" (John 20:17a). What this phrase seems to suggest is that the Risen One

---

26. Although in John's narration, Simon Peter and the Beloved Disciple are given a more prominent role.

27. The Greek word, *hapto,* can mean both "to touch" and "to take hold of" something or someone.

cannot be grasped,[28] that to grab hold of him is dangerous and forbidden. The Risen Christ who appears to his closest follower, Mary Magdalene, does not present himself within the confines of the familiar, but appears as changed, warning her not to grasp him, as if clinging constituted faithfulness. If a presence is proclaimed here, it is a strange presence indeed, represented more in absence and mystery than in the empirically familiar.

When the Risen Christ appears to his disciples, John's narration continues in this mysterious vein as it depicts Christ walking through locked doors (John 20:19–23). John recounts this tradition not to proclaim Jesus as a thaumaturgist, but to illustrate the unspeakable change wrought in the Risen One. John affirms not a straightforward, physical or empirical presence, but an enlivening, sustaining presence that bestows the gift of the Holy Spirit. The One who is present, in other words, is not present *as he was*, but as the One who calls his followers out from the room they have locked in fear, and into the world. He will be present *in the midst*[29] of them whenever they embody his ministry and message. Christ's presence, for John, is recognized in the absence of the familiar, on the threshold of a world of difference and change.

Luke-Acts articulates the appearance of the Risen Lord in a similar manner. Along the road to Emmaus (Luke 24:13–35), for example, Jesus' followers do not recognize him, even though the Risen One accompanies them along each step of their journey. They recognize him, rather, only at the journey's end as Jesus takes and breaks bread, blesses it, and shares it with them, only as he *embodies the practice* of his ministry.[30] This narration suggests that Christ's presence is recognized whenever his ministry of feeding, healing, and reconciliation is reenacted. Otherwise, his absence is most acutely felt.

Likewise, Saul's conversion, as narrated by Luke-Acts (Acts 9:1–19), records an appearance of the Risen Christ, but under especially odd circumstances. Saul does not see any physical

28. To borrow language from the Philippians Christ-hymn.
29. See ch. 5, p. 149, for an exposition of this turn of phrase.
30. Note how this recognition of the Risen Christ meshes with our interpretation of incarnation as embodiment. See ch. 3, pp. 74–80.

instantiation of Christ, but rather hears a voice and beholds an intense light. The *figura* of the Risen One is absent, and only in numinous representation, akin to Moses' encounter with God before the burning bush, is he recognized as present.

Finally, Paul's own depiction of the Risen Christ throughout his correspondence is slim on the details of presence. When Paul speaks of the resurrection, it is in characteristically brief terms, at times punctuated by an apocalyptic sensibility. The oldest extant description of the Risen Christ, found 1 Corinthians 15, is particularly terse: "Last of all, as to one untimely born, he appeared also to me" (1 Cor. 15:8). Apart from a bare pronouncement, Paul devotes no attention to the empirical presence of the Risen Christ. When he speaks of his own experience of the Risen One, moreover, it is not "in physical or psychological terms, but only with religious symbols."[31] The significance of the Risen Christ, for Paul, is not in terms of a physical presence that can be neatly contained, but as a lure that summons those who behold him into the sustaining power of God's Spirit. When Paul waxes apocalyptic about the resurrection (1 Thessalonians 4–5; 2 Cor. 12:1–5), his narration of presence does not depart from this strand. The specification of the Risen Christ is far less important than the power of resurrection faith, a "presence" given by God. The Risen Christ, no less for Paul than for Mark, is present not within the tried and true, but at the mysterious and dangerous threshold of change. The One who is present as the inaugurator of this change, accordingly, is also recognized as absent. Although Mark's narration of the empty tomb offers the most lucid example of absence in the New Testament, this theme weaves its way throughout the witness of Paul, Luke-Acts, and John. The appearance traditions, then, might be said to narrate the presence of absence, wherever the Risen One is recognized.

Strange as it might have sounded to many in the first century,[32] the proclamation of the resurrected Christ served as a

---

31. Johnson, *Writings*, 102.
32. In a Hellenic context of reverence for the old, stable, and unchanging, the Christian claim of resurrection—and the new life it implied—surely sounded dissonant.

continual invitation for the Christian community to open itself
to the new, the unfamiliar, the stranger. Mark's narration of
the empty tomb, and the recognition of the presence of absence in the appearance narratives, have the peculiar effect
of inviting those who read the story to hearken to the invitation of the future and the religious Other. Has this element
been lost in contemporary interpretations of the resurrection?
Have our reflections, in effect, served to close the empty tomb
in the demand to specify a concrete, risen presence? It is to
these questions, and to the attempt at a constructive theology
of resurrection, that we turn in the next section.

TOWARD A CONSTRUCTIVE THEOLOGY
OF RESURRECTION

Because overmuch has been made of resurrection presence
throughout Christian history, because such dramatic, miraculous content has been attributed to the claim of Jesus Christ
as risen, I begin these constructive reflections with a precau-
tion: the *absence* of Christ. If resurrection is interpreted only in
terms of presence, the risen Christ can become something that
is neatly contained, whether in the form of creedal orthodoxy,
a naive historicism, or in paradigmatic moments of individual
encounter with the kerygma. In each case, the presence of the
Risen One rushes to the fore, while his absence is unthematized
and ignored. Although this inauguration of absence represents
a substantial departure from much of the classic theological tradition, it also represents a recovery of some of that tradition's
more neglected aspects, particularly the *via negativa*. Acknowledging Christ's absence, moreover, is essential in our present
pluralistic age if we are to avoid a facile "presencing" of the
Risen One and the callous imposition of that One in other religious contexts.[33] The Risen Christ is the One who cannot be
contained by any presence, whether communal or individual,

---

33. This starting point, moreover, may have an even greater resonance in our
contemporary Western context, in which the absence of God and the viable position
of atheism are discerned most acutely.

and cannot be reduced to any instantiation or linguistic articulation of him. Though present within communities that profess his name, Jesus Christ "reveals" himself as the Absent One who remains beyond our grasp.

Resurrection as Absence

Beginning our reflections with the thematization of Christ's absence parallels the narrative thread of the Markan witness we have been following most closely. For Mark, the discovery of the empty tomb does not entail the definitive location of the risen Christ; rather, the tomb unveils Christ's absence. Mary Magdalene, Mary, and Salome expect to find Jesus of Nazareth within the confines of a neglected sepulcher, yet it is precisely in this space that they *do not* find him. He is absent, having already moved beyond the tomb's four walls.

This absence is reflected particularly clearly in the *via negativa*—a cornerstone to both the classic Catholic theology of God and the dialectical Protestantism of Barth, Tillich, and Luther—which stresses that our understanding of God arises insofar as we acknowledge what we *do not know* about God. Negation permeates any and every statement that human beings can make about the divine. Though we can never complete the sentence, "God is...," we can achieve greater clarity of our statements about God by thematizing what God *is not*. Edward Farley characterizes this approach well: "Language is world-oriented and world-saturated.... If God is the creative condition of the world and thus of human beings and their systems, none of the referents of language will express the actual being of God."[34] Nothing we say can enclose the mystery of God, while everything that we say about God reveals both the poverty of our language and what God is not.[35] Language about the resurrection, obviously, is no

---

34. Edward Farley, *Divine Empathy: A Theology of God* (Minneapolis: Fortress, 1996), 29. The *via negativa* finds ample precedence in the work of several classical theologians. It permeates the *Summa* of Aquinas, reaches a high note in the mystical theology of Pseudo-Dionysius, and finds twentieth-century voices in Paul Tillich's *Systematic Theology* and in Robert Scharlemann. See particularly Scharlemann, *Inscriptions and Reflections* (Charlottesville: University Press of Virginia, 1989).

35. Again, the echoes of deconstruction resound here. See Mark C. Taylor, *Nots* (Chicago: University of Chicago Press, 1993), ch. 1.

exception to the *via negativa,* but offers startling new relevance of the negativity of any and all statements about the Risen One. Absence is the "not" writ large over the empty tomb.

Resuming the kenotic theme we have been developing, the following proposal emerges: The kenotic Christ does not disappear with Jesus' crucifixion and burial, but emerges renewed in the nascent church's articulation of the Risen One. The One who unveils the kenotic pattern continues this movement even at the threshold of death by emptying himself of any exclusive spaces, by his absence from those spaces that claim him as theirs alone. It is precisely this kenotic dynamic that renders the Risen Christ incapable of being grasped and enclosed by those who confess him. The kenotic Christ is both the Risen and the Absent One who refuses to be contained by any articulation of him, who bursts the bonds of any localized presence.

Without the presence of absence, Christian claims run the risk of attempting to enclose those mysteries to which they refer. The presence of absence, then, needs to be the persistent iconoclastic companion of any resurrection claim, for absence is that which resists any authority—ecclesial, biblical, or theological—having the final word on God. The Risen Christ, in short, is absent from any particular, exclusive spaces; he is the One who refuses to arrogate privilege to himself or to the community gathered in his name. The Risen One is not a prefabricated presence to be resorted to at will for comfort or convenience, but a terrifying and mysterious absence who refuses to become merely a sop for the individual conscience.

The ground we are beginning to tread in these reflections is likely to raise eyebrows and perhaps kindle fear. Little here is offered in terms of cheap grace or coddling security, but rather, only a haunting image of an empty tomb and a suggestion of Christ's absence. Yet if we ignore these frightening aspects, we obscure the events to which Christian proclamation of the resurrection is connected: Jesus of Nazareth's horrific death, his abandonment by those who followed him, and his burial by strangers. The resurrection, if nothing else, is about the connection between the premature death of an abandoned man in first-century Palestine and the experience of a new life continuing after that death for those who remembered him. Such a connection is both frightening and surprising good news.[36]

Recalling the Marcan narrative, we note that fear is both the concluding note of the gospel ("for they were afraid" [Mark 16:8]) and the way in which Mark's readers are invited back into that story. To miss this fear, to rush headlong to a glorious appearance of the Risen Christ, obscures both Mark's intent and the Risen One's invitation to all. Fear is thus an appropriate response to the death of Jesus and his haunting absence, but also an avenue for the community's new life and remembering the particular life of the Risen One. Although it represents the appropriate place to begin our reflections, the absence of Christ is not the final word of the resurrection, for Christians also claim a presence manifesting itself even at the threshold of death.[37]

Resurrection as Presence

Having voiced the iconoclastic warning of the absence of the Risen Christ, we now turn our attention to the crux of Christian claims about the Risen One, namely, that Jesus Christ is present in the world even today. To proclaim the Risen Christ as present is not tantamount to restricting that presence to a specific locale, but to claim that the story of Jesus Christ continues, that

---

36. This element of fear has been resolutely ignored by contemporary consumer Christianity. In a culture of consumerism, there is nothing to fear (except, perhaps, the loss of one's purchasing power), only new comforts to crave and new diversions in which to immerse oneself. Whether this refusal to acknowledge fear represents a genuine dispelling of fear or the mere masking of it with more material goods is an unresolved question. What is certain, however, is that when the church aligns itself with the prevailing consumer winds, little room is left for the public profession of fear within its sanctuaries. Offered instead are the sundry diversions of softball leagues, potlucks, and seminars on "financial security."

37. The death of Christ makes possible his embodiment in the world for those who would follow him. Moreover, at the heart of the Christian claim is that there is no embodiment apart from the world. The risen Christ is known in the world, not in flight from it. If the death of Christ represents the transition from his openness to other human beings to his openness to the entire cosmos, then we might also say that the world itself bears the traces of this openness. If the risen Christ is to be known in the world, then the world itself might be seen as "the embodiment" of the Risen One. In short, the Risen One is present in the world. Peter Hodgson has made use of this theme in his recent systematic work, *Winds of the Spirit*, and in his earlier christological project, *Jesus—Word and Presence* (Philadelphia: Fortress, 1971). See *Winds*, ch. 16, and *Word and Presence*, 283ff.

it is not erased with the rolling of the stone in front of Jesus' tomb.[38]

This evocation of Christ's presence brings our kenotic model full circle; the empty tomb of the resurrection thus involves a return to life, a return to the more.[39] Christ's kenosis is not for the sake of itself; nor is emptying an end in itself. Rather, Christ's self-emptying is for the sake of *others*, embracing the world and extending abundant life to all. Without this corresponding sense of return, kenosis rapidly degenerates into self-abnegation, and in extreme cases, nihilism. Nothingness and absence, from the resurrection perspective, are not the final words in the cosmos; rather, as Abe and Hegel would remind us, kenosis is for the sake of fulfillment. If nothing else, the Christian claim of resurrection has always affirmed this—out of the darkness of a forgotten empty tomb, new life emerges.

What might we mean by affirming the presence of God in the Risen Christ? How can contemporary Christians describe the continuing presence of One crucified in first-century Palestine? Because the term "presence" has become somewhat slippery, we need to be careful in staking our claim. The *Oxford English Dictionary* offers some guidance, although its primary definition is more applicable to tangible entities than to the divine. Presence, accordingly, is "the state of being before, in front of, or in the same place."[40] Upon first glance, to claim Christ "in front of" ourselves would seem to objectify or reduce his presence to a quantifiable entity. Something other than objectification, then, must be the meaning of the Christian announcement of resurrection presence.

---

38. This aspect of our interpretation has parallels with Willi Marxsen's work. Marxsen writes that one way of expressing the truth of resurrection today is to say that "the cause of Jesus continues; or in the words of the hymn: 'Still he comes today'" (*The Resurrection of Jesus of Nazareth*, trans. Margaret Kohl [Philadelphia: Fortress, 1970], 141).

39. See Cyril O'Regan, *Heterodox Hegel* (Albany: State University of New York Press, 1994), 169. O'Regan is addressing here Hegel's broader concern with creation and incarnation, of which the resurrection is but one moment within larger "return" to the divine life. The imagery, nonetheless, is extremely helpful for a more focused examination of resurrection.

40. *Oxford English Dictionary*, 2nd ed., vol. 7 (Oxford: Clarendon Press, 1989), 393.

Two sources offer some help in delineating the contours of this slippery term: the legendary visionary tradition of Moses before the burning bush (Exodus 3), and Julian of Norwich's *Revelations of Divine Love*. Four characteristics of presence are prominent in even the most cursory survey of these texts. Each speaks of the divine presence as (1) mediated, (2) encompassing all aspects of time, (3) resisting enclosure, and (4) the bestower of love and peace. First, perhaps the most striking example of the mediation of God's presence is the legend of Moses on Mount Horeb. Moses does not stand face to face with God, but beholds God's presence through a numinous medium: the burning bush and the voice that resounds from it. "He looked, and the bush was blazing, yet it was not consumed" (Exod. 3:2b). Such mediation, according to many Hebraic traditions, was essential, since a direct apprehension of God would kill the beholder (Exod. 33:20). God, according to this example, is never directly present, but manifests Godself *through the world*.[41] The divine visage is hidden—yet present—in the face of an Other. It is behind and through this Other that the divine expresses itself.

Second, Moses' encounter with the presence of God encompasses the entire range of temporality. God does not only reveal Godself in the present to Moses, but identifies Godself as the "God of Abraham, the God of Isaac, and the God of Jacob" (Exod. 3:6), establishing continuity with the past and summoning it to present memory. God's grounding and sustaining presence also continues in the future, as the voice from the bush promises Israel's deliverance from the Egyptians and God's guidance to a land flowing with milk and honey. This future promise presents itself as a lure, as an invitation for a further encounter with the divine that is never fully realized (even when the Israelites arrive in the promised land). The God whose presence is promised in the future also reveals Godself in absence, because the divine presence can never be directly apprehended. To speak of God's presence in the future is to

---

41. Karl Rahner expresses this mediation as well: "We go out toward God only by entering into the world" (*Hearer of the Word*, trans. Joseph Donceel [New York: Continuum, 1994], 120).

claim that we are always on the way to God, a way marked by longing and separation.[42]

Third, the divine presence vehemently resists enclosure. Moses learns there is no way even to name God: God bespeaks the divine "name" as "I am who I am," or "I will be what I will be" (Exod. 3:14), an expression that is at the same time comprehensive and iconoclastic. God, and God's presence, simply are enacted and will be enacted. Any attempt to quantify or reify that presence is bound to eclipse the One whose presence is proclaimed.[43]

Fourth, and finally, the divine presence is attested in love. Few figures across the centuries have written of this theme with as much grace as Julian of Norwich. At the conclusion of her *Revelations,* Julian learns the reason and ground for her visions: "Who showed it to you? Love. What did he show you? Love. Why did he show it? For love. . . . So it was that I learned that love was our Lord's meaning . . . that before he ever made us, God loved us; and that his love has never slackened, nor ever shall."[44] God is present, for Julian, in the love of a Mother and in the love of others; Christ is, for her, the Mother who suckles her infant and shows mercy to those in need. God reveals Godself in love, as the abiding, sustaining provenance of life.

Gathering the wisdom of these two visionary traditions, we approach a rough understanding of what might be signified

---

42. This recognition of absence and longing is a key component to the Platonic conception of *eros,* an element that Wendy Farley recovers in her recent work. For Farley, to love another is to recognize the beloved's presence *and* absence. "The beloved is present as absent, so to speak. It is related to the lover not by sheer immediacy but by the echo left by its absence" (*Eros for the Other: Retaining Truth in a Pluralistic World* [University Park: Pennsylvania State University Press, 1996], 72). To love God, then, would be to celebrate God's presence and to recognize that God is never fully present, to long for God in the "echo" of divine absence.

43. Martin Luther, in a similar vein, offers a description of God's omnipresence without reducing God to the totality of entities in the world. "God in his essence is present everywhere, in and through the whole creation in all its parts and in all places, and so the world is full of God and he fills it all, yet he is not limited or circumscribed by it, but is at the same time beyond and above the whole creation" ("That These Words of Christ, 'This is My Body,' Etc., Still Stand Firm against the Fanatics," in *Luther's Works,* vol. 37, ed. Robert H. Fischer [Philadelphia: Muhlenberg, 1961], 59).

44. Julian of Norwich, *Revelations of Divine Love,* trans. Clifton Wolters (New York: Penguin, 1966), 109.

by the divine presence: God's presence is continually mediated through others, never apprehended directly, yet never reducible to its mediation. Summoning the past, empowering the present, and offering hope for the future, the divine presence cannot be contained, yet presents itself to us in the distinct configuration of love. As we will see, the Christian affirmation of resurrection also exhibits these characteristics, through its sacramental mediation as embodied love and its nonobjectifiable presence throughout time.

Resurrection Presence in the Form of Embodied Love

"Still he comes today." In announcing the presence of the Risen Christ, Christians are not claiming that Jesus of Nazareth is immediately visible, close at hand as a securing idol. His presence, like the presence of God, cannot be reduced to any entity in the world. Nonetheless, his presence can be affirmed as mediated through others in acts of embodied love. The Risen Christ is present wherever and whenever Jesus of Nazareth's ministry of open commensality and healing is faithfully re-membered. Thus understood, resurrection presence is nothing less than the recognition that God's grace comes to us embodied, granting new life to our hungry and bruised bodies. It is *other people*, then, who enflesh Christ's ministry; it is through them and their acts of feeding and healing that Christians come face to face with the Risen Christ. The theological tradition has expressed this encounter most clearly in its articulation of Christ's presence through the *sacraments* and the *community of the saints*.

The sacramental tradition within Christianity has always recognized the inescapability and preciousness of the human body. By designating certain rites as paradigmatic for witnessing the divine presence, this tradition is emblematic of the quintessential Christian claim: Word becomes flesh. It is not enough, according to a sacramental understanding, to announce, hear, and read the good news, for we must taste, see, and feel it as well. The sacramental tradition expands the Protestant hyperemphasis upon "hearing the Word" into a visual, edible feast: seen in ritual gestures, tasted in bread and wine, splashed in the waters of baptism. In Augustine's commentary on the Gospel of John,

he calls the sacraments "a sort of visible word."[45] This coinage
is a helpful one for designating what we mean by resurrection
presence. For in claiming the sacraments as visible words, we
also claim that they enflesh and re-member Jesus of Nazareth's
own ministry. The sacraments, then, are symbols with a dual referent: symbols of Christ's presence in the midst of our lives and
symbols of our calling to practice Christ's ministry and live out
his message. They put flesh on the bones of Jesus' own proclamation of the reign of God. A shared meal or a bath is where
Christians discern the presence of the Risen One again and
again. What I want to suggest, moreover, is that the presence of
Christ is evoked not only in the generally authorized Christian
sacraments, but whenever persons feed and heal one another in
love. Baptism and communion are thus not the only practices
that bespeak the Risen Christ's presence, but are paradigmatic
because they illustrate the chief characteristics of that presence:
embodied healing, nourishing, and love.

One of the striking aspects of the sacramental tradition is that
their announcement of Christ's presence is tied not to super-
natural occurrences but to the most basic of human acts: eating,
drinking, bathing, healing—the very practices that are most in-
tegral to the sustenance of human bodies. God in Christ does
not come apart from the ordinary and everyday, but in the midst
of them. It is not we who create this presence, moreover, but
the self-emptying God who gives of Godself by manifesting the
divine presence in concrete others. Resurrection presence con-
fronts us embodied; our eyes are opened to it whenever our
bodies are sustained in love.

Much of the history and debate surrounding the sacraments,
unfortunately, has had to do with restricting their number and
specifying the means in which Christ's presence is made known
through them. What becomes important, however, in an expanded view of sacramental presence, is not the number of rites
or means of that presence, but the way in which everyday acts
are performed. The miracle of the Risen Christ's presence is not

---

45. Cited in Carl E. Braaten and Robert W. Jenson, eds., *Christian Dogmatics*, vol. 2
(Philadelphia: Fortress, 1984), 291.

that it is to be connected only to specifically authorized rites, but that it permeates ordinary time. Whenever we are nourished and healed, whenever we are transformed by another's gracious act, Christ can come to us again.

The Risen Christ becomes present wherever the hungry are fed, whenever all are welcomed to the banqueting table. Paradigmatic of resurrection presence, the sacrament of communion is not only a memorial of Jesus of Nazareth's final meal with his disciples, nor is it only an anticipation of God's future; it is also the symbolic embodiment of Jesus of Nazareth's practice of open commensality, his extension of hospitality and food to all who would dine with him. The Risen Christ is present not as a ghost, but as a shared meal—the food "in front of" each guest—as real as the bread that nourishes and the wine that quenches. Christ becomes present not because of the elements themselves, but in the manner in which these elements are served and shared. It is not the words themselves spoken over the elements that make a meal a eucharist; it is not any bread and wine. Rather, it is the thanksgiving with which the words are spoken, the justice with which the bread is baked, the love with which the grapes are pressed, and the bounty shared with all that make the feast. Because the Risen Christ's presence is connected with the manner in which food is shared, and not strictly with the elements themselves, even "ordinary" meals can become occasions for glimpsing his presence.[46] The eucharist is a genuinely *open* meal, to which all are welcomed, by which we

---

46. The Danish film *Babette's Feast* offers one example of the sacramentality of a shared meal. The film tells the story of a dying religious sect whose aging members live austere lives and uphold a simple diet. Babette, a refugee from the French Revolution, arrives in their midst just as the community experiences the rend of schism and the pang of petty jealousy. The group obligingly employs Babette as a cook for fourteen years, during all of which she is regarded as an "outsider." After winning the lottery—the money that will finally bring her back to her homeland—Babette decides to prepare a sumptuous meal for the commune, a "thanksgiving meal" to which the sect reluctantly agrees. Convinced that the meal will lead to bacchanalian revelry, the group instead experiences—in and through the exquisitely prepared food—reconciliation, remembrance, and healing. They are reopened to each other as they celebrate their relationships and remember their past. The meal becomes, in other words, a kind of communion. After the meal, they learn that Babette has spent every penny of her lottery winnings to prepare this feast. Unquestionably, Babette's gracious act is what enables the community to reach out in love to each other again.

can be opened to one another,[47] and in which the Risen Christ comes to us. What a scandal it is whenever a person, particularly the religious Other, is excluded from it.

The Risen Christ also comes again whenever we reach out to each other in acts of healing. This is another way in which Jesus of Nazareth's embodied ministry is made real. As persons called to follow the One who refused to reduce the "sick" to their own illness, Christians are likewise called to extend human touch to others, to embrace those ostracized by the stigma of disease. Witnessed most distinctly in the sacraments of baptism and unction, these symbolic acts pay close attention to our bodies, cleansing and healing them. Like the eucharist, however, what is significant for recognizing the Risen Christ's presence in baptism or unction is not the elements themselves (the water or the oil), but the way in which the act is performed. By bathing and healing each other, Christians admit both their vulnerability and need for God's grace. To allow another to touch me in healing is to admit that I am not alone, that I need others to be opened to the mystery of God's love. As persons called to heal one other, Christians recognize the presence of Christ in acts of healing, whatever those acts may be.[48]

---

47. The Reformed practice of communion is particularly illustrative of this mutual opening. In most Reformed churches, parishioners do not receive the communion elements from the minister, but from their neighbors. Persons are opened to one another by feeding one another, by sharing the most universal gesture of hospitality and fellowship.

48. Paule Marshall's novel *Praisesong for the Widow* (New York: E. P. Dutton, 1984) narrates an unforgettable baptismal scene. Avey Johnson, a middle-aged widow who is grieving the death of her husband, embarks on a Caribbean cruise with two friends. In the middle of the journey, in a moment of panic, she jumps ship and finds herself among the local population on the island of Carriacou. As she sails in a small boat to the island, Avey succumbs to seasickness and loses bowel control. Only through the hand and bath of a stranger, Rosalie Parvay, is Avey nurtured back to life: "Avey Johnson tried protesting being given the bath. There was no need, she could do it herself, she no longer felt weak.... By way of a response, Rosalie Parvay simply reached over a hand from where she stood at the bedside and gently closed her eyes. 'Is no trouble, oui...' Gradually, under Rosalie Parvay's discreet touch and the welcome feel of the soap and water on her skin, Avey Johnson had found herself growing less opposed to being bathed. Now, there was the hushed singsong voice in the room, and this also helped ease her tension.... She gave herself over to the musing voice and to such simple matters as the mild fragrance of the soap on the air and the lovely sound, like a sudden light spatter of rain, as the maid wrung out the washcloth from time to time over the water in the galvanized tub" (pp. 219–21). Marshall's narration of this healing scene is evocative of baptism, which brings

We recognize the Risen Christ's presence in the sacraments—and in the sacramentality of everyday life—because these practices represent the embodiment of Jesus of Nazareth's ministry and message. The Risen Christ relentlessly seeks expression in the flesh. This is one important aspect of the classical veneration of the saints. For it is through particular others that Jesus Christ comes to those who would follow him. Without embodiment, the Word remains a rarefied and numinous ideal. In the words of Lawrence Cunningham, "The saint enfleshes Christian ideals in concrete historical situations and widely divergent historical epochs. Jesus enjoins the life of voluntary poverty 'for the Kingdom of God.' Saint Benedict, Saint Francis of Assisi, Saint Vincent de Paul, and the hidden saints of the Catholic Worker Movement show us how voluntary poverty should look at given times in our history."[49] We catch an intimation of Christ's presence in the unique faces of others: in the face of a poor woman who offers bread to a stranger, in the face of a spouse whose capacity for love expands with each shared day. The saint, as a manifestation of the Risen Christ, is not a distant "holy" person, but one who draws near in the midst of our everyday life.[50] The resurrection body extends to *all* bodies, and becomes most visible in those persons who recognize the claim of others upon them. The presence of the Risen Christ, in other words, is witnessed whenever the saints among us empty themselves on behalf of others. It is through these others that Christ's embodied love is made real.

In claiming the Risen Christ's sacramental presence and his expression in the community of saints, we are not suggesting that his presence is enclosed by these instances. Recalling the warning issued at the outset of this exploration, we recognize

---

about a renewed sense of life. "All the tendons, nerves and muscles which strung her together had been struck a powerful chord, and the reverberation could be heard in the remotest corners of her body" (p. 224).

49. Lawrence Cunningham, *The Meaning of Saints* (San Francisco: Harper & Row, 1980), 75.

50. Karl Rahner considers saints to be people "drawn out of and beyond themselves in love...who by the everyday conduct of their ordinary lives have achieved a dimension of life which is to an undreamt of extent absolute" ("All Saints," in *Further Theology of the Spiritual Life*, vol. 2, Theological Investigations 8, trans. David Bourke [New York: Herder & Herder, 1971], 25).

that the Risen One also presents himself in absence. If his presence is announced in others and in specific acts of embodied love, the empty tomb reminds us that these persons and acts are instances of an elusive presence. For even these faces and events cannot surround the One to whom they point. If we were to suggest that any occasion is exhaustively revelatory of resurrection presence, we would lose sight of the Risen One who goes on ahead of us, calling us to follow, and we would ignore those others whom he unveils. Nevertheless, to suggest the Risen Christ's elusive presence in concrete acts of embodied love is to acknowledge that presence as no less real. Christ *does* meet us in the face of the vulnerable other, however evanescent it may be.

Presence in the Past, Present, and Future

Just as the modality of resurrection presence manifests itself in specific acts of embodied love—resisting those spaces that would enclose it—the temporality of the Risen One also abhors exclusivism. Eluding the constraints of any one aspect of temporality, the Risen Christ both transcends and permeates ordinary time: in the remembrance of a *past* event that incorporates the tragedy and colossal suffering of human existence, in *present* communities in the world wherever this memory is embodied, and in the *future* as the ground of Christian hope, love, and openness to the Other.[51]

Christian proclamation of the Risen One has routinely made much use of the past. This recollection is critical in any contemporary interpretation of the resurrection, lest it become ahistorical. Unless our reflections upon the Risen One are tied in some way to the scandalously particular life and death of this carpenter from Nazareth, they will become simply the seeds

---

51. See also Hodgson, *Jesus—Word and Presence,* for a similar typology of the presence of the risen Christ. "I shall seek to understand the resurrection in the most comprehensive sense possible, as an event embracing all three modes of time but with a peculiar focus upon the present: the *future promise* of new life is based on the *past occurrence* of the raising of Jesus, the experiential basis of which is the *present faith* of the community, its encounter with him as the living agent of God who sends into mission" (p. 222). The present section of my work owes much to Hodgson's temporal analysis of "presence."

of speculative idealism, having no relation to the sufferings, trials, and tribulations of a particular life in a particular context. Our interpretation of the resurrection, therefore, must recall the distinct configuration of that life, as remembered by the community gathered in his name.

Although much has been made about the presence of Christ in the past, rarely is this presence tied to the particular memory of others. Many popular conceptions would suggest that Christ's resurrection represents the vindication of all suffering, a claim that has often obscured the tragic aspects of our collective history. Rather than being the definitive triumph over suffering, the resurrection, I would claim, is that which enables us to keep alive the memory of those departed voices crying in anguish and to pay attention to their voices today. The Risen Christ does not erase suffering, but keeps its dangerous memory painfully present. The voices of those trampled underfoot by the onward march of colonial exploitation and religious triumphalism continue to be heard in the stories they have left behind. Part of the Emptying Christ's return is a return to those stories, keeping them alive for the sake of life. The memory of the Risen Christ recalls the massive suffering and horror of human existence. It does not offer cheap answers to tragedy, but gathers together those fragmentary accounts and small voices of the victims. Johann Baptist Metz offers similar words along these lines:

> The real and all-inclusive history of suffering manifested in memory of Christian redemption includes the suffering of finiteness and of death as well as past suffering and the sufferings of the dead. . . . A Christian soteriology cannot be a casuistic cover-up for real suffering. . . . Above all, the silent suffering of the inconsolable pain of the past, the suffering of the dead continues, for the greater freedom of future generations does not justify past sufferings nor does it render them free.[52]

---

52. Johann Baptist Metz, *Faith in History and Society: Toward a Practical Fundamental Theology*, trans. David Smith (New York: Crossroad, 1980), 128.

The memory of the crucified and risen Christ keeps alive those voices that the victors of history would attempt to smother. Keeping alive these voices, the Christian outlook of crucifixion/ resurrection, moreover, has always affirmed that its God is a God of life, not death. If there is a "side" to be taken in this distinction, then the Christian motif will always be one of survival in the face of seemingly insurmountable and staggering odds, that we can go on because we must go on, that to relinquish one's life and one's struggle is to allow death to have the final word. It is in "going on" that the resurrection motif refuses to surrender the past, but returns to that past in hope and memory.[53]

The return of the Emptying, Risen Christ, however, is not only a matter of past memory; this return offers a fundamental conversion to the *present world*. Early Christian profession of the risen Christ displays an unambiguous concern with the present, that the Risen One changes those who are drawn into his presence. For Mark, the resurrection story does not conclude with an ascension, but by locating the Risen Christ squarely in this world, ahead in Galilee. "The Easter texts testify to a powerful change in Jesus, but they do it in order to empower the readers for new life and renewed ministry."[54] Mark's focus, in other words, is upon the difference that the Risen One makes *now*.

Christian affirmation of the presence of the Risen One does not amount to an opiate or a pacifying promise of reunification with the Lord in the sweet by-and-by. Resurrection, rather, announces a return to this world. In the words of Jürgen Moltmann, "Resurrection hope isn't concerned with another life. It has to do with the fact that this mortal life here is going to be different.... We experience resurrection through the rebirth to living hope. We experience resurrection through the love which already brings us to life here and now, and we experience resurrection through liberation."[55] The Emptying

---

53. In the words of Marjorie Suchocki, "The resurrection power of God does not annihilate the past, it transforms the past. That which was, is affirmed, but given a new dimension, a new context, a new direction" (*God, Christ, Church*, rev. ed. [New York: Crossroad, 1989], 114).

54. Smith, *Easter Gospels*, 15.

55. Jürgen Moltmann, "The Resurrection of Christ: Hope for the World," in D'Costa, ed., *Resurrection Reconsidered*, 81.

Christ invokes a return to life whenever his being-for-others is embodied, wherever love is made manifest, wherever hope is glimpsed anew. The claim of Christ as risen, then, addresses far more than the issue of Jesus of Nazareth's destiny. What is initiated in the ministry of Jesus reaches its culmination in the resurrection and thus becomes embodied in the church, whenever the church is faithful to its calling of following the Incarnate and Risen One. Once again, our vision bears the traces of a fairly wide incarnational sensibility. This focus upon the nascent church, the community that gathers in the wake of Jesus' crucifixion and resurrection, is an obvious one in the New Testament writings. For, apart from the appearance to Paul on the road to Damascus, and to John on Patmos, the Risen Christ always appears where two or more are gathered in his name. The Emptying Christ's return is primarily a return to a community enlivened and sustained by his abiding presence.[56] The Risen Christ is present wherever "church" is approximated.[57]

There is yet another dimension to the Risen Christ's pres-

---

56. This emphasis upon the community of faith within the pancosmic sweep of incarnation and resurrection finds theological precedent in the work of Hegel. For Hegel, the resurrection is the transition from the representation of God in the world (incarnation) to the inauguration of the Kingdom of Spirit. Resurrection typifies the dynamic movement of Spirit from Christ to the world. "The appearance of God in the flesh occurs in a specific time and in this single individual. Since it is an appearance of this kind, of itself it passes by and becomes past history. This sensible mode must disappear and rise again in the sphere of representation. The formation of the community has just this content—that the sensible form passes over into a spiritual element" (*Lectures on the Philosophy of Religion*, vol. 3, ed. Peter C. Hodgson [Berkeley: University of California Press, 1985], 221–22). The church thus renders present what was inaugurated in the Christ-event, the giving of God's self to a genuine Other. Karl Rahner offers an analogous view of church: "The historical continuation of Christ in and through the community of those who believe in him and who recognize him explicitly as the mediator of salvation in a profession of faith, is what we call church" (*Foundations of Christian Faith,* trans. William Dych [New York: Crossroad, 1978], 322).

57. It is important to place this caveat, wherever church is *approximated,* in our formulation. For as a human institution, the church is always subject to stumbling inadequacies, shortsightedness, and outright failure in confessing and following the Risen One. The church always stands in need of God's grace and continually demands reformation. In a very real sense, "church" is never witnessed in the world. What we experience in this all-too-human institution, rather, are faint glimmerings, barely audible intimations, and slight brushes with the presence of Christ. Yet their faintness does not render these brushes with presence any less real. Despite their imperceptibility, there are times when the presence of Christ is made real—most

ence in the world. In addition to incorporating his own past
and our collective past, and giving them a new direction in the
present church, the Emptying Christ returns as hope for the
future. To claim the Risen Christ as present in hope is not to
render him a repository for idle wishes and compensatory projections. Far from being a means of tender consolation, hope
is "the most radical exercise of the human spirit when subject
to the bitterest pain,...even though hope is present only in
him who first and foremost hopes on behalf of *others*—hopes
in the responsibility he takes for them, hopes in that love for
him whom we call God."[58] Hope is not optimism; it sees the
world in its messy detail, its staggering injustice, its unbeliev-
able suffering. Yet hope also believes that the world is not this
way inevitably, out of divine foreordination or because of fate.
Rather, hope envisions a different world, in which the bounty of
the world is shared with all, so that no one will "hurt or destroy
on all my holy mountain" (Isa. 11:9a). For Christians, moreover,
Jesus Christ is the One risen into this bounteous vision. The resurrection itself is a radically hopeful affirmation: somehow, in
some way, out of the ashes of death there is a return to life in the
new birth of the ecclesia. Mark, therefore, narrates the resurrection as much in terms of promise as present confirmation: Mary
Magdalene, Mary, and Salome are told that they will encounter
Jesus in the future, ahead of them in Galilee. The Risen Christ
forms the content of their hope and empowers them for the
journey ahead. By remembering what happened in Jesus Christ,
then, Christians sustain hope for the future, and through such
hope, remembrance of others is nourished. The Risen Christ is
not simply present as a historical artifact or in terms of one's
immediate, personal encounter with the kerygma, but as the
embodiment and aim of the longing and hope of creation.

Resurrection hope is not the longing for specific, tangible
entities, but for God and God's presence with us. Because the
Christian affirmation of resurrection concerns *God*, it main-

acutely in situations of radical openness to other human beings and in openness to
the world itself.

58. Rahner, "Ideas for a Theology of Death," in *Theology, Anthropology, Christology,*
Theological Investigations 13, trans. David Bourke (New York: Seabury, 1975), 176.

tains radical openness to others and to the world itself. As Wolfhart Pannenberg has said, "The Christian perception of what happened in Jesus will always retain an openness to the future."[59] Throughout classical theology, this openness to the future has been connected with the *parousia*, the promise that Christ will come again. This connection between resurrection and eschatological expectation, though often overlooked in a demythologized age, is essential to uphold, for, without this openness to the future, Christian affirmation of the Risen One becomes the quirky syncretism of Judaic and Hellenic religious themes, interesting as a relic of history but stripped of its ability to nourish hope. The content of Christian hope is necessarily future-oriented, for the proclamation of the Risen One has the ability to open Christians to both the wonder of the world and the mystery of God. The Risen Christ thus turns our attention to concrete others by returning to *this world* in the hope for God's future.

The Risen One and Christian Discipleship

Mark's narration of the empty tomb, we have noted, has remarkably little to say about Jesus Christ other than the bare proclamation that he has been raised, is not "here," and that he is going on ahead of those who seek him. This paucity of detail concerning the status of the Risen One is contrasted by the abundant implications this claim has for Christian discipleship. Mary Magdalene, Mary, and Salome are instructed to tell others what they have heard, and to follow the Risen One along the road to Galilee. It is in following the Risen Christ that the Christian claim of resurrection is most fully actualized. Mark's narrative, in other words, has as much to do with Christian praxis as it does with the otherwise isolated question of "what happened to Jesus."

Elisabeth Schüssler Fiorenza has recognized this aspect of Mark's Gospel as astutely as anyone on the contemporary scene: "The Easter message is a proclamation that requires

---

59. Wolfhart Pannenberg, *Jesus—God and Man*, 2nd ed., trans. Lewis L. Wilkins and Duane A. Priebe (Philadelphia: Westminster, 1968), 108.

action rather than confession. It is future-oriented rather than backward-looking: the women 'seek' Jesus among the dead but are told that the tomb is empty."[60] The Risen One's presence in the world is witnessed whenever the memory of what was inaugurated in Jesus of Nazareth is faithfully "en-acted" and "em-bodied" in community. The movement, in other words, is consistently from Christ to the world. The claim of Christ as risen, then, means that the ecclesia is responsible for following the One who has "gone ahead." For the Risen Christ does not confine himself to the familiar, but empties himself of those confines that would enclose him, engaging the world and calling upon us to follow. The tomb remains empty, but the world of difference is invitingly open to us.

The demands of resurrection discipleship not only require the Christian to be open to the world, but also place that openness squarely within the context of life. If nothing else, the dynamic of resurrection is about the stunning emergence of life even in the face of death-dealing odds. Christian proclamation of the Risen One, then, must occur in solidarity with the flourishing of life in God's world. Schüssler Fiorenza addresses this aspect of discipleship pointedly: "G*d and the Resurrected One can be found only among the Living Ones."[61] It is because the Risen Christ goes on ahead of the women, because he leaves the dank confines of a forgotten sepulcher, that he emerges in solidarity with the living and on behalf of those who have died. Those who confess Christ as the Risen One thus need to align themselves on behalf of life as well—a stance that surely will evoke a critical posture against those structures in society that would deny the flourishing of all life.[62]

The discipleship entailed in professing Jesus Christ as risen, however, is not exhausted by solidarity with the oppressed. In

---

60. Schüssler Fiorenza, *Miriam's Child, Sophia's Prophet*, 123.
61. Ibid., 127.
62. The affirmation of Christ as risen ipso facto evokes solidarity with the "least" of society, the poor and suffering—including the planet itself—who are denied the abundant life that Christian faith proclaims. Casting one's lot with the Risen One means that much remains to be done that is *our* responsibility under God's grace. In Schüssler Fiorenza's words, "Resurrection does not simply spell the survival of the soul but requires the transformation of the world as we know it" (ibid., 121).

proclaiming the Emptying Christ as the Risen One, Christians point to a pattern of discipleship in which kenosis reemerges. Here, in the Christian life, is where our kenotic model comes full circle. Emptying ourselves of privilege and our own presuppositions and expectations, we might be overtaken by the wisdom of God.

We have already noted the likely connection between the kenotic imagery in Philippians 2 and the Sophia tradition. Might such attention to the wisdom of God be hovering in the background of early Christian proclamation of the empty tomb? It is precisely this connection that Schüssler Fiorenza makes in her recent work. According to her provocative interpretation, it is precisely because of the story's open-endedness that the connection with Sophia is all the more suggestive. For the wisdom of God is not something that can be confined to a tidy set of propositional formulae. It will not reduce itself to our own definitions, but overtakes us and eludes our grasp.

Wisdom Christology is perhaps the oldest strand of christological reflection. Its traces weave throughout Paul's letters (e.g., 1 Cor. 1:24), the prologue of John's Gospel, and the letter to the Hebrews. Because of its early provenance, claiming its connection with the Markan narrative is all the more possible. At the very least, the Markan community was familiar with the wisdom tradition. Schüssler Fiorenza makes this connection even stronger: the Sophia tradition is that which is "proclaimed by women" in the wake of the resurrection "event." This early connection of the *figura* of Jesus Christ and the empty tomb with the Jewish wisdom tradition was eventually obscured by subsequent emphasis upon appearance narratives and a starker focus upon the cross. Yet some of the earliest traditions, Schüssler Fiorenza claims, "understood the mission of Jesus as that of a prophet of Sophia sent to proclaim that the Sophia-G*d of Jesus is the G*d of the poor, the outcasts, and all of those suffering from injustice."[63]

What is significant for our purposes is that the space in which this wisdom of God comes to us is an ambiguous one, immea-

---

63. Ibid., 140.

surably open to the future. The risen Christ empties himself
of all confines and restrictions, appearing only *ahead* of those
who come to meet him. Those who would follow are likewise
instructed to tread this road to Galilee and to empty themselves
of anything that would confine the One they confess as Lord.
Only by emptying oneself of such preconception can the Christian be open to the wisdom of God, the wisdom Jesus Christ
embodies,[64] a wisdom that unveils an immensely wider world.

The Risen Christ and Religious Pluralism

On one level, for Christians, the uniqueness of the Risen One
can hardly be disputed. As the culmination of Christ's self-
emptying, as the suggestive whisper of an "absent presence" of
God, as the nourishing and sustaining presence of hope in the
midst of darkest despair, the Risen Christ unfolds both a world
and a worldview for Christians. Christian theology, in short, loses
its distinctive identity if it ignores the scandal of resurrection.
Without it, the Christian God is no longer a God of life, and
those who would close the tomb forever are given the final word.

   Yet the One who embodies both world and worldview, as the
Risen One, cannot rest within the confines of Christian theology alone. For when Christians affirm Christ as risen, they are
plunged into three currents that run counter to any form of
religious triumphalism. First, the risen Christ is an *absent* presence that can never be contained by *any* formulation about him.
Thus, the final word of the Christ-event will never be uttered;
any talk about the resurrection, likewise, must evince this provisional, absent character. Acknowledging the poverty of our own
expression of the Risen One, in other words, invites the contributions of *all* (particularly those who do not profess Jesus
as the Christ). Second, the Risen One manifests himself as the
One who goes on *ahead*. As the One who cannot be confined
to the past (including past dogma!), the Risen Christ promises
to be revealed only in the future, in the world, on the road

---

64. Elizabeth Johnson has suggested an approach for contemporary Christology
that draws extensively on the wisdom tradition. See *She Who Is: The Mystery of God in
Feminist Theological Discourse* (New York: Crossroad, 1992), 156–61.

to Galilee. Those who would follow this One are likewise compelled to open themselves to that world. Third, the affirmation of Christ as risen focuses our attention upon the *permanence of change*. Paul underscores this change with his moniker of "spiritual body,"[65] describing the resurrection as a transformation of familiar, terrestrial embodiment. If such change underwrites the inaugural formulations of resurrection, then why should contemporary articulation of the Risen One ignore this change and seek instead to establish the Risen Christ as a frozen absolute? Why should the Christian affirmation of Christ as risen so stubbornly resist change, particularly in the encounter with other religions? Such resistance, I would argue, runs counter to the permanence of change that resurrection itself suggests.

Perhaps the most compelling reason to consider the encounter with non-Christian religions in evaluating resurrection claims, however, is evident in the trajectory of those claims themselves. Christian claims about the resurrection do not enclose themselves upon a singular figure in first-century Palestine. Rather, the claim of Christ as risen unfolds, for the Christian, an immeasurably wider world in which the summons of God's grace is irresistible. The breadth and comprehensiveness of this grace, moreover, is so great that it would be equivalent to resisting God's grace if we were to shut ourselves off fully from any segment of humanity that stands within that world. The claim of Christ as Risen, in short, opens for the Christian an immeasurably more spacious world, in which the only things that are promised are the certainty of change, the ubiquity of grace, the constancy of love, and the glimmer of hope. The Risen Christ can indeed invite Christians to hearken to the hushed invitation of the religious Other, and may even launch Christians into the realm of interreligious dialogue. Such conversation, however, can only serve to *change* those who embark upon it, a change that is evident most fully in Christian praxis. Confessing the

---

65. See 1 Cor. 15:42–58. This unspeakable change is also suggested in the Gospels, where those disciples who encounter the risen Christ do not recognize him at first glance. Recognition is evoked only when the Risen One partakes in familiar actions: the breaking of the bread, the calling to fishermen at sea. See John 21:1–14; Luke 24:28–35.

Emptying Christ as incarnate and risen, Christians are likewise directed to relinquish their own privileges in the face-to-face encounter with radically different persons and communities. It is to these practical consequences of Christian confession that we turn in the next chapter.

CHAPTER V

AND WE SHALL BE CHANGED

O NE OF THE RECURRING ARGUMENTS of this work has been that Christian confession is consistently bound up with the life of discipleship. *What* Christians believe and how they articulate those beliefs in the form of doctrine have direct consequences—for good or ill—in *how* the Christian life is conducted. Doctrine, in other words, makes a difference not only in how we formulate our convictions about God, Christ, and the church, but also in how we live out those convictions and respond to God's presence in an increasingly pluralistic world. Throughout much of the history of Christian theology, doctrine has exhibited a regulative function, instating appropriate boundaries and norms within which orthodox speech can take place. The Nicene Creed and the Chalcedonian formula, according to this view, are remarkable not in their exhaustive definition in matters of belief, but in the invitation they offer for further reflection on these matters and their ability to guide that reflection.

For example, when Christians recite the words of Nicaea and claim Jesus Christ as "begotten not created, of the same reality as the Father...who for us humans and for our salvation came down and was incarnate, becoming human,"[1] they are not claiming that these words are all there is to say about the Incarnate and Risen One. Rather, this open-ended language requires us to say *more* about those events and occasions that are paradigmatic in the Christian life.[2] The event of Jesus Christ in-

---

1. The Nicene Creed, as translated in Peter C. Hodgson and Robert H. King, eds. *Readings in Christian Theology* (Minneapolis: Fortress, 1985), 205.
2. Indeed, many of the classical christological creeds refrain from exhaustive

vites an unceasing profusion of linguistic, liturgical, and artistic expressions. Christian doctrines, accordingly, help establish the parameters within which this expression continues; they form the "rules" that shape and guide identity and activity in the Christian community.[3] This regulative view of doctrine suggests that Christian professions of faith are something more than the isolated convictions of a solitary individual; rather, those professions are continually held accountable to the larger community of the church and to the cumulative wisdom of our predecessors in faith (the history of theology). Doctrines, which are one result of this inherited tradition, suggest that we need *others* to express our convictions; they hold us accountable to those others and to the traditions of which we consider ourselves a part.

If it is accurate to say that doctrines establish boundaries or parameters for "orthodox" speech, as George Lindbeck suggests, then certain expressions are ipso facto excluded from the field. Taking the Nicene Creed again as an example, it would be inappropriate to claim Jesus Christ as the Son of God who donned flesh as a Docetic disguise but never became human or suffered. To claim as much would be to eclipse the full humanity that the language of the creed explicitly affirms, even though it does not define that humanity. A regulative view, moreover, does not claim doctrinal "rules" as rigid absolutes. Rules are effective only insofar as they are recognized by those who mouth them; as they guide communities, they are continually being reevaluated and reinterpreted. A *living* community must have vibrant norms that are always open to new expression. Doctrine, in other words, loses its ability to guide the Christian life when it becomes a matter of wooden definition; the community that adopts ossified rules quickly falls moribund.

---

definition—and mediate opposing positions—by their ambiguous language and imagery. Although the creeds exclude some interpretations of Christ's person (Docetism, for example), they also invite more than one valid interpretation. For a further exploration of the function of christological creeds, see the excellent essay by Walter Lowe, "Christ and Salvation," in *Christian Theology: An Introduction to Its Traditions and Tasks*, ed. Peter C. Hodgson and Robert H. King (Minneapolis: Fortress, 1994), 226–30.

3. See George Lindbeck, *The Nature of Doctrine: Religion and Theology in a Postliberal Age* (Philadelphia: Westminster, 1984), for a recent development of this view.

Although the view of doctrine as "rule theory" has been an effective one throughout the history of the church, and despite its recrudescence in contemporary work such as Lindbeck's, I believe that this interpretation of doctrine is partial and misses two important trajectories. First, the rule view tends to obscure the change that doctrines invariably undergo. The *metanoia* that Christians are wont to claim has never been simply a conversion to a new community shaped by tried and true rules; rather, it is a conversion to a *new life*, of which the regulative community is only a part. The beliefs and expressions that give voice to that new life will invariably fall short of any exhaustive expression, and the forms in which it is expressed undoubtedly will change. The new life is not about stultifying sameness across the centuries, but the gift of a new beginning. Second, although it is clear that such expressions of the new life are not an "anything goes" matter, the rule view of doctrine tends to envelop Christian witness in the confines of the familiar and exclude those who are not a part of the identifiable Christian community. Only those within the church are to hold each other accountable to those rules, while those beyond the pale are left to their own devices—they have nothing to add and from them we can learn little. Contrary to this view, I would claim that doctrines—particularly christological doctrines—are relentlessly "ec-centric" (moving out from the center), that they are not the guiding norms for one's religious backyard alone, but fling the Christian beyond the white picket fence into an immensely larger world.

Thus, the problem with the regulative view of doctrine is that it does not adequately acknowledge the *practical* import of Christian confession. Christian belief, in other words, makes a difference—both to the distinctive and ever changing shape of Christian identity and to the attitudes and actions Christians undertake in a world of difference. This work has focused on perhaps the most distinctively "Christian" of the major doctrines: Christology. We have examined two prongs of this doctrine—incarnation and resurrection—and suggested that a deeper probing of these claims cannot rest within the confines of the identifiably "Christian" church. Christian confession of the Emptying Christ is not a centripetal movement that encloses those of like mind in a world of their own; rather, it is a centrifugal dynamic that underscores the reality of otherness and the need for difference.

This practical change inaugurated by the Emptying Christ, I would suggest, is threefold: First, it shifts the focus of Christian *discipleship* from a relatively simple moral matter of "following" Jesus to a much deeper concern with the ethical claim of the religious Other, the metaphysical recognition of interrelationship and the demand of difference in following Christ. Second, this rearticulation suggests that the *practice of interreligious dialogue* itself is changed. The relentless call of the religious Other questions the traditional model of "dialogue," if by that we mean the detached exchange of competing religious truth claims. What is suggested instead is a model of dialogue-and-solidarity and a conception of religious "truth" that embraces the aesthetic, opening us to the beauty of different, particular others. Third, our study has suggested that *doctrine* itself changes, particularly with reference to Christology. The religious Other, as we will see, does not stand on the periphery of christological doctrine, but at its very center. To exclude those others, as many doctrinal articulations do, is to render Jesus Christ nothing more than a parochial figure.

Because Christian doctrine often has served to exclude the religious Other, the guideposts along this route are few and far between. In much of what follows, I will draw upon the work of Dietrich Bonhoeffer and Simone Weil, persons grabbed simultaneously by the crux of the good news and by the plight of others suffering in their midst. Contemporaries in Europe during a time of upheaval and cataclysm, these thinkers did not consider the Christian gospel to be a pacifier for the individual conscience; rather, a turn to Christ was at the same time a turn toward others. For each, the cost of this solidarity was substantial, resulting in Bonhoeffer's execution at the hand of his Nazi tormentors, and Weil's slow, withering death because of her refusal to accept any privilege over the dismal conditions of imprisoned workers in her own country. Both writers present a vivid example of the connection between thought and praxis, and of the conviction that how one envisions God and Jesus Christ makes a difference in how life is conceived in light of them.

THE DIFFERENCE KENOSIS MAKES IN DISCIPLESHIP

One can argue the case that in a culture of consumer Christianity, the meaning of discipleship has degenerated into trite moralisms. What the consumer mentality craves in an era of plurality and ambiguity is simplistic answers that ostensibly mesh with the life and ministry of Jesus. One manifestation of this consumer itch is the oft heard retort "What would Jesus do?" as if the life of discipleship could be boiled down to an array of straightforward responses to hypothetical scenarios. Under this model, discipleship becomes a correlation between dilemmas one may encounter in the "real world" and a supposedly appropriate "Christian" response. Jesus thus becomes the supreme rule giver or moral exemplar who unveils a life of discipleship that can be neatly arranged in terms of following those rules and examples. Such a model is unavoidably individualistic and rarely addresses the deeper systemic issues that underlie the moral dilemmas that Christians face. Instead, this portrayal of discipleship supplies cheap answers in increasingly ambiguous times.

In response to the prevailing popular winds that would construe the life of discipleship narrowly in terms of moral obligations, I would offer a fuller exposition that includes a sense of obligation and willingness to be claimed by others, but that also suggests a *metaphysical* dimension to the Christian life. The call of the Other is not simply a matter of following hard-and-fast rules, but suggests that my well-being is bound up with the Other's well-being, that we need each other and our undeniable differences to live the abundant life the good news proclaims. What the life of discipleship entails, as a response to the Kenotic One, is the emptying of the individual, moral self in order to find a larger self in solidarity with others. This alternative construal of discipleship suggests that the Christian life is comprehensive and cannot be distilled to a tidy set of questions and answers. Suspicious of privileged conditions and privileged answers, the life of discipleship questions anything— even religion itself—that would mute the clarion call of others in our midst.

The Ethical Dimension

One facet of this comprehensive life is the ethical, undoubtedly the aspect of discipleship that has been stressed most strongly in recent years. What I mean by the ethical dimension of discipleship is not simply the obligations that ensue in following Jesus Christ, but the pattern of life-with-others that emerges when the self empties itself of its own cherished "center." Following Christ thus reflects not an individualized focus on my attitudes and actions toward others, but a deeper recognition of the Other qua Other—and the solidarity of others that results therein. The turn to Christ is at once a turn toward human others in their particularity and difference.

This conception of the life of discipleship is a direct correlate of the kenotic themes we have been developing. To profess the Emptying Christ is to suggest that the dynamic of kenosis has resonance in Christian praxis as well as creedal affirmation. Nancey Murphy and George F. R. Ellis claim as much in a recent work: "The point, then, is that the proper response to a kenotic God is a kenotic relation to God and to all of God's creation. It begins as a theological attitude, an awareness of our status relative to God, that enables an emptying of our pride in relation to our work, our achievements, and the fellow humans we encounter in our lives."[4] The "difference" kenosis makes, if adopted as a model of discipleship, is that it empties the self's own privilege and isolation, liberating that self for life-with-others.

Dietrich Bonhoeffer offers one example of how this life-with-others might be carried out. In a sermon composed within the confines of a prison cell on the occasion of his nephew's baptism, Bonhoeffer writes: "[We] prove ourselves worthy to

---

4. Nancey Murphy and George F. R. Ellis, *On the Moral Nature of the Universe: Theology, Cosmology, and Ethics* (Minneapolis: Fortress, 1996), 196.

survive by identifying ourselves generously and unselfishly with the life of the community and the sufferings of our fellow-men."[5] Bonhoeffer thus challenges his audience, which includes the contemporary generation, to break the barnacles of self-attachment and allow others to have a claim upon oneself. The ethical dimension of discipleship is not a paternalistic existence *for* others, as if I might help or aid others occasionally in their affliction, but a permanent existence *with* others, and being affected and changed in that process.

Once we conceive of the life of discipleship in terms of *being-with*, however, we cannot slither behind the screen of stultifying sameness. The life that is lived with others, in contrast to the paternalist's, recognizes the irreducible difference of the others with whom one builds that life, the concrete detail and uniqueness of the faces around oneself. No one has thematized this alterity better than Emmanuel Lévinas, whose work we encountered briefly in chapter 2. Lévinas's musings on ethics and otherness provide a philosophical framework for how we might construct a kenotic ethic. Despite Lévinas's obvious inattention to the question of discipleship per se, his consideration of ethics as "first philosophy" offers one example of the claim of others upon oneself, and of a life molded by their summons.

For Lévinas, the *face* of the Other is what signifies both radical alterity from me and kinship with me. The face is at once both hauntingly different, evoking the reality of otherness, and vulnerable, inciting me to preserve this difference because the Other is related to me. In creation, "the kinship of beings among themselves is affirmed, but at the same time their radical heterogeneity also. . . . In the face to face the I has neither the privileged position of the subject nor the position of the thing defined by its place in the system."[6] The face presents an Other to whom I am bound, whose alterity vanishes—along with my own capacity for relationship—if I vaunt myself over that person. The summons of the face, in other words, is not a matter

---

5. Dietrich Bonhoeffer, *Letters and Papers from Prison*, trans. Reginald Fuller, Frank Clark, et al. (New York: Macmillan, 1972), 299.
6. Emmanuel Lévinas, *Totality and Infinity*, trans. Alphonso Lingis (Pittsburgh: Duquesne University Press, 1969), 293.

of choice. It is not simply that I allow myself to be affected by the Other; rather, relatedness and the claim of the Other are preconditions of authentic human being.[7]

The radicalness of Lévinas's proposal is that the claim of the Other is so pervasive that this Other is *prior* to myself. Lévinas suggests that relational anthropology does not amount only to the emptying of the self in order to recognize the Other; rather, the Other is *already there*, calling me to him or her even before I am. It is not the case, for Lévinas, that "I" exist, ergo I am obligated to others; rather, it is more accurate to say that *others* exist, ergo "I" stand in relation to them and am summoned by them. In the beginning, in other words, are the relationships that constitute me, to which I owe my very existence. In Lévinas's words, "The intersubjective relation is a non-symmetrical relation. In this sense, I am responsible for the Other without waiting for reciprocity. . . . It is precisely insofar as the relationship between the Other and me is not reciprocal that I am subjection to the Other."[8] My response to the Other, my willingness to exist in solidarity with him or her, in this sense, is always a posterior act. It occurs because the relationship with the Other is always present before me: I "am" insofar as I recognize the relatedness and obligations of the multifarious faces around me.

If we combine the wisdom of Lévinas's relational anthropology with our preceding reflections on Christology, it becomes clear that the genuinely radical nature of Christian discipleship is not its adherence to rules or norms for "Christian" behavior, but rather, its willingness to *empty* itself of any such rules that would leave one secure in one's own sphere. In professing the One who "incarnates" being-with-others, Christians are called to recognize the reality of otherness, the claim of the Other

---

7. It is in this regard that ethics is "first philosophy" for Lévinas. In an interview with Philippe Nemo, Lévinas responds, "I mean to say that a truly human life cannot remain life *satis*-fied in its equality to being, a life of quietude, that it is awakened by the other, that is to say, it is always getting sobered up, that being is never—contrary to what so many reassuring traditions say—its own reason for being" (*Ethics and Infinity*, trans. Richard A. Cohen [Pittsburgh: Duquesne University Press, 1985], 122). The self, accordingly, is never an isolated monad, but continually co-constituted by others.

8. Ibid., 98.

upon them, and the interrelation that constitutes abundant life in God's world. The ethical paradigm in glimpsing this life, in other words, is the kenotic self that would empty itself of anything—even rules and religion—that obscures the reality and claim of the Other who is already there.[9]

The Other, in short, does not exist for my own convenience; neither does she or he exist as one to be converted to my mode of thinking or believing. As the one who refuses to be restricted by any label I would apply, any definition I would impose, the Other remains an inexhaustible mystery to me. In Lévinas's words, "The face is present in its refusal to be contained. In this sense it cannot be comprehended, that is, encompassed.... The Other remains infinitely transcendent, infinitely foreign."[10] The reality of otherness does not serve to confirm my own privileged sense of identity, for to recognize something besides oneself as *real* is to acknowledge that "I" am not a self-sufficient creature. What discipleship constitutes, in its comprehensiveness, is the radical opening of the individual life to the unfathomable depth of others in their uniqueness and intricacy. To recognize others as *real* allows us to be surprised by others and to admit that we are never alone, however much we may search for an island of solitude. The ethical dimension of discipleship, in this sense, is nothing less than the recognition that human persons are made for each other, that each person affects every other, that whatever would seek to sever or injure this relatedness invariably reverberates throughout corporate life.[11]

This inescapable factum of interrelationship means that each human being, in his or her uniqueness, is irreplaceable in this world of difference. Each concrete Other is, in the words

---

9. We will explore the idea of a "religionless Christianity" shortly.

10. Lévinas, *Totality and Infinity*, 194.

11. This view of Christian discipleship is implicit in Martin Luther King Jr.'s "Letter from a Birmingham City Jail." Few writings of the last half-century have voiced the comprehensiveness of the Christian life as vividly as this classic document. "I am cognizant of the interrelatedness of all communities and states. I cannot sit idly by in Atlanta and not be concerned about what happens in Birmingham. Injustice anywhere is a threat to justice everywhere. We are caught in an inescapable network of mutuality, tied in a single garment of destiny. Whatever affects one directly affects all indirectly" (quoted in *A Testament of Hope: The Essential Writings of Martin Luther King, Jr.*, ed. James Melvin Washington [San Francisco: Harper & Row, 1986], 290).

of Simone Weil, "something sacred to which [we are] bound
to show respect."[12] Anything that would deny the sacrality of
others, therefore, is contrary to the way of self-emptying that
Jesus Christ embodies. To deny the irreplaceability of the Other
is to claim that "I" am superior to that Other, to vaunt my
own privilege at the expense of others, to live over others
instead of with them. The ethical dimension of Christian discipleship, in this sense, is that which seeks to preserve the
reality of interrelationship and the inexhaustible mystery of the
concrete Other.

The Metaphysical Dimension

Our brief examination of the ethical component of discipleship
has suggested that "following Christ" is not tantamount to ad-
hering to a fixed set of rules that govern our relationship with
others. Echoing our exegesis of Philippians 2, we have suggested
that the life of discipleship is characterized by its turn toward
others in compassion and love. The ethical component of Christian life is neither simply a life *for others* nor is it the bestowal of
Christian "virtue" upon others. Rather, it suggests something far
deeper: recognition of the Other *as Other*, as someone unique
and mysterious, and as such, beautiful and sacred. The ethical
dimension of Christian discipleship is what opens "me" to the
reality of "you." It frees the self from the prison of individualism
by emptying the self of all pretensions of self-sufficiency, thus
unveiling the primacy of interhuman relation.[13]

Most treatments of Christian discipleship have sought to affirm as much throughout the history of theology. They have
sought, namely, to underscore the supreme value of the Other
qua Other, and that the Christian posture is one that aligns itself
with the Other, or at least on behalf of the Other. Such is the *obligation* of Christian discipleship, that other human beings have a

---

12. Simone Weil, "Draft for a Statement of Human Obligations," in *Selected Essays,
1934–1943,* trans. Richard Rees (London: Oxford University Press, 1962), 220.
13. Douglas John Hall offers a similar view of the nature of discipleship and,
indeed, reality itself: "What is most important for us—what is *real*—is not what
individual entities are made up of but what transpires *between* entities, *between* persons" (*Professing the Faith: Christian Theology in a North American Context* [Minneapolis:
Fortress, 1993], 500).

claim upon oneself. This focus, however, addresses only half of the issue. The "difference" that the kenotic approach makes is that it construes discipleship both ethically *and* metaphysically. Here is where our study deepens the Pauline insight, by suggesting that kenosis illuminates not only our ethical responsibilities with others, but the development of the self-in-relation as well. For it is only the "emptying self" that approaches wholeness: in the surprising dynamic of kenosis the self that relinquishes its supposed independence gains a wider self co-constituted with others. Standing at antipodes to the isolated, monarchical self, the emptying self is continually open to change and the unexpected incursion of God's grace. This self cannot exist alone because it needs others and change for its own well-being.

Even the experience of confinement cannot destroy the fundamental relatedness of human be-ing. In fact, the forced isolation of the self from others—often found in prisons—generally intensifies the need for others.[14] Dietrich Bonhoeffer recognized this inescapability of relationship as acutely as anyone of his generation, and came to this recognition while imprisoned, separated from those he loved. Appropriately, he ties together the most stubborn ethical demand of discipleship ("Be perfect, therefore, as your heavenly Father is perfect" [Matt. 5:48]) with this recognition of interrelation. Interpreting "perfection" akin to "wholeness,"[15] Bonhoeffer writes, "We can never achieve this 'wholeness' simply by ourselves, but only together with others."[16] The claim of Christian discipleship, then, is not that it is somehow a more "ethical" existence; rather, the claim is that following Christ can open one's eyes more fully to the Other, so that she or he is not merely acknowledged, but recognized as someone *with* me, as someone with whom I am bound in an inescapable network of relation.

That the Christian affirms this interrelationship is not, in

14. It is not surprising that the most extreme form of punishment in many prisons, the option of last resort, is solitary confinement. Such isolation, if prolonged, can result in insanity. The self, if left solely to itself, devolves and destroys itself. Starved of being-with-others, it can no longer be.

15. The Greek word *teleios*, used in Matt. 5:48, is a rich adjective, connoting both "perfection" and "completion."

16. Bonhoeffer, *Letters and Papers*, 200.

itself, unique. Indeed, strains within each of the classical religious "ways" recognizes that individual well-being is bound up with interhuman and ecological flourishing.[17] What *is* unique, from the Christian perspective, is that each concrete Other can become an occasion for glimpsing Christ, for sensing God's concern with humanity and humanity's relationship with God. As Matthew writes, "For I was hungry and you gave me food, I was thirsty and you gave me something to drink, I was a stranger and you welcomed me.... 'Truly I tell you, just as you did it to one of the least of these who are members of my family, you did it to me'" (Matt. 25:35, 40b). The difference that the Christian affirms is that the life of discipleship is marked by being-with-others, and that in this solidarity Christ comes to us again. According to this vision, the centerpiece of Christian conviction, Jesus Christ, can be recognized only *in* and *with* distinctly different human others. Christ comes to us, not alone, but as we turn toward others in following him. The metaphysical claim of Christian discipleship, then, is that the self is a truncated self if it exists apart from others, if it seeks only the refuge of the familiar. In contrast, it affirms along with Martin Buber that the human being "becomes an I through a You."[18] If we assert an "independent" self, then the result is not only a distorted sense of self apart from others, but a distorted view of discipleship, so that "following" Jesus devolves into an individual assent to rules—and a warped conception of faith—assent to propositions for the sake of personal salvation.

The kenotic dynamic of discipleship, then, empties the individual self of any privileged "center." It recognizes that Irenaeus's vision of each human fully alive cannot be achieved when each individual remains ensconced in a private backyard. Even from the confines of his prison cell, Bonhoeffer recognized that the life of discipleship could only be construed as

17. Certainly, the Buddhist conception of *pratityasamutpada*, which we explored in chapter 2, offers a vision of ecological interrelation, as do the Hebrew creation narratives and this pearl of wisdom from the *Tao Te Ching:* "Heaven abides; earth lasts / They last and abide / By not living for themselves. / Hence they live forever" (Lao-tzu, *Tao Te Ching*, trans. Herrymon Maurer [New York: Schocken, 1985], 47).

18. Martin Buber, *I and Thou*, trans. Walter Kaufmann (New York: Simon & Schuster, 1970), 80.

being-with. "It's remarkable how we think at such times about the people that we should not like to live without, and almost or entirely forget about ourselves. It is only then that we feel how closely our own lives are bound up with other people's, and in fact how the centre of our own lives is outside ourselves, and how little we are separate entities."[19] What is striking about Bonhoeffer's conception is that what is most essential to the self is found *outside itself.* This claim throws into question every solipsism and cherished Western presupposition that the individual self is of permanent centrality and the ultimate criterion of truth. It acknowledges, rather, that I can become myself and know myself only *through* the others.

Admitting the impoverishment of the isolated, monarchical self and accepting the constitution of a wider, relational self is a tardy theological echo of what the biological sciences have been claiming for centuries: *all* forms of life need each other for their very be-ing; interrelation is writ large throughout the ecological tapestry. A relational anthropology, moreover, accepts the permanence of change that results from such interrelation. For to claim that I am co-constituted by the Other is to claim that my relation with that Other changes who "I" am. The relationship of the "I" to the "You," in other words, is characterized by constant flux and growth. One never rests in a settled place with the Other, but grows through continual change with another. Relationships and creatures, in a word, *live* through this change; if they exhibit stagnancy, they wither and die.[20] As one surveys the spectrum of life on earth, it is not fixity and perduration that stick out from the record, but the universal preponderance of change. The enduring, fixed self is both a biological and theological illusion, for both the ecological life that the biologist observes and the abundant life that the theologian is wont to address are marked by constant mutation and growth. Life itself depends on such change—the continual, responsive engagement of the self in a wider network of others.[21] Or, to

---

19. Bonhoeffer, *Letters and Papers,* 105.
20. As evolutionary biologists would tell us, those species that exhibit the best-suited adaptive change to their environments survive across generations.
21. We must recognize that this relational conception does not erase the signifi-

place this observation in more explicitly theological terms, the richness of the Christian life can be measured by its degree of "conversion" to others,[22] its response to others' joys, trials, and struggles, and its willingness to be changed by others in that response.[23]

The Fruit of Kenotic Discipleship

As the dynamic of kenosis wends its way through the lives of disciples, no single aspect of corporate life is exempt from it. If there is truly a "cost" of discipleship, it is the voluntary casting aside of privilege. Putting into practice the ideal offered in the Philippian Christ-hymn, this relinquishment calls into question the entire Western ethos of entitlement in which First World Christians find themselves. In a culture that cultivates privilege for those "who have earned it," fosters a bewildering parade of cutthroat competition for limited goods, and justifies those who emerge victorious, there is no stance more countercultural. The emptying self not only ignores the distinctions and tribalisms that a culture of competitiveness creates, but also proposes a radical alternative to that culture itself. Relinquishing all privilege, the kenotic vision evokes a *life of others* (solidarity) rather than life over (privilege), life for (charity that presupposes a cul-

---

cance of the self. Indeed, one cannot talk about relation unless there is a self that can participate in such relationships. What I am suggesting here is that relationship does not swallow the self, but that the self is co-constituted by relationships with others as "subjects." Whether one is speaking of fellow human beings, other mammals, insects, or even protozoa, concrete others do not exist solely *for me*, but in their own right *as others*. For a similar treatment of the relational self, see Sallie McFague, *Super, Natural Christians* (Minneapolis: Fortress, 1997), esp. chs. 5, 7.

22. Note how this locution is an *inversion* of the popular conception of Christian discipleship. The Christian life is not marked by others' conversion to Christianity (my way of belief), but my conversion to others. The "proselytizing I" must surrender its own privilege in faithful discipleship.

23. There is perhaps no more powerful example of the change that occurs in the individual self in relation to others than the phenomenon of human love. More than any other aspect of human life, love illustrates that individual lives flourish when shared with an Other. In love, we admit our genuine need for another and that we ourselves are changed with that Other, by being open to the mysterious grace of that Other's very being and the surprise of life together. The Other comes to us in love as a gift not to be grasped, objectified, or projected upon, but in his or her alterity, interestingness, and reality. Paraphrasing St. Augustine, to love something truly is to recognize it as *real*, to want it simply "to be." See *Confessions*, trans. R. S. Pine-Coffin (New York: Penguin, 1961), book 13.33–38, pp. 344–47.

ture of privilege), or even life with (in which "we" represent the center).[24] The practical consequence of confessing the kenotic Christ is a life of discipleship that questions anything—even religion itself—that perpetuates the violent cycle of disparity.[25]

The relinquishing of privilege extends most directly to the church, for there is perhaps no better example of the misplaced assertion of superiority and the evasion of responsibility than the church that ensconces itself within its hallowed walls. What the kenotic life of discipleship envisions is a wider view of church: not an institution apart from the world, but a group called into a solidarity of others. Simone Weil has scathing words for those who would place church allegiance ahead of responsibility, the escapists who refuse to turn toward the earth: "Imperfection comes from attaching yourself to the Church as to an earthly country.... The children of God should not have any other country here below but the universe itself, with the totality of all the reasoning creatures it ever has contained, contains, or ever will contain. That is the native city to which we owe our love."[26] The universal claim of the church is not its position of privilege in relation to all other assemblies and institutions, its demand that *all* might be "saved" through it; rather, its universality is its willingness to be in the midst of that world, its call to be the *"ek-klesia,"* the community called out (*ek-*) into the world, not into itself.

What is striking on the contemporary American scene is how rarely the church lives up to its name. In a culture of consumer Christianity, the church models itself more as a house of refuge than a community called forth into encounter with

---

24. This "life of others" is not meant to contradict our previous designation of discipleship as "being with others"; rather, it is meant to further specify the meaning of discipleship, to de-center the "I" who exists with others.

25. The gist of this proposal is found in a recent article by Anselm Min, who writes, "This solidarity is not 'our' solidarity 'with' 'others,' where 'we' implicitly constitute the privileged center of reference to which 'others' have to be referred but the solidarity 'of' others, where no group is a privileged center, where all of us are 'other' to one another in religion, culture, language, and ethnic origin, yet also summoned as others to enter into the solidarity of a 'we' by working together to create common conditions of dignity by the dialectic of recent history" ("Dialectical Pluralism and Solidarity of Others," *Journal of the American Academy of Religion* 65, no. 3 [fall 1997]: 589).

26. Simone Weil, *Waiting for God* (New York: Harper & Row, 1973), 96–97.

others. Many middle- and upper-class churches have become sops for bourgeois fears, institutions that justify privilege instead of castigating it. Reflecting our society's predominant self-absorption of how "I" can better "myself," the church becomes more an *"en-klesia"* of navel-gazers. Certainly, Bonhoeffer anticipated this trend, and his words against it are harsh: "Here and there people flee from public altercation into the sanctuary of private *virtuousness*. But anyone who does this must shut his mouth and his eyes to the injustice around him.... [Free responsibility] depends on a God who demands responsible action in a bold venture of faith, and who promises forgiveness and consolation to the man who becomes a sinner in that venture."[27] "Church," in short, loses its meaning when it becomes its own justification for privilege, when it chooses to "follow Christ" by closing its eyes to those others beyond its walls.

Perhaps the most basic demand of a kenotic ethic, the paramount example of this relinquishing of privilege, is the practice of nonviolence. Violence extends the trajectory of privilege to its extreme, blatantly asserting itself over others: because "I" am justified in my stance, I can use any means necessary to perpetuate it. Indeed, the logic of violence claims that I can destroy those who threaten my own privilege and "right." So enmeshed are we in a culture of violence that it is difficult to imagine a world bereft of it. Indeed, much of our nation's attention is currently focused not on the elimination of violence from our streets, but on the justified use of it.[28] The dynamic of self-emptying, however, runs explicitly counter to this near-ubiquitous behavior: it offers an alternative to the violent cyclone that eventually engulfs everything in its path. As Murphy and Ellis note, "The practice of nonviolence,...specified

---

27. Bonhoeffer, *Letters and Papers*, 5–6.
28. The proliferation of laws in recent decades widening the scope of "justifiable homicide" is but one example of the logic of violence. In some states it is now legal for a homeowner to shoot a suspected burglar fleeing his or her house. The current torrent of punitive laws—three strikes and you're out!—offers ample evidence for our culture of violence as well. Our response to crime focuses little on prevention and more on incarceration. We build more prisons and fewer schools; death row continues to grow as a supposedly commensurate response to the violence we have gestated.

to focus on...kenotic actions, is a social practice aimed at radical change in the moral character of the participants—a shock treatment to reverse the direction of a deteriorating social situation."[29] Instead of asserting that might makes right, the appropriate response to a kenotic depiction of God in Christ is to question anything that would vaunt superiority at the expense of another. Nonviolence, in other words, is the *method* in which a kenotic ethic of solidarity is most readily discerned.

Most Christian appeals for nonviolence focus almost exclusively upon the interhuman sphere. Diagnosing the sickness of violence and militarism, which invariably sets person against person in an escalating spiral of rage, several contemporary theologians have advocated a pacifist stance as an antidote to the sickness. Most of these writers have roots—confessionally or sympathetically—in the Anabaptist tradition.[30] Often appealing to the norm and life of Jesus, their works offer an unambiguous plea for both the removal of the rhetoric of violence from Christian theological discourse and the excision of its cancer from everyday life. If this radical, pacifistic alternative cannot be realized on a global scale, then the church at the very least is called to embody an alternative in its speech and action. In the midst of a violent and fractured world, the ecclesia can represent a radically new way of being.

Most recent assessments of violence, however, tend to bypass what certainly is the most universal of all examples of its cancer: humankind's violent depredation of the ecosphere itself. The near-exclusive focus upon the violence humanity inflicts upon itself has averted our glance from the scars of biotic extinction, the most flagrant example of humanity's own will to power, the arrogant assertion of our own "privilege."[31] The scars of this

---

29. Murphy and Ellis, *Moral Nature of the Universe*, 159.

30. Prominent among this recent collection of work are Murphy and Ellis, *Moral Nature of the Universe;* John Howard Yoder, *The Politics of Jesus* (Grand Rapids: Eerdmans, 1972); and Stanley Hauerwas, *The Peaceable Kingdom* (Notre Dame, Ind.: University of Notre Dame Press, 1983).

31. In a recent work, Marjorie Suchocki interprets original sin as violence, or rebellion, against creation. Her work offers a sorely needed adjustment of the theological lens and turns our attention to the violence we have wrought against the planet itself. See *The Fall to Violence* (New York: Continuum, 1995), 16–46.

violence have become so familiar that we have inured ourselves
to them: global warming, the elimination of wilderness areas,
ozone depletion, and the gradual disappearance of biodiversity.
The insidious dynamic of ecological violence invariably wends
its way back to those who inflict it; no matter how hard we try
to insulate ourselves in the air-conditioned comfort of larger
all-terrain vehicles, it redounds to us, resulting in a diminished
quality of life and a bleak future. Slowly but surely, we are killing
ourselves, others, and the very planet we inhabit.

Undoubtedly, stopping the violence in our dire situation is
possible, but will require more than the mere stanching of the
earth's suppurating wounds. What is required, as most any cli-
matologist or ecologist will tell us, is a radical conversion to the
earth and the relinquishing of our highly consumptive habits.
We can no longer exert authority or privilege over those more
vulnerable aspects of creation simply because we can, but must
empty ourselves of our greed, overconsumption, and insatiable
desire. Perhaps because the burden upon us, in the face of
such urgency, is so heavy—it will certainly cause discomfort to
those who heed its call—so few have paid it much attention.
The cost to our high standard of living is simply too much. Yet
no more obvious impetus for a kenotic ethic of solidarity and
nonviolence exists than the ubiquitous groaning of the planet
itself, particularly for those of us in the First World.

The Ec-centric Movement of Discipleship

The consequences of adopting a kenotic ethic of solidarity and
nonviolence are unavoidably ec-centric; that is, they remove
the church from any assumed *center*. Claiming as much, however, distances our interpretation of discipleship from other
current Christian exponents of nonviolence, such as John Milbank and Stanley Hauerwas. Viewing the Christian church as an
alternative society to the world's power structures and its "on-
tology of violence,"[32] these theologians advocate a recovery of
the church's disruptive and subversive message: a norm of love

---

32. See John Milbank, *Theology and Social Theory* (Cambridge, Mass.: Basil
Blackwell, 1991).

that establishes fairly well-defined boundaries between "church" and "world." Fidelity to Jesus Christ, according to each of these thinkers, places the disciple in a relatively small sect opposed to the world's destructive and violent propensities. The "center" of this sect is the ministry of Jesus Christ, his destabilizing vision, and the confessions that arise in response to him. Believers and followers of this vision form a nucleus around this center, while the "world" stands only at the periphery, bound as it is by a different lord. Although the writings of Hauerwas and Milbank represent the most academic strand of this interpretation of discipleship, its influence is pervasive, and is found wherever those would claim discipleship as "membership in" an alternative group, distinct from the world as such. Christ, according to this vision, stands not so much at the center of the planet or the "village" (Bonhoeffer), but at the center of the church.

The tack that I have been advocating, however, throws into question any conception of discipleship that interprets it *primarily* in this sectarian manner. For as kenosis breaks the barnacles of self-attachment and heeds the call of others, the life of discipleship cannot rest within the narrow confines of the church, even if the church is viewed as an "alternative society." Recognizing Christ more "in the midst"[33] of life rather than at the center of a slim segment of that life, discipleship is marked more by polyphony than monotony, by polycentrism rather than monocentrism, and a conversion to the earth rather than a conversion to an alternative society.

Simone Weil is one exponent of a vision of discipleship that stands in stark contrast to a more sectarian view. Notice how, for Weil, this vision is constructed along kenotic lines:

> To empty ourselves of our false divinity, to deny ourselves, to give up being the center of the world in imagination, to

---

33. Jesus' first resurrection appearance to the disciples, as narrated by John, centers on this turn of phrase: "Jesus came and stood in the midst" (John 20:19, KJV). Stephen Hancock offers a helpful interpretation of *eis to meson* in a recent sermon. "In the midst. Of what? Of the group? Yes. But in the midst of everything else as well. In the midst of the fear, the discouragement, and the weariness he stood. In the midst of all this guilt and all this grief. In the midst of this very ordinary place and this most typical low time Jesus comes and stands in the midst of it all" ("In the Midst," preached at Second Presbyterian Church, Nashville, April 19, 1998).

discern that all points in the world are equally centers and
that the true center is outside the world, this is to consent
to the rule of mechanical necessity in matter and of free
choice at the center of each soul. Such consent is love. The
face of this love, which is turned toward thinking persons,
is the love of our neighbor; the face turned toward matter
is love of the order of the world, or love of the beauty of
the world which is the same thing.[34]

Relinquishing the center is, however, a destabilizing move, certainly riskier than the comparative security that a move to
sectarianism may offer. Such a move places the Christian life in
the midst of a polyglot and pluriform world, a world in which
confessional Christian claims are not self-evident. Christians,
because of their explicit confession of the Emptying Christ,
are thrown out of the sect of the same into solidarity with
others who are different, and are forced to show the *relevance*
of those confessions as they live, move, and have their being in
an immeasurably wider world.

The Christian life cannot be chiefly about fellowship with
those who share the same beliefs. Such a narrow conception
of discipleship runs contrary to the scandal of Jesus' ministry:
his ignoring of any distinctions that set persons against one
another—Gentile against Jew, master against slave, husband
against wife, parent against child.[35] The demands of kenotic discipleship, on the other hand, question any form of privilege and
division that arise in the world, including the church's own religious tribalism. The church, in other words, must empty itself
of the facile claim that it alone has all the answers; it must cease
viewing the Christian life upon a narrow path that leads directly
to its own sanctuary and instead travel a road that hearkens to
the presence of God in the midst of a polyglot world.

Such a vision of the Christian life is *polyphonic,* and has resonance with all of life in its intricate detail and difference. Rarely

---

34. Weil, *Waiting for God,* 159–60.
35. In chapter 3 we examined Jesus' proclamation of the reign of God and his
practice of open commensality. See also John Dominic Crossan's work in this regard
in *Jesus: A Revolutionary Biography* (San Francisco: HarperCollins, 1994), ch. 3.

approached in contemporary theological reflection, this vision is broached in some of Bonhoeffer's letters from prison. "Christianity puts us into many dimensions of life at the same time; we make room in ourselves, to some extent, for God and the whole world. We rejoice with those who rejoice, and weep with those who weep.... Life isn't pushed back into a single dimension, but is kept multi-dimensional and polyphonous."[36] The Christian life can make a difference to more than those simply gathered in Christ's name. This is the genuine meaning of Jesus Christ's universality: not that Christ is necessarily proclaimed as Lord by all, but that his life and message has resonance with all of life in its messy detail, its pluriform facets and multiple contexts. It is not that his name *must* be uttered in joy in the streets of Soweto at the end of apartheid or in agony in the slums of Calcutta, but that it *can* be uttered and that it transforms those who do utter it. Yet, in proclaiming and following this One, Christians are opened radically to the contexts—and to others within those contexts—in which such utterance takes place. Emptying the self, the one who follows Christ is moved, affected, and changed by the world. The proclamation of Christ *ipso facto* takes place in openness to the world.

As Bonhoeffer writes during the last throes of war in Europe, God's reign and call is "as wide as the earth."[37] It calls us to embrace not chiefly those who are like us, but to evade the comforting strains of the familiar and be claimed by others. A kenotic church would admit that it needs others for its very existence, that to ignore those others would be to domesticate Christ's destabilizing call upon us. Unless the "Godward" turn is simultaneously a turn toward others and the world itself, the life of discipleship loses its comprehensiveness, becoming a form of escapism and a shedding of responsibility. The ec-centric movement of the Christian life, rather, recognizes that conversion to Christ is at one and the same time a conversion to others.

---

36. Bonhoeffer, *Letters and Papers*, 310–11.
37. Ibid., 304.

A "Religionless Christianity"?

A final consequence of the kenotic practice of discipleship, consonant with the ec-centric movement we have highlighted, is the emptying of religion itself, the relinquishing of religion's own claims to absoluteness and security. In an era in which "religion" tends to pit human beings against one another,[38] it is perhaps time to entertain this seemingly unchristian option.

Dietrich Bonhoeffer, in a letter to Eberhard Bethge, wrote of this possibility and thus anticipated much in our contemporary situation of pluralism and ecological catastrophe:

> The time when people could be told everything by means of words, whether theological or pious, is over, and so is the time of inwardness and conscience—and that means the time of religion in general. We are moving towards a completely religionless time; people as they are now simply cannot be religious any more. Even those who honestly describe themselves as "religious" do not in the least act up to it, and so they presumably mean something quite different by "religious."[39]

Inasmuch as we can gather from Bonhoeffer's fragmentary notes, he considered the era of "religion" to have reached its end for at least two reasons: First, the death-dealing crises of his day demanded that Christians align themselves with life, alongside those of multiple religious—and atheistic—persuasions. The preservation of life, in other words, takes precedence over questions of religious "uniqueness" or "definitiveness." Second, because of these crises the time of "inwardness" was finished. Religious reflection alone could not adequately address the life-and-death issues of the day; in fact, reflection alone could even obstruct the action needed to save the lives of other human beings. Insofar as we are enmeshed in a situation of the planet's

---

38. In contexts as diverse as Sri Lanka, Northern Ireland, and Palestine, "religion" has often provided the veneer under which a host of national, racial, and ethnic hostilities have festered. The countless number of religious wars and struggles that have erupted over the past few decades offer abundant evidence that religious misunderstanding is increasing at an alarming rate.

39. Bonhoeffer, *Letters and Papers*, 279.

own life and death, and inasmuch as contemporary religious reflection can at times obscure the exigencies of our time, Bonhoeffer's words echo with particular force in our own context as well.

These words, however, fall particularly hard upon theologians. As persons immersed in the language and imagery of faith, Christian theologians are naturally invested in the *difference* their work makes. Precision of expression, the suitability of religious symbols, the philosophical rigor of one's interpretation of God, Christ, and church—all are the proper concerns of the theologian. Yet these venerable enterprises are never ultimate in themselves; they are always partial expressions of what Tillich calls the "New Being in Jesus as the Christ."[40] Any articulation of that new life, of the symbols that inform it, is bound to reflect the theologian's own parochialism and myopia. In an era in which Christian fundamentalists claim the primary symbols of faith (God, Christ, church) as exhaustive truths, and in which many mainline academic theologians engage in obscure discussions remote from contemporary issues and needs, Bonhoeffer's words serve as a poignant reminder of the point of theology: to better guide and inform the *life* of *faith*. When theology becomes either an arcane language game for a privileged few or a blind recitation of absolute truths, it has lost sight of its mission. Bonhoeffer never suggests that our "religionless time" dispense with theological reflection; rather, he urges that we make that reflection genuinely responsive to its context. If the discipline of theology empties itself of some of its more glaring pretensions, it may better inform the new life *and* make a difference.

The danger of theology or "religion," in other words, is this: The "right" doctrine and the exact precision of one's theological articulation, even the proper reverential act can, like anything else, quickly become the object in which one places security and trust. The security of those objects is what Bonhoeffer's stance so resolutely questions. What is of chief

40. Paul Tillich, *Systematic Theology*, vol. 1 (Chicago: University of Chicago Press, 1951), 50.

importance in this new way of life is not the rigor of one's expression, but one's willingness to suffer and *be changed* by others
in the world. In Bonhoeffer's view, the Christian "must live a
'secular' life, and thereby share in God's sufferings.... It is not
the religious act that makes the Christian, but participation in
the sufferings of God in the secular life. That is *metanoia:* not in
the first place thinking about one's own needs, problems, sins,
and fears, but allowing oneself to be caught up into the way of
Jesus Christ."[41] The specific religious posture of myself and the
Other, in this sense, makes a difference, but not an ultimate
difference: in a situation of crisis, what matters is the degree
of openness to those who are most vulnerable. The Emptying
Christ, as the One who incarnates the turn toward others, makes
clear the cries of the vulnerable in our midst.

Emptied of individualism and inwardness, a *religionless Christianity* evokes a return to the earth, to its groaning for justice
and its plea for healing, because this return approaches the
heart of the good news. The struggles, travail, and longing of
the planet *matter,* not as a way station along a solitary journey
into God, but as the manner in which the vulnerable God of
incarnation makes Godself known to creation. Yet it is precisely this depiction of a suffering, kenotic God that much
of Christian "religion" has obscured. Instead of drawing the
connections between creation, incarnation, and the concrete
demands of Christian discipleship, many strands of Christian
theology have otherwise been concerned with perpetuating the
Christian religion's own ascendancy, legitimacy, and privilege,
both institutionally and intellectually. The concern has been
more with personal salvation and the survival of the Christian
religion rather than faithfulness to Jesus' practice of "open
commensality" (Crossan) and openness to the Other that our
vision of incarnation, resurrection, and discipleship has been
advocating.

What would a posture of religionless Christianity look like?
Bonhoeffer's brief letters offer only a few scattered clues. Continuing the theme of his epistolary fragments, I would offer the

41. Bonhoeffer, *Letters and Papers,* 361.

following interpretation: Religionless Christianity is certainly not the surrendering of Christianity's (or any other religion's) own particularity. It is not the subsuming of a particular religious stance as if a more adequate perspective could be reached in abstraction from that stance. A religionless posture is not one that exists above and beyond the concrete manifestations and confessions of any one religious tradition. It is not the privileged gaze of the one who, familiar with the plurality of religious paths, resides beyond them and concludes that all paths lead in the same direction. A religionless posture, in short, is not a generalized commitment to others, devoid of particular confessional commitments.

Neither, however, is the religionless posture an elevation of the particulars of one's own religious tradition. Particularity is to be celebrated as a reflection of the diversity of creation but is not, in itself, the highest good to be praised. The religionless stance recognizes the particularity and partiality of one's own tradition, but recognizes that only *through* this particularity does one emerge in solidarity with others. The confessional claims of the Christian tradition, for example, perhaps best evidenced in its own "scandal of particularity," the incarnation, do not converge back upon themselves to the confines of the ecclesia and the elevation of Christian "truth" above all others; rather, these claims continually radiate outward, moving from Christ to the world, drawing those who would follow this One away from the narrowly private sphere toward the continual call and need for others. Though a generalized commitment to others[42] may invoke an analogous solidarity of others, the more one abstracts oneself from particularity, the greater the danger that one obscures the *difference* between individuals and traditions.

The posture of religionless Christianity, on the other hand, recognizes that particularity and partiality can never be overcome. No "God's-eye" vision for human beings is possible or even desirable. The posture recognizes that it is best through

---

42. For example, John Hick's approach to the world religions or Kant's version of the "ends principle."

particular commitments and confessions that we encounter others as *different and real.* A particular commitment recognizes that it alone does not possess the sole means of truth, but that it needs *others* to approach the universal aims of wholeness and abundant life for all. For example, the particular commitment of following Jesus Christ and his embodied proclamation of the reign of God does not close Christians off from others, but places Christians upon a threshold of genuine difference, and this vision of justice and peace can only be embarked upon if one works with others who embody different proclamations. A religionless posture recognizes that difference is real, desirable, and inescapable; otherwise, the proclamation of the reign of God drowns in a sea of monotonous sameness. Any single religious commitment that we articulate in the midst of our pluralistic world is bound to reflect the particularity and partiality in which we stand. We will never possess the sum total of religious truth or an adequate understanding of what Christians have called the "mystery of God," even if we explicate it along kenotic lines! Yet this lack never excuses us from the work that needs to be done on behalf of this world. Only through particular commitments do we approach a fuller understanding of this mystery and the others with whom we live.

A religionless Christianity, in other words, is not the surrendering of one's distinctly Christian faith, nor is it the giving up of "being Christian" in order to better serve others. It does not consider "Christianity" to be a temporary way station along the road to fuller solidarity with others. What religionless Christianity does relinquish, however, is the smug security of its own language, interpretations, and traditions as sufficient in themselves. "Religion," in short, is the elevation of these particulars to the status of universals, as mandated once-and-for-all-time expressions of truth. A religionless Christianity empties itself of any of these pretensions to absoluteness. It maintains its language and traditions, but does so with the continual awareness that these expressions are ever partial, ever fragmentary articulations of the universal, eschatological vision of justice, peace, and wholeness in which one is taken up when one becomes a follower of Jesus Christ. A religionless Christianity finally admits that otherness and difference are prerequisites for abundant life in God's world. It admits that Christians *need others* not only to be "better Christians," but to be better human beings. In this sense, a religionless Christianity will question anything— even the claims and traditions of the Christian religion—that blocks recognition of otherness. In many cases, following Jesus Christ may place the disciple in the strange position of questioning the multifarious triumphal claims that have coalesced around the One whom Christians claim as incarnate and risen. Such is the difference that kenosis makes in the life of Christian discipleship, that we may be required to empty our religious proclivities toward absoluteness in the name of being more "faith-ful" followers of Jesus Christ.

THE DIFFERENCE KENOSIS MAKES IN DIALOGUE

Having surveyed the difference that kenosis makes as one moves from professing Christ to following him, and having noted the centrality of others in the transition from Christ to the world, we now turn to the concrete demands of interreligious encounter. What does our approach have to say about the *nature* of interreligious interchange? Is it the simple celebration of difference for its own sake? Or, does this encounter necessitate the demand for seasoned judgments on the truth and adequacy of divergent claims and worldviews? Does the kenotic approach, in short, equip those who adopt it with any criteria for making judgments, or does it render the interreligious encounter an "anything goes" matter?

I will suggest that a kenotic approach does not empty us of the capacity for making judgments, but better enables us to think and act responsibly in a pluralistic world. Emptying makes a difference not only in how we extend ourselves toward others, but in *how we come to know*. It has *epistemological* as well as ethical significance. This epistemological difference is best reflected in the change it brings to bear on questions of dialogue and truth. As we will see, the change is significant: questioning whether academic dialogue alone is an adequate model for

interreligious interchange and whether "truth" is an adequate
category in itself.

An Epistemological Shift

The apotheosis of reason and the celebration of the individual are both legacies of the Enlightenment. Knowledge, so
the familiar mantra rings, is the key to liberation, perhaps a
modern-day translation of John's dictum that "the truth will
make you free" (John 8:32b). The more the human person
knows, the more she or he is an independent person, free from
the suffocating constraints of ecclesial and imperial authority.
According to the Enlightenment paradigm, the restless, autonomous individual learns through dint of his or her own will,
through experience and reflection upon that experience. In
a conflictive and confusing world, the individual mind is what
offers the promise that we can better assess "truth" the more we
trust our own reason and not the dictates of alien authorities.[43]

   The dynamic of kenosis, however, suggests an alternative view
of knowledge. It is not so much the accumulation of experience
and reflection that builds certainty; rather, *relinquishment* is key.
Nancey Murphy and George F. R. Ellis offer a helpful summary
of this view: "The epistemological consequence... is that self-
renunciation is not only the key to ethics—to orthopraxis; it is
also the key to knowledge—to orthodoxy. Renunciation of the
will to power is a prerequisite for seeking the truth."[44] What is
suggested in this alternative epistemology is not the autonomy
of the individual mind, but its *need for others*. No matter how
much the truth may set us free, the self is not what guarantees
that truth. For knowledge emerges not in the isolated machi-
nations of the individual mind, but in the continual interaction

----

   43. Note how this is a popularized account of knowledge and truth. The Enlightenment theorists rarely disavowed the role that communities and history had
upon the individual's coming-to-know. When they urged others to "know thyself,"
they were not jettisoning the role of the interpretive community, but offering a
much needed alternative to ecclesial and imperial abuse. Nevertheless, for Kant
and Descartes, the "other mind" constituted a "problem." Only in regard to oneself
alone could one be certain.
   44. Murphy and Ellis, *Moral Nature of the Universe*, 139. "Learning requires a willingness to give up what one holds dear, whether this be self-aggrandizing views of
reality or simply pet scientific theories" (ibid).

with others of difference. If knowledge depended solely on the individual, it would degenerate into solipsism; when the self empties itself of any pretensions to complete autonomy, however, truth exhibits a wider purview—making a difference to self *and* others. A kenotic theory of epistemology thus invites the self to "make room for others" (Weil) as human persons come to know themselves *and* others. As we will see, this recognition makes a world of difference to the practice of interreligious dialogue.

A Critique of "Dialogue" and an Alternative Model

One of the issues lingering on the margins of our discussion of Christology has been *religious truth*. Ostensibly, one of the advantages of the kenotic approach I have been presenting is that it offers a fresh understanding of truth, that truth is not something to be grasped and affirmed at all costs, as if we possessed it individually, but that truth and knowledge emerge when we empty ourselves of the privilege of knowing more than others. A kenotic conception of truth questions any competitive stance in which one demonstrates the superiority of his or her convictions over those of an Other. This alternative approach has potentially significant effects in the arena of interfaith encounter, questioning the adequacy of dialogue alone as a mode for interreligious understanding.

From a kenotic perspective, the dialogical model has its limitations. The problem with using it alone is that many forms of dialogue veer toward a propositional, competitive view of truth: competing positions are explicated, defended, and attacked at conferences by their generally privileged proponents. The model, moreover, is generally an elitist one: those who are deemed competent enough to sit at the conference table are a few esteemed representatives of each religious tradition, educated mainly in the West, with the leisure to devote long periods of time to studying their own traditions and those of others. If "dialogue" is construed along these lines alone, what results is an impoverished understanding of the nature of both religious truth and interreligious encounter. Our kenotic model, on the other hand, affirms that *otherness* is a prerequisite for

truth and that understanding is reached as much through the
mutual sharing of *confession* and *practice* as it is through the
rarefied exchange of academic dialogue.

Because our approach questions any propositional, competitive theory of religious truth, it is important to trace the
contours of its foil, interreligious apologetics. Though not
representative of the sum total of the dialogical approach,
apologetics does take to the extreme those trends to which our
kenotic model most seriously objects. The work of Paul Griffiths, as outlined in a recent book, *An Apology for Apologetics,*[45]
is representative of this important strand. Although Griffiths's
work offers new avenues for the exploration of religious difference, it eventually falls short of the continued engagement of
difference that a kenotic approach embodies.

Griffiths's approach assumes a *propositional* view of truth: "Religious claims to truth are typically absolute claims: claims to
explain everything; claims about the universal rightness and ap-
plicability of a certain set of values together with the ways of life
that embody and perpetuate them; and claims whose referent
possesses maximal greatness."[46] Religious claims are statements
about the nature of reality that can be demonstrated true or
false, depending on their consonance or dissonance with the
wealth of experience by those who maintain them, and by how
well they hold up to logical scrutiny. Such claims are open to
endless examination, both by those who maintain them and
by those who stand outside the fold. These claims are communally normative as long as they withstand the scrutiny of those
who would question them. If claims are demonstrated to be
false, and those who maintain them recognize this incoherence,
then the believing community must rearticulate the "truth" it
seeks to express, so as to better orient believers' lives and better
demonstrate the *content* of their beliefs.

A particular religious tradition's truth claims are best encapsulated, according to Griffiths, by its doctrine-expressing
sentences, "which are taken by the community either to make

45. Paul Griffiths, *An Apology for Apologetics* (Maryknoll, N.Y.: Orbis, 1991).
46. Ibid., 2.

And We Shall Be Changed 161

or to entail claims about the nature of things, or claims about the value of certain courses of action."[47] A tradition's doctrinal sentences express what is most central to its vision, forming the bricks and mortar out of which a particular house of religious truth is constructed. Once an assemblage of doctrinal sentences is brought into contact with another, alternative religious structure, their respective truth convictions are bound to clash. Griffith's approach acknowledges that doctrinal difference is genuinely real, and attempts to engage this difference by a renewed emphasis on the much maligned discipline of religious apologetics.

Griffiths states this conviction in a concise thesis: "If representative intellectuals belonging to some specific religious community come to judge at a particular time that some or all of their own doctrine-expressing sentences are incompatible with some alien religious claim(s), then they should feel obliged to engage in both positive and negative apologetics vis-à-vis these alien religious claim(s) and their promulgators."[48] When participants in dialogue gather together, then, they need to learn each other's language, and demonstrate the (in)effectiveness and (in)coherence of each other's reservoirs of religious truth. Interreligious apologetics, according to Griffiths, best addresses the reality of religious difference by encouraging all participants to demonstrate the veracity of their own set of doctrinal propositions.

By reviving interest in interreligious apologetics, however, Griffiths is not advocating the renewal of Christian triumphalism. Productive apologetics can take place only if the scandalous accompaniments of classic apologetics (cultural superiority, economic exploitation, and colonialism) are abandoned. Apologetics, in other words, can take place only when each participant in dialogue has an acknowledged voice, an equal claim to the articulation of truth. Otherwise, apologetics becomes a thin mask for exploitation: "Apologetics must, to the extent possible,

47. Ibid., 9.
48. Ibid., 3.

be divorced from the threat, implicit or explicit, of military, socio-economic, or cultural oppression."[49]

Thus, apologetics must be carried out within the framework of mutual openness to the languages shared at the dialogue table. We engage in apologetics with the intention of learning from our partners, and in the hope that they might learn from us. For the postmodern apologist, every doctrine is at the same time sacred and subject to revision. We "apologize" for our faith because we know that there is much in our language that demands further modification. In Griffiths's words, "The expectation of learning and of problem-solving will thus be among the primary motivations and expectations of the proper apologist."[50]

Where might the productive give and take of interreligious apologetics take place? It is no coincidence that Griffiths considers the academy to be the preeminent body for fostering such critical engagement. "The academies of the West (perhaps especially in the USA) are institutions whose ideals are such that they make the perfect location for the development and application of a proper apologetic."[51] The embodiment of the apologetic ideal, therefore, is the customary exchange of academics conversing with other academics, taking place not in houses of worship or in places of struggle and suffering, but within the revered walls of the country's best institutes of higher learning. Only in these places, it seems, can noncoercive, non-proselytizing, and informed dialogue take place on "neutral" ground.

If we dig below the surface of Griffiths's proposals, however, it becomes evident that the "ideal" embodiment of interreligious apologetics is far from neutral. It privileges those who have the means to devote themselves to long periods of study and to cultivate the degree of linguistic sophistication necessary for

---

49. Ibid., 63.
50. Ibid., 82. Nothing in one's own tradition is beyond revision. "Appropriation and creative borrowing are just as important as engagement in positive and negative apologetics; neither need exclude the other, just as long as both are taken with intellectual seriousness and argumentative passion" (ibid., 107–8).
51. Ibid., 79.

the polemical exchange of dialogue. In short, his proposals privilege those persons in the West (primarily white males of moderate to extensive means) with the adjudged "competency" to speak and listen disinterestedly. It is not simply the apologetic approach that issues forth in such privilege, but the model of dialogue *alone* that cultivates the discrepancy between those deemed able to participate and those left on the fringes. For the very nature of dialogue is to invoke academic privilege, to favor those who can speak and argue most effectively.

This assumed competency to speak is precisely what our kenotic model is bound to dispute. A kenotic sensibility would require participants to empty themselves not only of self-interest, but of their cherished sense of academic privilege as well. Such an approach would certainly throw a wrench into the well-established system of Buddhist-Christian meetings, and the like, in which papers are presented, criticisms ventured, and a rich conversation is promised to those privileged enough to understand it. A kenotic approach would not dismiss all such academic exchanges as irrelevant; rather, it would question these exchanges as the only—or even the most important—manifestations of interreligious encounter. Learning from one another involves more than the understanding of a new religious vocabulary and academic disputation of its validity and coherence. It involves, in addition, the sharing of one tradition's *practice* with another.

Kenotic dialogue, therefore, occurs at a much deeper level than the familiar academic discussion. Instead of assuming that understanding arises in direct correlation with a disinterested exchange of doctrine-expressing sentences, a kenotic approach suggests that transformative understanding occurs whenever persons partake in one another's religious practice, whenever they share them with conviction. I learn from an Other when I empty myself of my own customary practice and am drawn by another's text or ritual. Such an exchange is not the random smorgasbord so familiar to many in the New Age movement, in which persons appropriate whatever they desire from an Other as long as it suits their needs. Because this sharing of practice occurs at the *invitation* of the religious Other, rather, we encounter the Other on that person's own soil and—as much as possible—within his or her own religious cosmology. Simone Weil offers some enigmatic words that reflect the wisdom of this alternative: "The study of different religions does not lead to a real knowledge of them unless we transport ourselves for a time by faith to the very center of whichever one we are studying."[52] We cannot, in other words, "understand" another tradition only in the detached mode of an academician, no matter how frequently we engage in "dialogue" with the religious Other. We understand more fully, rather, when we are claimed by another tradition, when we are grabbed by its confessional core. Such occurrences, naturally, happen only from time to time in actual encounter, on those rare occasions when one becomes a *participant*—alongside others—in another tradition.[53] A kenotic approach views academic dialogue as only one aspect of interreligious interchange. It encourages, more importantly, the mutual engagement of religious practice.

A second difficulty with the predominant dialogical model, of which Griffiths's approach is one representation, is that it assumes a certain academic distance from confessional claims. The motivation for dialogue, under the predominant model, stems primarily from the contemporary, religiously pluralistic context and the pressing need for understanding and cooperation in the face of momentous social and ecological crises. In order to work together on behalf of peace and justice, persons of different religious traditions must learn to talk to one another and remove themselves, to a certain extent, from those confessional claims that they hold most dear. Only if we are able to hold confessionalism in abeyance can we be open to the wisdom and truth of

---

52. Weil, *Waiting for God*, 183–84.

53. Oddly, these exchanges are likely to take place on the supposedly partisan ground of one tradition's worship or sacred space. Such locales offer the best opportunities for one to encounter the religious Other *as other*, and perhaps the only opportunity for one to be claimed by that other's practice. In my own recent experience, two instances stand out as embodying this kenotic ideal: a Good Friday sermon preached by Rabbi Stephen Fuchs at Second Presbyterian Church, Nashville, and the celebration of a joint Seder meal/communion service on Maundy Thursday in the same congregation. Both provided challenges for Christians and Jews to encounter one another as others and learn from each other by participating in each other's rituals.

another religious tradition, only then can dialogue be a genuine exchange and not a thin mask for religious triumphalism.

The approach that I would offer, however, sees the roots and motivations for interreligious interchange occurring at an even deeper level. Our contemporary context undeniably demands dialogue in the name of humanity's and the planet's survival. Yet, as our kenotic approach to incarnation and resurrection have suggested, there are *confessional* reasons for Christians to embark upon dialogue as well. As we have seen, at the heart of Christian doctrines of incarnation and resurrection we find not ourselves, but the call of others and the demand that we be claimed by that call. A focus upon the Emptying Christ, in other words, finds the dialogical imperative not only in the contemporary context, but at the core of what Christians believe. Christians are called to relinquish their own pretensions at ultimate religious truth (but not their core confessions) to accept the invitation of the religious Other, and to be transformed by that invitation. If there are genuinely confessional reasons for Christians to engage in interreligious encounter, then it is not simply the case that we should hold those confessions in abeyance, as the predominant dialogical model implies. Rather, Christians (and Buddhists, Jews, Muslims, and Hindus, for that matter) should affirm those confessional claims that stand at the very center of their respective religious cosmologies.[54]

If participants in dialogue distance themselves from core confessions,[55] then the distinctiveness of religious traditions not only subsides under a current of sameness, but also dialogue itself loses its essential religious motivation. The contemporary

---

54. I can speak at this point only from a Christian perspective, and would suggest that there is an abundance of confessional reasons for Christians to encounter others as others. I can only assume—and think it is a justifiable assumption—that there are genuinely Buddhist and Jewish confessional reasons for such encounter as well, insofar as these traditions also affirm the reality of otherness.

55. Examples of a "core confession" would be the Christian claim of Jesus Christ as the Incarnate One, the Jewish conception of God's Covenant with Israel, or Buddhist teaching on Enlightenment. A core confession forms part of the internal cluster of beliefs, narratives, and practices that maintain a religious group's present identity by preserving some continuity between its collective past and its vision for the future. Typically, a core confession helps form what is most distinctive to a particular religious tradition, and most divergent from other traditions.

context of ecological catastrophe and massive social injustice requires us to recognize dialogue not as a peripheral concern, but as a pressing, central concern. In the name of our collective survival, we need to understand each other. But as this study has suggested also, religious confessions themselves are essential to dialogue, standing not on the periphery of the conversation but at its very core. Religious confessions draw us not inward, but outward toward others. We uphold these confessions because they remind us that we are *never* alone.

What draws and captivates me, then, is the beauty of the Other *as other*, the person of difference who stands not on the margins of my own confessional commitments but at their very center. The religious Other presents herself or himself both as a stranger whose difference is real and as an intimate whose destiny is bound up with my own in an interrelational cosmos. For Christians, Christ is the way unto a world of difference—its diverse religious traditions, its scandalously particular historical and socioeconomic contexts, its varying cultures. The "way of Christ," in other words, does not revolve around itself, but radiates outward and hearkens to the call of others.

The transformation that this kenotic assessment of Christology has wrought, then, upon the stage of interreligious encounter is a major shift from a simple cognitive assessment of religious claims to a wider appreciation of the *beauty* of the religious other. The model of dialogue alone may provide a necessary forum in which the cognitive claims of world religions are evaluated, but as we have seen, the cognitive is but one dimension of the religious life. One consequence of our kenotic model, then, has been to empty academic discussion of its supposed adequacy and to recognize the necessity of the *aesthetic* dimension. Anselm Min, in a similar vein, has suggested that the future of interreligious encounter depends on its "breaking with logocentrism and intellectualism, which are always interested in reducing the other to the same, and shifting our ultimate concern from the intellectual to the aesthetic."[56] Only

---

56. Min calls his alternative proposal "dialectical pluralism." See "Dialectical Pluralism," 603.

this wider concern can do justice to the comprehensiveness of the religious life.

Judgment and Aesthetics in Interreligious Encounter

The turn to aesthetics may seem at first glance to be an evasion of responsibility. Rarely in contemporary discourse, it seems, is an appreciation of the *beautiful* connected with one's moral obligations. Indeed, one of the unfortunate and unwitting legacies of the Enlightenment has been the presumed independence of the aesthetic and ethical spheres. In the Christian context, moreover (despite Kierkegaard's pleas to the contrary), the ethical is generally considered more elevated than the aesthetic. The good Samaritan was lauded not for his appreciation of nature's bounty as he walked along the path, but for his attention to the need of a stranger.[57] In such an atmosphere, some might suggest that the aesthetic is at best a distraction— and at worst an evasion—from our ethical responsibilities and the pressing need for formulating judgments in a pluralistic age. The approach that I am advocating, however, surrenders none of these necessities; rather, it suggests that our appreciation of the beautiful is bound up with our understanding of truth *and* our obligations toward others. A kenotic approach to interreligious encounter does not mean that we have emptied ourselves of all capacity of making judgments, although it does imply a shift in *how* we make those judgments.

Wendy Farley, in her recent work *Eros for the Other*, offers some suggestions for how we might "retain truth in a pluralistic world." The world of difference that Christians profess and into which we are thrown can be a bewildering one in which the traditional anchors are uprooted. Nonetheless, this situation does not cast us adrift in the ludic sea of postmodern relativism. According to Farley, there are guides by which we can make judgments: "The reality of others provides criteria for what is good or evil, for what is interestingly different, and

---

57. The example is taken from the Cole Lecture given by Edward Farley, "Beauty as the Beast: The Uphill Path to a Theological Aesthetics," at Vanderbilt Divinity School, October 16, 1997. The following section owes much to Farley's work, particularly in its reappropriation of Jonathan Edwards's conception of beauty.

what is damaging and cruel."[58] It is the Other *as other*, then, who emerges at the center of my moral compass. Whatever is affirming and sustaining of the life of that Other points toward what Christians (and others) affirm as good and true; whatever violates and destroys otherness we must resist as falsity. I catch an intimation of the "truth," of the "good," when I recognize the Other as real, when I empty myself of the privilege to speak *for* that person and allow his or her own voice to speak. In the realm of interreligious interchange, then, "truth" is not so much the assessment of the veracity of one claim over against another, but the *unveiling of otherness* around us.[59]

The criterion of otherness suggests that "truth" is not presented as a given absolute, but emerges in encounter with others. It suggests, furthermore, that we *need others* in order to arrive at judgments, because we cannot judge as if we were alone. As Farley writes, "I interpret truth as something available through ongoing effort, undertaken as a practice, in dialogue with others and in relationship to the unceasingly changing and infinitely complex concreteness of existence."[60] Truth, in other words, does not enclose upon itself, but radiates outward, encompassing the reality of otherness and the vibrant movement of life itself. If we attempt to absolutize truth according to what we "know," whether in the form of religious pronouncements or pet philosophical themes, we claim that truth is something we "possess."[61] If, on the other hand, we acknowledge that we can never attain the truth by ourselves, that we must continually seek it, that we *need others* in this search, then we will recognize truth as something that emerges in bits and pieces, in practice and solidarity, whenever we empty ourselves of the pride that would

---

58. Wendy Farley, *Eros for the Other: Retaining Truth in a Pluralistic World* (University Park: Pennsylvania State University Press, 1996), 38.

59. One of the connotations of the Greek word for truth, *aletheia*, is precisely this sense of disclosure or unveiling. Martin Heidegger has written extensively on this theme. See "On the Essence of Truth," in *Basic Writings*, rev. ed., ed. David Farrell Krell (San Francisco: HarperSanFrancisco, 1993), 115–38.

60. Farley, *Eros*, 186.

61. Whitehead would call this absolutization the "fallacy of misplaced concreteness."

claim truth as ours alone, and recognize the call of others in our midst.

One of the consequences of recognizing truth as something that emerges along the way with others is that we recognize those others not only as real, but also as beautiful in themselves. Because the Other is essential to any comprehension of the good and true, we begin to open our eyes to the irreducible detail of the Other—the contours and wrinkles of this person's face, the uniqueness of that person's manner of speech and movement. The Other is beautiful not as a *means* to truth, but simply by virtue of the fact that *he or she is,* and that without that Other I am alone. The shift here is a subtle one that recognizes the interdependence of truth and beauty, recognized in kenotic practice. In the words of Simone Weil, "The intimation of the beauty of the world, that which corresponds to the absence of finality, intention, and discrimination in it, is the absence of intention in ourselves, that is to say the renunciation of our own will."[62] We see the beauty of others when we refuse to absolutize ourselves or any one thing at the expense of another. The Other, without whom I am a solipsistic monad, who travels the truth with me, is beautiful because she or he is other.

The Other, summoning us to recognize the aesthetic dimension of truth in his or her own face, also encourages us to hearken to the beauty of the good. The *ethical,* in other words, exhibits an aesthetic dimension. Few thinkers have addressed this interconnection, and questioned the Enlightenment's bifurcation of ethics and aesthetics, as thoroughly as Jonathan Edwards. For Edwards, true virtue—or embodiment of the "good"—is a "propensity and union of heart to being simply considered,"[63] the "agreement or consent of being to being,"[64] or the openness of self to others. Although Edwards is speaking primarily of the human person's openness to God—the "good" is the heart's "consent" to God's will—this consent is also echoed whenever the human person opens himself or herself to others,

---

62. Weil, *Waiting for God,* 178.
63. Jonathan Edwards, *The Nature of True Virtue* (Ann Arbor: University of Michigan Press, 1969), 8.
64. Ibid., 100.

to the beauty of the earth itself. The heart recognizes the beauty
of others when it delights in the fact that *they are*. Thus, to know
and do the good in relation to the Other is at one and the same
time to recognize that person's beauty.[65]

Difference, truth, the good, and beauty are thus bound together as threads of an intricate tapestry. Since each can be
approached only in community with others, we are called not
merely to tolerate the plurality of human existence, but to embrace it. Such is the sustained argument of Farley's *Eros for the
Other*. "A capacity to recognize and love plurality is one criterion
by which a conception of truth must be judged. It is a criterion
imposed by reality itself in accord with its pluralistic and infinitely diverse embodiments."[66] Difference, in other words, is
real, a thing of great beauty, a measure of what is good and true.

This recognition and love of the plurality of human existence, however, does not leave us floundering in a postmodern,
ludic play of difference in which every perspective and stance
is tolerated. To claim that truth must embrace plurality does
not translate into an incapacity to make moral and ethical
judgments. An embrace of difference does not mean one has
to tolerate the intolerable. Though the recognition of plurality certainly renders such ethical judgments more difficult
for everyone who acknowledges it, perduring values are nonetheless possible. Robert Kane's recent work, *Through the Moral
Maze*,[67] is an excellent study in the necessity of grappling with
our pluralistic world and its myriad truth claims in coming to
seasoned moral judgments. Contrary to the popular assessment
that an embrace of plurality leads to foundationless relativism,
or even moral indifference, Kane argues that opening oneself
to *all* points of view is a prerequisite for knowing and doing the
good. Kane tentatively adopts a Kantian ethic with a few mod-
ifications: we are to treat every human being as an end, not
as a means, as long as their actions serve to uphold the "moral

---

65. In Perry Miller's words, "For Edwards, the Puritan in pioneer America, the
definition of the ethical is beauty" (*Jonathan Edwards* [New York: William Sloane
Associates, 1949], 290).

66. Farley, *Eros*, 17.

67. Robert Kane, *Through the Moral Maze* (Armonk, N.Y.: North Castle, 1996).

sphere" of life, that situation "in which everyone *can* treat everyone else as an end."[68] When a particular individual's actions
violate that moral sphere (i.e., when someone treats someone
else as a *means*) then one is compelled to respond in ways that
thwart the abuser's intentions and promote the one who is being objectified as an end. We are open to all points of view in
this search for the truth, then, as long as each point of view
enables the flourishing of the Other as other. Once a person's
actions violate this "ends principle," we are compelled to resist
them in the name of truth.

Taking an example fairly close to home, suppose that a Christian's belief that salvation comes through Jesus Christ alone
motivated that person to share the "good news" with others.[69]
Indeed, gripped by such conviction, the Christian has no choice
but to share it with others. In itself, this conviction is neutral in
regard to otherness; the sharing of this conviction, however,
may take one of two forms: one that is respectful of otherness
and another that is a violation of it. If the Christian, motivated
by conviction, tells others the "good news" in an atmosphere
in which those others' convictions and personhood are hon-
ored, then she or he is treating them as *ends,* as others valuable
and beautiful in themselves. This example of respectful sharing
may take multiple forms: conversation, assisting those in need,
and working with others in ways that benefit the common good
(building agricultural infrastructure, safe housing, and other
facilities that better enable the flourishing of human life).[70]
Whatever form this conviction takes, however, what is paramount is that the Other remain at the center of the Christian's

---

68. Ibid., 22.
69. I am focusing on this narrow soteriological perspective—*solus Christus*—
because it has often led to the persecution of adherents of other religious traditions.
Although it continues to be a common view, it does not by any means represent the
most adequate Christian perspective (as this work has shown).
70. This work is generally characteristic of missionary activity. Note how the criterion of "otherness" effectively regulates how one's convictions are implemented.
What is primary in such work is the respect of the Other as other, and the fostering
of the flourishing of that Other. The sharing of the "good news," as it were, takes
place in the midst of this work, as the others with whom the missionary works begin
to ask what motivates or guides him or her. The criteria of otherness does not necessarily question the enterprise of missionary activity per se, although it criticizes
numerous ways in which this work is carried out.

lens as a unique, indispensable human being. When the Other becomes simply an object to be converted, the Christian has violated the Other's beauty and truth.

This violation can likewise take multiple forms, most of which are familiar in Christian history. At one extreme is the example of forcible conversion, witnessed in the Crusaders and Conquistadors. Though ostensibly motivated by a soteriological conviction, these conquering figures followed them without regard for the personhood of those they encountered. The Other became not a person of unique beauty, but a clay figure upon whom they could impose their desires and convictions. Although forcible conversion is the most exaggerated form of this violation, it can also take invidious, subtler forms—occurring wherever Christians stop their ears to the claims of others, whenever the "good news" drowns out any strains of difference in the global chorus.[71] Whenever this occurs, what results is not the sharing of the good news, but the blind assertion of my version of it. Wherever such violation occurs, whatever form it takes, Christians and others are compelled to resist it in the name of the truth and beauty of the Other. This imperative may place Christians in the odd position of preserving the integrity of the Christian message by resisting the scandalously exclusive forms in which it is often presented.

Recognition of the aesthetic dimension of truth and ethics has substantial consequences as Christians come to grips with the claims of other religious traditions. The consequence is not a detached appreciation of the plurality of traditions as if they constituted the resplendent colors of the same religious rainbow. This kind of aestheticism views difference as a scandal and beauty only in uniformity. As I have suggested, however, a kenotic sensibility—one that de-centers the self—glimpses beauty as bound up with difference. The beauty of the Buddhist tradition, for example, is not that it points in the same general

---

71. Again, the examples abound. In 1998 the Southern Baptist Convention issued a statement claiming that all Jews stand in need of the grace of Christ. Such blanket statements, irrespective of others' contexts, can only amount to a violation of otherness, to say nothing of the further injury that they do to the cause of interreligious understanding.

direction as Christianity, but that it forms an alternatively viable way of living, breathing, and acting in the world. Buddhism, in its multiple schools and traditions, exhibits a beauty that is wholly its own, with vastly different hues and dimensions with which most Westerners are not familiar. The beauty that Christians profess, as a direct consequence of their confession of the Emptying Christ, is a reflection of the genuine difference between religious traditions, not their similarity. When Christians open themselves to the beauty of the Other, they also open themselves to the beauty of the Other's religious tradition—the heart of his or her own orientation in the world. Beauty, like reality itself, has many faces.[72]

For Christians, this focus upon the aesthetic dimension of truth throws them back upon the very core of Christian confession. The dynamic of kenosis is not only de-centering, as it casts Christians upon the threshold of difference and calls them to love the beauty of the Other *as other;* it redounds to the Kenotic One himself, the proclaimer of the good news. Freed from an obsessive concern with the "truth" of their own religious claims, Christians might then recognize the incarnation as a *beautiful event.* The embodiment of God in the world, as witnessed in the *figura* of Jesus of Nazareth, is not most adequately described as the definitive disclosure of absolute religious truth, but as a beautiful gift of boundless love. The beauty of the incarnation is God's intimate concern with what is other than God, as most concretely illustrated in Jesus of Nazareth's openness to the vulnerable and rejected ones around him.

What is genuinely beautiful and truthful in the life of discipleship, then, is our own capacity to be opened and transformed by the Other. Professing the One who embodies God's concern with what is other than God, Jesus Christ, Christians are rendered open to others as they make that profession. Christians are called to recognize difference, to be claimed by others, to open themselves to the beauty of others, and to *love* others in

---

72. Interestingly, it was her intense appreciation of the "secular" and other religious traditions that prevented Simone Weil from identifying herself with the institutional Christian community: "The love of those things that are outside visible Christianity keeps me outside the Church" (*Waiting for God*, 95).

their difference. Yet by being so claimed and opened, Christians are *changed* by others. For the nature of love is to change whoever is affected by its embrace. As a tradition that proclaims the change of a vulnerable God who extends Godself and identifies Godself with creation, the change of a man proclaimed as the Incarnate One who is so deeply affected by others that he endures the most ignominious death on a cross, and the change of *metanoia* for those grabbed by his life and ministry, Christianity—in its multiple forms—embodies this change.

The life of discipleship, then, is not marked chiefly by following generalized commands, but by openness to the sheer beauty of the Other, simply because *she or he is.* The "difference" that kenosis implies for interreligious encounter, then, is the change from detached "dialogue" to a more sweeping embrace of the beauty and truth of others *as others.* Christianity may in one sense be called "the way of Jesus Christ," insofar as its disciples orient their lives according to the memory of the life and ministry of the Nazarene, but it may equally be called the "way of others," insofar as adherence to that memory empties the self of its privilege and autonomy, bringing the unique faces of others to the fore.

The Difference Kenosis Makes in Doctrine

Our reflections throughout this work have been an extended exercise, I would claim, in doctrinal theology. They have attempted to make better sense of the church's proclamation that Jesus Christ is the Incarnate and Risen One of God, with particular attention to our present context of religious pluralism. By "doctrine" I mean the church's *teaching,* its instruction on those clusters of beliefs that form the core of its distinctive identity. Typically, church doctrine is expressed in the form of pithy creeds and brief statements of faith. Doctrine may take the form of a short sentence, such as "Jesus is the Incarnate Son of God." The significance of doctrine is not its exhaustiveness, as if these statements alone constituted what is essential to the Christian faith,[73] but its ability to maintain some continuity within the church over time as the church responds to the gracious gift of new life witnessed in the event of Jesus Christ. The function of doctrine, in this sense, is not to proclaim timeless, unchanging truths, as if the church could offer an authoritative definition of the mysteries of Christian faith, but to establish parameters within which an identifiably "Christian" witness to these mysteries can take place. An analogous view of doctrine is shared by George Lindbeck, who writes, "Church doctrines are communally authoritative teachings regarding beliefs and practices that are considered essential to the identity or welfare of the group in question.... They indicate what constitutes faithful adherence to a community."[74] Doctrine, in short, preserves the continuity of Christian witness across the centuries in the form of brief teachings that demand further interpretation.

Theology, then, is the *interpretation* of the church's decisive and distinctive teachings, in constantly shifting contexts. As Karl Rahner reminds us in the quotation cited at the beginning of this work, "It is the task ... of the theologian in particular to repeat the old questions in a new way, so that they may really have a new and vital understanding of the old questions."[75] Doctrine, then, is not enough for maintaining the character and structure of Christian identity across the centuries, for its teaching demands the unique voices of each generation riveted by the gospel in unexpected ways and places. The church's teaching grabs those who would hear it in contexts as diverse as the slums

---

73. Indeed, all church doctrines demand further interpretation. The bare-bones teachings of the church, although they endure through time, require fresh voices and new articulations in ever changing contexts. Some of the language of church doctrine, in fact, may allow a rather large umbrella under which appropriate Christian "speech" may take place. See my previous reflections on the Nicene Creed and formula of Chalcedon, pp. 131–32.

74. Lindbeck, *Nature of Doctrine,* 74. Lindbeck, however, would doubtless recoil at my own language of the "mysteries of faith," since such locutions connote an "experiential-expressive" approach to religion and theology. Though I am unwilling to forgo the wisdom of the experiential approach, I am in accord with Lindbeck's main point, that doctrines function as broadly defined "rules" under which identifiably "Christian" interpretation can take place. Nonetheless, as my subsequent criticism of Lindbeck's position will point out, an exclusively "rule-oriented" approach to doctrine has pitfalls of its own.

75. Karl Rahner, "Dogmatic Questions on Easter," in *More Recent Writings,* Theological Investigations 4, trans. Kevin Smyth (Baltimore: Helicon, 1966), 122.

of São Paulo and the comparative isolation of the Australian outback. The doctrinal claim that "Jesus Christ is the Incarnate One" provides continuity—within these contexts—with those voices who have echoed it throughout the centuries, while the interpretation of that claim requires particular attention to the contexts in which that claim is uttered. Our work thus far, then, has been an exercise in *doctrinal theology*, insofar as it has focused on a specific teaching of the Christian church—Jesus Christ is the Incarnate and Risen One—and as it has interpreted this teaching in the present situation of religious pluralism.

Have our reflections on the Emptying Christ generated any impact upon the way in which doctrine itself is conceived? Is a *doctrinal* perspective on the interreligious question even necessary? Is Lindbeck's conception of the "nature" of doctrine adequate in a religiously pluralistic age? Or are there ways in which our view of doctrine changes as Christians open themselves to others, at the behest of their own most distinctively Christian claims? It is to these questions that we turn our attention in this final section.

A Doctrinal Perspective in the Company of Others

One response to the interfaith question is that a doctrinal perspective is unnecessary. Those who would argue as much might suggest that the practical consequences of Christian confession that I have outlined in this chapter—solidarity, nonviolence, and an aesthetic appreciation of the truth of the Other—are possible without delving into the intricacies of doctrinal theology. Indeed, we might have arrived at this same set of postures toward the religious Other more easily apart from any reflection on the church's incarnation and resurrection claims. Such a response might further claim that explicitly Christian doctrinal convictions most often prove to be barriers to a stance of solidarity with others, pitting Christianity against other traditions. From this perspective, the universal demand for openness to others, in the name of the human race's and the planet's collective survival, must be trumpeted *first*. Once we have turned our eyes to the pressing context that we inhabit, observed its crises, and proffered means of addressing them, we may subsequently shift our attention to doctrinal concerns. The interpretation of doctrinal convictions, then, is an appendage to more pressing contextual concerns—interesting perhaps for intra-Christian discussion, but hardly germane to the need for practical stances in an age of ecological catastrophe.

In response to this assessment, I would voice a "yes" of my own. It is most certainly the case that the practical stance of solidarity, nonviolence, and openness to others can be arrived at (and perhaps more easily) when it is done independently of the Christian worldview. And it is most certainly the case that the present context demands such response—in the name of survival—regardless of what Christians might say about the "identity" of Jesus Christ. Indeed, the fact that such practical matters can be approached from any number of religious angles only furthers the cause of interfaith dialogue and cooperation in the interest of planetary survival. Yet I would also respond that it is *not* the case that doctrine is a peripheral concern to these matters, particularly for Christians. As we have seen, there is no broaching of a "universal" demand apart from the particular, embodied, historical locations and persons affected by that demand. For Christians, as we have seen, the *universal* demand of openness to others is connected to a *particular* figure in first-century Palestine, around whom this demand is most acutely sensed. Christians proclaim a particular, paradigmatic, and decisive manifestation of a universal claim of openness toward others and the reign of God in their assertions about the person of Jesus Christ. In this sense, doctrine is not peripheral—for Christians—in an age of religious pluralism.

Another result of this study has been to show that Christian doctrine, and the way that it is conceived, make a difference in the practical stance of discipleship. The questions "What do I believe?" and "How do I live?" do not exist independently, but mutually inform each other. Indeed, it may even be the case that the former conditions the latter more strongly than the reverse. One's beliefs are not merely one's own private affair, regardless of how much religious privatism has seeped into the contemporary scene. These beliefs affect—for good or ill—one's actions, attitudes, and behavior in an increasingly pluralistic world. In this sense, "personal faith" is more myth than reality, and public stance (or lack of a stance) is the manifestation of corporate faith. The *kind* of Savior that Christians proclaim has direct bearing on the *kind* of followers Christians seek to become. Christology thus makes a difference to Christian identity and discipleship. Whether one sees solidarity, nonviolence, and openness to the Other as bound up with who Christians believe Jesus Christ is, or whether one sees these concerns as detached from one another, depends on whether one views the Christian faith as something "private" for the consolation of lonely, individual souls, or whether it reflects a coherent *way of life* embedded within the world in response to God's grace.

I have focused upon that cluster of doctrinal affirmations that surround perhaps the most "Christian" of beliefs, that of Jesus Christ as the Incarnate and Risen One of God. This focus is essential for Christians because belief in Jesus as the Christ serves perhaps more effectively than any other doctrinal locus as a continual reservoir of Christian identity and continuity. I have focused on Christology because the contemporary context demands a Christian response to the exigencies of the day. Any appropriately Christian response must in some shape or form be connected with this *figura;* otherwise, the Christian contribution to global crises vanishes in a vapor of religious generality. It is in response to the "event" of Jesus Christ and in their own interpretation of that "event" that Christians exhibit continuity with their foremothers and forefathers, and in that response that they present themselves as attuned to contemporary concerns.

Finally, I have focused particularly upon Christology because it, perhaps more than any other doctrine, has proven the greatest barrier to interreligious conversation. In many cases, the proclamation of Jesus Christ as the Incarnate and Risen Son of God has served much like a badge of orthodoxy, with the express intent of exclusion: the trumpeting of a unique and triumphal Savior, universal in scope. Such confession marks off territory within which those who confess him as Lord are members of the beloved community, while those who do not fall beyond the pale of salvation. The Christian "response" to adherents of other religious traditions then becomes either a matter of indifference (ignoring those beyond the fold), or of intense proselytism (to "save the lost"). Neither response, we should note, is an acceptance of the Other as real, intrinsically beautiful, or even as someone with his or her own voice. Indeed, christological confession can cause Christians to be afraid of otherness, so that the only response is the stopping of one's ears or the forcible conversion of the Other to my own point of view.

One question that has framed my work more than any other is whether christological confession necessarily results in the exclusion of the religious Other. The answer that I find most satisfying is an emphatic no; indeed, it seems more of a distortion of faith in Jesus as the Christ and of Christian doctrine to claim that the One who embodies openness to the Other calls upon his followers to ignore, exclude, or view that Other simply as an object of conversion. What I have demonstrated, I hope, is that an intense focus upon core christological convictions (incarnation and resurrection) serves as an avenue not of exclusion, but of openness toward others, particularly the religious Other. The Emptying Christ, as we have seen, empties christological doctrine and theology of some of their more dominating features.

Christian Doctrine as Accountability

Doctrines exhibit a *theological* function. They offer the wisdom of centuries of reflection upon the core convictions of the Christian faith. We read and are moved by their strains not simply out of blind allegiance to the past, but because these voices from the past continue to have resonance today. They offer examples of interpreting the reality of the new life in Jesus Christ, and challenge us to articulate that reality in fresh ways today. Christological doctrine announces, in abbreviated form, the "fundamental" features of the person and work of Jesus Christ. Doctrinal theology, then, is not a self-sufficient enterprise, but is subservient to a wider purpose: expressing and communicating the new life offered in the divine disclosure of Jesus Christ.

Doctrines, however, also have a *regulative* function; that is,

they establish parameters within which appropriate Christian
speech is made possible. Doctrines, in other words, hold Christians accountable to one another. They serve as guides by which
the Christian church charts its course in a puzzling and multi-
faceted world. One of the most significant explorations of the
regulative function of doctrine in recent years is Lindbeck's *The
Nature of Doctrine*. Lindbeck's approach is helpful for our present
project insofar as it suggests that Christians pay strict attention
to doctrine in the name of their own community's identity, but
limiting in its restricting of the regulative function of doctrine
to the Christian community alone. As we will see, one consequence of a kenotic conception of Christ is that *others* hold us
accountable as well.

Lindbeck's central argument is that doctrines serve as rules:[76]
"The function of church doctrines... is their use, not as expres-
sive symbols or as truth-claims, but as communally authoritative
rules of discourse, attitude, and action."[77] Doctrines, in other
words, hold Christians accountable to their own communities
and collective history. Any Christian response to the exigencies of the current day must exhibit some consonance with the
modality of Christian confession.

This project adopts Lindbeck's regulative view of doctrine insofar as it glimpses christological doctrine as not possessing an
invariant meaning across the ages, but as it sets in place certain
types of expression that govern Christian witness in the world.
The two linguistic "rules" that I have isolated are the claims of
Jesus Christ as the *Incarnate* and *Risen* One. What each of these
affirmations means in a religiously pluralistic age, as we have
seen, has amounted to a departure from some "triumphal" interpretations. Insofar as this has been the case, the project has
pointed toward the reality of *doctrinal change*. Nonetheless, my
interpretation has retained much of the traditional language
of incarnation and resurrection, because such language holds

---

76. This argument is, we should note, *nontheological*. Part of Lindbeck's motivation
stems from his desire to move theology out of the intellectual ghetto and into
conversation with the social sciences. Such a move is best inaugurated by a nontheological approach.

77. Lindbeck, *Nature of Doctrine*, 18.

Christians accountable to their own collective history, to the wisdom of those who have gone on before them. A "Christian" response to an age of religious pluralism requires, at the very least, some kind of consonance with the integrity of historical Christian witness. Such consonance is possible, I would argue, through the continued employment of broadly Christian categories of speech, which in the case of Christology involves both claims of Jesus Christ's incarnation and resurrection. Insofar as this project has accepted the regulative role of these forms of speech, it has pointed toward the reality of *doctrinal endurance* across the centuries.

Lindbeck's view of the regulative view of doctrine, however, becomes problematic as soon as he turns his eyes to the question of communal identity in a wider world. His focus, in some respects, is communally introspective, yielding much fruit for intra-Christian witness, but little in terms of the Christian community's engagement with a wider, religiously pluralistic world. Lindbeck writes of the importance of being *within* a particular religious community: "One must be, so to speak, inside the relevant context; and in the case of a religion, this means that one must have some skill in *how* to use its language and practice its way of life."[78] Doctrine, in this sense, is regulative only for those who share it. It can be appreciated and engaged fully only by those who have been nurtured and sustained by its familiar strains and cadences. Though such acknowledgment prevents Christians (and others) from imposing their language upon others, it also tends to shift the focus away from those who speak religiously different languages. What is important, in Lindbeck's eyes, is the continued, responsible use of doctrine within the Christian community without the engagement of those beyond its supposed walls. Those who are not so inculcated, we are led to believe, have neither the competence nor the exposure necessary to make a doctrinal difference. The unfortunate consequence of this approach, it seems, is to leave each religious tradition, as it were, in the familiar surroundings of its own backyard.

---

78. Ibid., 68.

In some senses, Lindbeck's approach verges on sectarianism. He writes of the need for "communal enclaves that socialize their members into highly particular outlooks supportive of concern for others."[79] Although his view does not epitomize "Christ against culture" (H. Richard Niebuhr), and includes an awareness of those outside the Christian fold, his regulative view is predicated on a communitarian ethos that nurtures those who share the same religious language. Concern with the language of others thus becomes an ancillary concern. If there is a sense of interreligious dialogue for Lindbeck, it is to help others better speak their own language: "One of the ways in which Christians can serve their neighbors may be through helping adherents of other religions to purify and enrich their heritages, to make them better speakers of the languages they have."[80] Though such an approach is clearly not sectarian in the strictest sense, one is left wondering what holds the greatest sway in Lindbeck's perspective: the call of the Other, or the demand for the tradition's own internal linguistic consistency. From my own reading, it seems that the second concern ultimately wins out in his approach, limiting the scope of interreligious dialogue and dampening the call of the religious Other.

Here is where I have the greatest difficulty with Lindbeck's approach, here where his proposals run at cross-purposes to the transformative potential of interfaith encounter. As our project has shown, an intensely doctrinal focus does not send us with excessive concern into the confines of our own churches, belaboring the coherence of our own religious language; rather, it sends us outward. Christian doctrine is not a sectarian matter, but a *worldly* matter; it is through christological doctrine, moreover, that the call of the religious Other is most loudly heard. The lure of doctrine, it would seem, draws Christians in precisely the opposite direction from what Lindbeck's work implies. It is not simply the case that doctrines serve only as *rules* for "belief-ful' communities; rather, they function also as *vehicles of communicating the new life* that Christians have been

---

79. Ibid., 127.
80. Ibid., 61–62.

echoing for centuries. This new life cannot be enclosed by rules, but rather, seeks expression in language that continually stretches its own categories and usage. The new life that Christians proclaim cannot be contained by the church's own private language; nevertheless, the church is compelled to articulate it in some way, and this articulation is what we might consider as "doctrine." But because this language will never be able to enclose the realities toward which it points, the church is drawn continually outward. Attempting to express this new life, Christians are drawn away from sectarian confines and into the world.

Because Christian doctrine brings the church out of its own private sphere, the assessment of doctrine is not a matter of intra-Christian discussion alone. Certainly, doctrines help Christians hold each other accountable, but because they draw Christians into encounter with others, doctrine also calls *others* to hold Christians accountable. The dynamic of kenosis also suggests that our language alone is inadequate, that it needs to be emptied of its supposed self-sufficiency, and that Christians need the contributions, criticisms, and assessments of others to express more fully the new life that we proclaim. Indeed, because we are wedded to our doctrines most tightly, often others can best discern the lacunae and inconsistencies within our own language. We need others not so we can be religiously eclectic, but so that we might become *better Christians*, better respondents to the new life in Christ.

Doctrinal Ec-centricity and Christological Reflection

This last recognition explodes any understanding that suggests that doctrine is a matter for Christian discussion alone. There is something about doctrine itself that is *ec-centric;* it is the means by which Christians—as Christians—open themselves to others, by drawing us out of our own privileged centers. What stands at the center of doctrine is not the self, or the Christian community, but the proclamation of a new life grounded in the life and ministry of Jesus Christ. This new life, moreover, does not collapse upon itself—or even the question of "Christian identity"—but relentlessly seeks and continually hearkens to the call of others.

The Christian claim about the person and work of Jesus Christ is scandalously particular: a historical manifestation of God's grace is *universally* significant. The claim, in other words, is that something wider is maintained in this person, something of significance to the world itself, something to do with God's universal, eschatological reign. Have our christological reflections on doctrinal ec-centricity amounted to a surrendering of this wider scope? Does it mean that Christian universalism is no longer a tenable position in a religiously pluralistic age? Yes and no. Certainly, Christians can no longer proclaim Christ's universalism at the expense of the genuine otherness of those with whom we are called into existence. To do so would obliterate the difference that Christ's embodied ministry and memory make real. Any articulation of Christ's universality that seeks to dominate others needs to empty itself in our age, not simply in the name of respect, tolerance, and survival, but in faithfulness to the One whom Christians proclaim.

Yet this project does not suggest the surrendering of Christian universalism. Indeed, what it suggests is that the Christian "scandal of particularity" be glimpsed within a wider purview—one that takes into account not only familiar voices, but those heretofore ignored. For a genuinely held *universal* will admit that any articulation of it is prone to shortcomings. If Christ is of ultimate significance for Christians, then Christians will be compelled to share their articulation of him with others; but because Christ is universal, they will open themselves to others in that exchange. Such is the dynamic of interreligious encounter: participants encounter each other with universal (not parochial) claims of pressing urgency, but in exchanging them they become aware that their own expressions cannot enclose the universal by which they are seized. Sharing a "particular universal," surprisingly, may open Christians and others to unspeakable change.

I would suggest that this recognition bears correspondence with the crux of what Christians proclaim about incarnation: the God emptied and revealed in Jesus Christ is not about dominating sameness and mindless repetition of doctrinal formulae. To suggest as much is to confine Jesus Christ to the past, and to claim that faithfulness to him is a matter of adherence to what has been said by previous generations. The Christian claim, I would venture, has always been more than this and to confine anything to the past is to render it for all intents and purposes dead. The crux of Christian proclamation, instead, has been about something more: of abundant life for all, witnessed paradigmatically in the life, death, and resurrection of Jesus of Nazareth. In that proclamation of Jesus as the Christ, Christians are ceaselessly open to others and to the future. Faithfulness to Christ is not simply a matter of adherence to our collective past, but is reflected most clearly in our degree of openness to others and our willingness to be claimed by them in new situations.

I have chosen in the present work to focus upon one doctrine, probably the most problematic of Christian doctrines when faced with the present urgency of interreligious encounter: Christology. I have suggested that an intensely doctrinal focus does not lead to the absolutization of the Christian doctrinal point of view, but leads directly into encounter with others and openness to their claims. I suspect that a similar focus upon other pivotal Christian doctrinal claims—about God, the church, the Holy Spirit—will point in a similar direction. To suggest otherwise would be to render Christian universalism a mere parochialism. To do justice to these other pivotal doctrinal formulations, however desperately needed, is the fodder for further work.

The particular doctrine that I have focused upon, moreover, has been viewed through a particular lens: emptying. I have selected it among all other lenses because of its breadth (it is a biblical image common coin to most Christians, and exhibits a lengthy history of theological reflection), because of its resemblance to a prominent Zen Buddhist theme (*sunyata*), and because of the urgency with which it focuses the claim of the Other. The image of *kenosis* not only exhibits consonance with the theological past, but also is sorely needed in our own day. And, I would venture, it is not simply *one image* of Jesus Christ, but perhaps the single most appropriate image for our time, particularly in the West. In a milieu marked by the arrogation of "my" privilege over "yours," in an age that reflects the absolutization of the self—damn the planet and everyone else—in a society that often asks the questions "What can *I* get?" "What does this mean *for me?*" but rarely "How do I affect *others?*" the imagery of self-emptying is a much needed alternative to privileged Western hubris. A focus on the kenotic Christ, in short, de-centers the self to make room for others.

Undoubtedly, the imagery of the Emptying Christ can hardly be presented as a timeless absolute; to claim as much would be to enclose Christ within our own terminology and to offer an idol of our own making. More importantly, however, this imagery is appropriate and urgently needed in a Western context of consumer rapacity. It may provide a ray of hope in which Christians might finally relinquish their own sense of privilege in a religiously pluralistic world. Insofar as my reflection upon this image accomplishes this aim, it provides one way in which Christians might better embody those claims to which we give credence: God's love touches all, and God's reign includes all. A focus upon the Emptying Christ can illuminate the wider world in which we live, and can better equip us to survive and flourish with others on a planet beset on many sides by death. Kenosis offers one shape of hope for the future. To sustain such hope in the midst of suffering, destruction, and the arrogation of self-privilege is but one aspect of the new life that Christians have always proclaimed. The time has now come for the articulation of that hope in the company of the religious Other, and to add yet another voice to the distinctive, yet ever changing shape of Christian identity in a pluralistic world.

CHAPTER VI

CALLED BY THE OTHER

O NE OF THE MOST IMPORTANT CONTRIBUTIONS of both feminist and postmodern critiques of classical theology is the realization that the world we inhabit is a *constructed* world. Reality is not simply given to us, unadulterated, if we only have eyes to see it; rather, what we perceive as "real" is filtered through a complex sediment of inherited interpretation and our own cherished presuppositions. The constructed nature of reality extends not only to philosophical and theological knowledge, but to *all* knowledge. Even the natural sciences, which prior to this century hid behind a myth of objectivity, amply evince a constructive bent. Scientists construct models of reality that fit the preponderance of data, which are maintained as long as they correspond with the accumulated data of experimentation. Once one's data questions the regnant model of reality, the model must be modified, or in extreme cases, jettisoned. Niels Bohr's model of the atom, for example, proved adequate and illuminating for a time, until the emergent discipline of quantum physics rendered his model questionable. Likewise, contemporary models of the universe surely will be modified as further research and exploration uncovers heretofore unknown strata of the cosmos. This recognition of the constructed nature of reality—in all disciplines, and in all forms of human life—reinforces the somewhat simple dictum that *what* we see is conditioned unambiguously by *how* we see.[1]

If we recognize that no datum of "reality" is exempt from the interpretive gaze, this is not to say that all constructions and interpretations are equally adequate. As the example of atomic

---

1. See Sallie McFague, *Metaphorical Theology*, (Philadelphia: Fortress, 1982), ch. 3, for a helpful discussion on the use of models in contemporary social and natural sciences.

theory shows, interpretive models must be able to maintain themselves as coherent with the data of accumulated experimentation. Interpretation, in other words, must prove itself consistent with experience. Throughout these reflections I have consistently employed a *relational-kenotic* model, a model that is both *necessary* and *appropriate* for our time. Though it is hardly novel to the business of theology, a relational understanding of God, the world, and the interhuman offers the most adequate lens for our observation of the ecological cosmos. To deny relationality is to perpetuate a model that obscures the difference necessary to ecological being and becoming. To deny relationality fosters the illusion that each one of us is an island, removed from the complex web of interpretation, history, and experience that postmodern and feminist thought have so resolutely uncovered. Our claims, however, throughout this work have been even more specific, suggesting that *emptying-in-relation*[2] implies the closest possible relation and identification with the Other without the annihilation of self-identity or difference. Like any other model, this relational-kenotic approach is a constructed one; it claims no facile one-to-one correspondence between "how the world is" and our interpretation of that world. What it has suggested, however, is a way of construing "reality" that is conducive to the flourishing of each facet of the ecological whole.

Even this single model exhibits a variety of ways in which it might be employed. Part of the suggestiveness of the kenotic model, it seems, is that it invites a wide array of response and application. In much of the preceding work I have offered several of these responses simultaneously; indeed, that has been part of the purpose of the work: to invite conversation among differing configurations and interpretations of "emptiness" in our religiously pluralistic world. To the extent that it has operated on these several levels, the project has lacked some specificity regarding its imagery. Yet, because this project has not employed one interpretation of kenosis to the exclusion of all others, it has

---

2. Or, the paradox of "finding oneself" by "losing oneself," through the surrender of false security.

been helpful in furthering the case of interreligious encounter.[3] After all, only through conversation with others do the specifics of one's own religious model emerge in fuller detail. It is to this "lack" that we turn in these closing pages. In the space that remains, I will construct a fivefold typology for how self-emptying might be interpreted ontologically: (1) as an interpretation of the transitory and elusive nature of existence in general; (2) as a recognition of the mysterious "otherness" of God, about whom we must empty ourselves of any speculative flights; (3) as an interpretation of God's simultaneous dependence/independence in relation to creation; (4) as an unnecessitated, free possibility of God's grace; (5) as a mediation between God's "necessity" and "freedom" to be with others, revealed most powerfully in the cross.[4] One way of understanding this typology is to claim a greater Christian specificity for kenosis as we move from #1 to #5. Obviously, interpreting kenosis as a manifestation of the transitory nature of "reality" (#1) has stronger resonance with Buddhist claims of the illusory nature of the self than does a claim about the cruciform self-giving of God (#5). Regardless of how one interprets kenosis ontologically, however, kenosis displays a *moral* status as well. A recognition of a self-emptying pattern in the cosmos itself (whether ideally or descriptively) has the moral result of freeing individuals from the prison of solitude, into greater solidarity with others, in fuller cognizance of the interrelated universe. This common moral theme in vastly divergent interpretive possibilities provides a point at which worlds and worldviews both converge and clash, a point that will continue to foster the life of interreligious encounter for the foreseeable future.

---

3. During the early stages of this project, I found myself faced with a choice: I could offer either a specific construal of kenosis, which would reflect my own theological preoccupations and dampen the voices of other interpretations, or a more open-ended interpretation that invited conversation and alternative construals. Because I wanted to stress the promise of interreligious encounter, however, I opted for the latter.

4. For the basic structure of this typology I am particularly indebted to Eugene TeSelle, who, through a critical reading of an earlier draft, urged me to "eke out a position" on an interpretation of kenosis in relation to the plethora of contemporary and historical readings of it.

COSMIC EMPTINESS AND KENOTIC TRANSITORINESS

Perhaps the most basic interpretation of kenosis is to claim it as one manifestation of the cosmos's transitoriness. More specifically, it represents the freeing of the "self" from all fleeting sources of attachment—material things, money, status, even the "self" itself—so that one can exist with others in harmony. Here is where the consonance between a "Christian" interpretation of kenosis and a "Buddhist" recognition of emptiness reaches its high point. Part of the dynamic of both Buddhist enlightenment and Christian salvation is to be emptied of any kind of false security, in order to be freed for more abundant living. The movement of kenosis is to de-center the "self"—and anything else—from any privileged place of permanence.

The Buddhist tradition has routinely made more of this dynamic than its Christian counterpart. Indeed, it extends the razor of emptiness to *everything:* the "self" must empty itself, not only to exist in greater harmony with its surroundings, but because there is really no such entity as the "self." One of the most famous formulations of this kernel of wisdom is found in the *Milindapanha.* Milinda, the king, and the venerable Nagasena engage in a dialogue that begins innocuously with the king asking the sage his name. This seemingly banal question launches an extended discussion on the illusory nature of the self and the emptiness of anything we would "thingify": "Your majesty, I am called Nagasena . . . it is, nevertheless, your majesty, but a way of counting, a term, an appellation, a convenient designation, a mere name, this Nagasena; for there is no ego here to be found."[5] As the conversation continues, Nagasena shows how the self cannot be made reducible to any aspect of the body, its perceptions, sensations, or even its consciousness. Nor is the self the composite of these aspects. Its very "being" is elusive and cannot be specified precisely. Part of the problem, from a Buddhist perspective, is that we too often attribute a perduring quality to the "self" when it simply cannot be maintained. To "empty" the self, then, is a proper response to the "non-

---

5. Sarvepalli Radhakrishnan and Charles A. Moore, eds., *A Sourcebook in Indian Philosophy,* (Princeton, N.J.: Princeton University Press, 1957), 281.

thingifiable" nature of the "I," indeed, of everything. As the *Visuddhi-magga* notes, "In the absolute sense there is no living entity there to form a basis for such figments as 'I am,' or 'I'; in other words, ... in the absolute sense there is only name and form."[6]

A Buddhist interpretation of self-emptying urges us to liberate the self from all illusion, including our own perception of ourselves. It frees the self, and others, from the prisons of the labels that we so desperately want to affix upon things. Only when we recognize the transitory nature of cherished "categories" can we exist in greater responsiveness to others, with increased awareness and openness to the world itself. If we consider this response as *kenosis*, it is at its most basic level a proper response to *the way things are*. As the Buddhist would remind us, a cosmos of dependent co-origination is premised not on the absolutization of any one "self," but on the emptying of any one source of privilege, so that the compass of the interrelated whole is more keenly glimpsed.[7]

KENOSIS AND THE OTHERNESS OF GOD

The first interpretation of kenosis offers much in terms of cross-religious comparison. Both Christianity and Buddhism offer strains that point to the evanescence of all entities, and say that the source of suffering (and sin) can be traced to excessive attachment to anything. The other four interpretations of kenosis are at least implicitly *theistic*, and, insofar as they offer a model

---

6. Ibid., 285. Or, as a poem from the same source notes,

> Misery only doth exist, none miserable,
> No doer is there; naught save the deed is found.
> *Nirvana* is, but not the man who seeks it.
> The Path exists, but not the traveler on it. (Ibid., 289)

7. Although Buddhism has developed this strain of interpretation (interrelationship and the freeing from illusion) more significantly than Christianity, there are strands within the Christian tradition that echo similar themes. For many Christian theologians, most notably Augustine and Luther, the liberation from sin represents an analogous freedom from attachment. It is the turn from a fleeting, impermanent "good" to God, the relinquishing of the self as the center, and the finding of one's center in God. From the Buddhist perspective, however, the turn toward God might be seen as an unwarranted longing for attachment, even if it seeks security in the "ultimate."

for understanding the divine, begin to sound dissonant from a Buddhist perspective. A second option for interpreting kenosis is to say that it represents the inherent "otherness" of thought and its object, a trajectory that is reflected in thinkers such as Feuerbach and others concerned primarily with the "natural world" in contradistinction to speculative theology. This approach focuses almost exclusively upon the sensory world; it argues that those things and events "here below" offer more than enough to occupy our attention. We must empty ourselves of our speculative musings in order to take seriously humanity's way of being in the natural world and nature itself. If "God" is broached in this perspective, it is only insofar as God comes into being *through* the world.[8]

The value of this second approach is that it pays strict attention to the exigencies of the day. It urges us to grapple seriously with the issues and events that have the most direct impact upon the world and those who inhabit it. Insofar as such an approach is "theological," it claims that thinking about "God" is not an abstract endeavor, divorced from the day-to-day occurrences of this world. Most liberation theologians reflect some of the wisdom of this perspective, as does Luther's theology of the cross. Both of these approaches, though separated by a 450-year bridge, urge speculative thought about "God" to empty itself, and to focus upon the revelation of God *in* the world: in Luther's case in the suffering of Christ, and in the liberationist's case, the cruciform suffering of the poor in the world and their emancipatory struggle. The "being" of God is a mystery and a cognitive impossibility; we must empty ourselves of any pretension to describe it, and instead turn our attention to the things of this world that make a difference, and how God might be

---

8. Ludwig Feuerbach, however, would dismiss even this suggestion. All theology, for him, is anthropology—a projection of the best human aims and intentions upon an elusive divine realm. Talk about "God," in this sense, is talk about the noblest aspects of humanity. What is needed, according to Feuerbach, is the redirection of such thought away from the heavens and back to earth. Theology is not an erroneous discipline; it is a *misdirected* discipline. See *The Essence of Christianity*, trans. George Eliot (New York: Harper & Row, 1957), xxxiii–xliv. Some of the left-wing Hegelians, including D. F. Strauss, however, continue to uphold the necessity of theology and would deny that all God-talk is idle human projection.

reflected therein. In sum, this perspective glimpses God either at the *limits* of the sensory world or embedded *in the midst* of it, but refuses to turn its attention *beyond* that world. The approach that I have been offering throughout this work accepts much of the insight of this second interpretation of kenosis—insofar as it has focused upon the *difference* "here below" theology makes, and insofar as it has suggested (particularly though dialogue with Buddhists) how Christian theology might "deontologize" its own claims about God—yet it has also wanted to say something more about God. The most significant weakness of this interpretation, then, is that it invariably invokes the cloud of mystery when speaking of the divine. Although mystery lies at the core of many Jewish and Christian affirmations about God,[9] both Christians and Jews are unlikely to rest in that affirmation alone. For God's *relatedness* is also claimed at the center of each tradition, forming the foundation of the Jewish conception of election and the Christian idea of incarnation. Even if we cannot "know" the being of God in Godself, we might offer a model or analogy of what this relationship is like, for, without God's *relation* to creation, neither incarnation nor election makes sense. The final three interpretations of kenosis move in this direction, offering tentative suggestions for how the God-world relation might be conceived.

KENOSIS AND THE NECESSITY OF DIVINE BE-COMING

A third option is to claim that God's relation to creation exhibits simultaneous independence and dependence. God is other than creation, fundamentally distinct from it as author and ground, but God also "needs" the cosmos, and is not actualized fully except through relation to the "other" (creation). This strand of theology is reflected most prominently in the work of Hegel, and reemerges this century in process thought and in

---

9. The mystery of God is reflected in strands as diverse as the unpronounceable Tetragrammaton and the *via negativa*, to name only one example from each tradition.

some of Rahner's work, notably *Spirit in the World*.[10] God, according to this vision, is no less "God," but reveals Godself more fully in intimate relation with what is other than God, through covenant and incarnation. It is fundamental to the nature of God to empty itself of aseity and autonomy, in order to exist more fully with the other. Kenosis is not incidental to the divine life but fundamental to God's very being. God's self-emptying, in other words, epitomizes authentic relatedness and the highest degree of self-development. What is posited of God, moreover, is reflected throughout creation wherever interrelationship is most keenly glimpsed, whether in human relationships or within the realm of nature. This approach recognizes that "I" need the Other for my own self-development, that authentic human being emerges only with concrete earth others. Whenever persons empty themselves of supposed autonomy and privilege to exist with others, they become more fully human beings.

This interpretation wends its way prominently through the present work. As my constructive reflections on incarnation, resurrection, and discipleship have attempted to show, it is fundamental to the enterprise of Christian theology to delineate relationships between God and the world and between human beings. Such relatedness is best glimpsed through a model of emptying-and-return that sees one's attention to the Other and one's own identity as inextricably bound together. The need for the Other reflects both the poverty of the autonomous self and the richness of reciprocal relation. Insofar as my reflections have addressed this need, they bear much in common with Rahner's and Hegel's theological projects.

THE GRACE OF GOD'S SELF-EMPTYING

The fourth interpretation of kenosis shares much in common with the previous suggestions, but differs in at least one important respect: it glimpses God's relation to creation not chiefly as one of "need," but of God's unconditionally free grace. God, according to this interpretation, is utterly sufficient and related

10. Karl Rahner, *Spirit in the World*, trans. William Dych (New York: Herder and Herder, 1968), esp. ch. 2, "Sensibility," and ch. 3, "Abstraction."

in Godself, but extends Godself to the Other in creative and sustaining love. The "self-emptying" of God in the world is thus a *possibility* but not a *necessity* of God's "being." God's self-emptying is not the diminishment of God or a more explicit revelation, but one of the ways in which God expresses Godself. Perhaps the most prominent exponent of this position in the twentieth century is Karl Barth, who claims, "God Himself is the irresolvable and at the same time that which fills and embraces everything else. God Himself in His being for Himself is the one being which stands in need of nothing else and at the same time the one being by which everything else came into being and exists."[11] Part of Barth's motivation, and of others who would uphold this tack, is to preserve the "Godness" of God as the "One who loves in freedom." To suggest that God "needs" creation, according to this perspective, is to domesticate the divine, to reduce God to an object of our own projections. God in no way "needs" us, but chooses to relate to us in freedom.

Certainly, there is much in this perspective that merits applause: the stubborn refusal to reduce God to the projections and vagaries of human beings is one aspect, as is Barth's focus upon the *gracious* quality of God's own self-giving. If kenosis is not a *free* act, then it becomes a descriptive model devoid of ethical punch. The radicality of self-emptying, it seems, is not that it is necessitated, but that it is voluntary—a freely undertaken means of expressing a fuller, more authentically related life. Any interpretation of kenosis, if it seeks to maintain its ethical import, must maintain this voluntary, indeed gracious, aspect.

What is difficult about Barth's position, however, is that it places God's *nonrelatedness* at the apogee of theological discourse. By placing God's aseity *before* God's relation to creation, Barth exalts the monarchical individual model above all others. Relatedness, it seems, is only secondary to God's nature, emerging as an appendage to the One who is utterly complete in the divine Self. The counterpoint of the present work, in contrast, has been the suggestion that God is not primarily the One

---

11. Karl Barth, *Church Dogmatics*, vol. 2, part 1, ed. G. W. Bromiley and T. F. Torrance (Edinburgh: T. & T. Clark, 1956), 458.

sufficient in Godself, but the supremely related One. For only as supremely related can God be moved by the pattern of incarnation and crucifixion that Christians proclaim. Relation is primary, not secondary, to the vulnerable God of Bethlehem, Good Friday, and Easter.

THE KENOTIC FULFILLMENT
OF A RELATIONAL GOD

Because relation is primary to God, the difference between God's "necessity" and "freedom" may ultimately disappear. This mediating position is the final ontological interpretation of kenosis. The fulfillment of the relational God, symbolized by the emptying of God into creation, is not imposed by an external constraint, but is the result of the free and gracious activity of the One who wills to "ex-ist" with others. This freedom, moreover, is not mere caprice, but the necessary extension of God's relatedness. God needs an Other for God's self-realization, yet this need is not *required* by an Other, but is constitutive of the supremely related One's gracious freedom. The *nature* of God's freedom is to seek an Other; the nature of God is to bestow grace.

The cross, as the chief symbol of kenosis, sharpens our focus in this interpretation. The God who empties Godself in Christ on the cross is not constrained by necessity—for example, the demands of divine justice, as in Anselm's atonement theory. Neither is this self-emptying the extension of the One who is utterly complete in the divine Self. Rather, the "at-one-ment" revealed in the cross is the revelation of God-with-us, the fulfillment of a relational God who empties Godself in all of creation. This kenosis on behalf of us is *grace*, extended not because we require it or have "earned" it, not because it is God's caprice to extend Godself in this manner, but because it reveals *who God is* and calls us back to *who we are*—beings made for relation, beings made for God. Our response to God's self-emptying—whether in the form of doctrine, the life of discipleship, or the practice of dialogue—takes on a kenotic hue, because this response reflects more closely the persons God calls us to become. If there is an interpretation that has woven its way most prominently throughout these reflections, surely, it is this one.

These five types of kenotic interpretation do not exhaust all the possible ways in which the model of self-emptying might be applied to interhuman relations, the cosmos, and God. They are, at best, brief characterizations of the major strands of "emptying," chiefly in relation to the Christian tradition, but also with reference to Buddhism. As I have organized them, one notices the increasing *specification* of the emptying model. Whereas the first example is a general description of the elusive and transitory nature of every entity in the universe, the third, fourth, and fifth focus the *subject* of self-emptying squarely upon one agent—God. As one moves away from the first example (which shows much resonance across Buddhist and Christian lines), the potential for interreligious collision increases. Indeed, the last three examples offer much that a Buddhist conceptuality would surely dispute—not simply because of their explicit theism, but also because of the *perduring nature* that they attribute to God. Such convergence and collision, however, is precisely what interreligious encounter, at its best, evokes. As faith meets faith, one discovers both common thematic elements and ways in which themes diverge. One result of employing the kenotic model, for Christians, is that we recognize the common theme of aberrant self-absolutization (which is one root of sin for Christians and one cause of suffering for Buddhists) as that which needs to be emptied, and the dissonance that the Christian articulation of the "emptying God" sounds in ears attuned to Buddhist emptiness.

CONVERGENCE, COLLISION, AND THE CENTRALITY OF THE OTHER

Regardless of how one configures kenosis ontologically, however, a commonality emerges in terms of its *moral* status. This, perhaps, is the greatest convergence that emerges when Buddhists and Christians encounter one another: the demand of self-emptying in the name of our responsibilities for one another and our recognition of the interrelationship of all,

sentient and inanimate beings. The moral significance of kenosis is that it leaves no single being alone.[12] Recognizing the
illusion of self-absolutization, persons are called to relinquish
any privilege that would "elevate" the self at the expense of
others.[13] The moral dimension of kenosis, in other words, calls
us to open our eyes to others. It suggests that the Other has a
claim upon myself as strong as my own. It is a call, in short, to
compassion—not simply because my own well-being is bound
up with the Other's well-being, but because the Other, as other,
is sacred. Whether the fruit of this kenotic movement is "Christian love" or "Buddhist compassion,"[14] the result is similar: it
draws persons away from the illusion of self-sufficiency into
fuller community with others.

This overcoming of illusion, this liberation from the tyranny
of the "I," amounts to a greater recognition of *relatedness* and
the positing of a new form of community. Suspicious of the
absolutization of "the One" (myself) and the totalization of "We"
that ignores difference, this recognition of otherness *embraces*
difference as that which reflects the reality and sacredness of
the Other. Each one of us is different, yet related, called into
community on behalf of the flourishing of each other. Faced
with planetary extinction or global flourishing, the viability of
the future depends upon difference, for identical beings cannot
live long without others. On this much, Christian and Buddhist
worldviews are in agreement: each life is an interrelated life,
and if life is to sustain itself, it must empty itself of the prison

---

12. We have already explored the moral dimension of kenosis in some detail in
chapter 5. To minimize repetitiveness, I will highlight only the most salient points
of that argument.

13. The demand here, though it sounds innocuous, could hardly be articulated
more radically. For in renouncing anything that places some human persons over
others, the moral demand of kenosis castigates the entire Western culture of privilege, which predicates the "rewards" of the few at the expense of the toil and
suffering of the many. What is questioned, in other words, is the entire network of
social, economic, sexual, and environmental relations that objectify the Other for
the "benefit" of the self. The scope of this demand is far-reaching, touching every
aspect of human life on earth.

14. See Aloysius Pieris, "Christianity in a Core-to-Core Dialogue with Buddhism,"
in *Love Meets Wisdom*, (Maryknoll, N.Y.: Orbis, 1988), 110–35, for a more extensive treatment of Buddhist/Christian understandings of *agape* and *gnosis*, and their
respective convergence and divergence.

of self-absolutization to exist *with* others.[15] The convergence of these kenotic themes is felt most strongly in the exigencies of everyday life and in issues of survival: life as we know it and the addressing of those exigencies are impossible without others.

The temptation from the Christian perspective, however, is to *substantialize* that which is common to both Buddhist and Christian diagnoses of the human condition. Although both Buddhists and Christians are prone to identifying the "source" of sin and suffering to be inordinate attachment of the self to itself, and in their respectively unique ways urge that "self" to empty itself of pretension and privilege, the Christian continually wants to say more. The Christian, in brief, is likely to attribute the genesis of *self*-emptying to Christ's own kenosis, or even more comprehensively, to the emptying of God in creation. To claim as much, certainly, is warranted from a Christian perspective, for if Christians were to surrender all talk about God and Christ in the name of interreligious convergence, we would be ignoring the *difference* of our own articulation of the beloved community.

Christianity *can and must* continue to voice its unique perspective on the human condition under God's grace, yet it must also recognize that its own perspective may sound dissonant and even unwarranted from other perspectives, particularly the Buddhist's, inasmuch as it voices God as a totalizing All to which we should cling.[16] A kenotic perspective, as we have seen, offers a lens through which worldviews both converge and clash. Yet

---

15. Within Christianity, there are many ways of expressing this new form of community. One is Paul's image of the "body of Christ," in which those who gather in Christ's name follow the Emptying One, surrender self-privilege, and focus upon the well-being of others. Another image is the "beloved community," which has its roots in the Johannine corpus and finds powerful twentieth-century voices in Howard Thurman and Martin Luther King Jr. Particularly for Thurman, the well-being of the community depends on its willingness to reach out to others: "It is being felt and slowly realized that community cannot feed for long on itself; it can only flourish where always the boundaries are giving way to the coming of others from beyond them—unknown and undiscovered brothers.... Men, all men belong to each other, and he who shuts himself away diminishes himself, and he who shuts another away from him destroys himself" (*The Search for Common Ground* [Richmond, Ind.: Friends United Press, 1986], 104).

16. I have already suggested how dialogue with Buddhists might bear fruit in the Christian doctrine of God by uplifting apophatic strands and reconfiguring the related otherness of God. See ch. 3, pp. 67–73.

amid this consonance and cacophony exists a demand for further encounter: as unique persons bound together in a single
web of life, we can only live *with* each other; this solidarity is
where we both learn from our differences and recognize that
difference is fundamental to life itself.

In one sense, our exploration of the Emptying Christ is far
from the definitive word on anything—Christology, God's relation to the world, or interhuman relations. What it has offered,
rather, is a model—appropriate for our time—through which
Christians might glimpse one of their own core affirmations of
faith, that Jesus Christ is the Incarnate and Risen One. This
kenotic exploration has shown us that the Other, particularly
the religious Other, does not lurk on the fringes of Christian
confession, but at the very *center* of it. If there is a definitive
change in the way Christian doctrine is configured, surely this
recognition is it. For if the Other lies at the center of one's
own confession and proclamation, then Christian doctrine no
longer is a matter of our own private religious concern. Jesus
Christ, the Emptying One, does not present himself for Christians' own self-legitimization, but is present wherever others
are embraced as different and real. If Christians are called to
"encounter Christ," then such encounter does not take place
solely within the narrow confines of the past or even among
the present community of the faithful. Rather, encounter with
the Emptying Christ is present most prominently whenever we
meet the Other face to face, an encounter that continually lies
before us and lures us into the future.

As we have seen, the good news that Christ is risen, as it
places Christians upon "the road to Galilee," is liable to place
us in the midst of the unfamiliar and the unexpected. As they
tread this road, Christians are reminded once again that life
in Christ is not characterized by oppressive similarity, but by
boundless difference and the unexpected incursion of grace in
God's world—a grace that meets us in and through others. What
emerges as definitive from this study, in other words, is that the
religious Other is indispensable for both a fuller recognition of
that life and the opening of our eyes to that world. Without the
Other, we stand alone.

INDEX

Book Notes

Citizens and Exiles:
Christian Faith in a Plural World
Michael Nazir-Ali

What comprises a Christian response to our swiftly changing multicultural world? How can steadfastness to one's own faith be enhanced by an understanding of differences? What part can Christians play in moving the interfaith agenda toward a ministry of reconciliation? Michael Nazir-Ali's outstanding, honest, and readable contribution to the debate will enable and encourage Christians to maintain the integrity of their faith while remaining open and accepting of others.

0-8298-1356-X, 198 pages, paper $16.95

Common Ground:
A Priest and a Rabbi Read Scripture Together
Andrew M. Greeley and Jacob Neusner

In this revised and updated edition of the acclaimed *The Bible and Us,* Father Andrew Greeley and Rabbi Jacob Neusner present their characteristically candid and often provocative interpretations of the history, context, and meaning of scripture. *Common Ground* reveals how a rabbi understands Christ, Mary, and St. Paul and how a priest views creation, Abraham and Sarah, and the prophets. This new edition includes chapters on the gender of God and how the authors' minds have changed over the years.

0-8298-1120-6, 334 pages, paper, $16.95

Listening to the Least:
Doing Theology from the Outside In
Ian A. McFarland

In *Listening to the Least,* Ian McFarland demonstrates how the church can claim its legitimate authority without being authoritarian. Christianity claims to teach with authority, but it has supported serfdom, slavery, the oppression of women, anti-Semitism, and other moral wrongs. The author argues that the church teaches with authority only by encouraging authority to be questioned by those who least share in it.

0-8298-1283-0, 166 pages, paper, $15.95